LOVE
on
TRIAL

Our Supreme Court Fight
For the Right to Marry

KRIS PERRY AND SANDY STIER

ROARING FORTIES
PRESS

Berkeley, California

Roaring Forties Press
1053 Santa Fe Avenue
Berkeley, CA 94706
www.roaringfortiespress.com

Cover design by Jeff Urbancic and Nigel Quinney. Interior design by Nigel Quinney.

Cover photographs courtesy of Diana Walker.

Library of Congress Cataloging-in-Publication Data is available

978-1-938901-65-2 (print)
978-1-938901-70-6 (ebook)

*To our parents and all parents who love
and accept their children as they are;
and to our children,
who are the greatest joy in our lives.*

———————————————

Eternal vigilance is the price of liberty.

— Thomas Jefferson

Contents

Before We Get Started . . .

This is our book about our fight for the right to marry.

It's a right, we think, that everyone should have, but we never expected to play a role in trying to make that happen. Then we did. Life is funny that way, full of surprises. And we never expected, once we'd won that right, we might have to fight for it all over again. One thing is for sure: we can't take that right for granted. Not now. Not ever. But that seems to be the way when it comes to human rights. When you think the war is won, think again. You have to be prepared to fight every day.

Well, we won our fight, with the help of a lot of other people, who were with us and even more so, who came before us. And along the way, we knew that if we won, a lot of other people would benefit. And that, if we lost, a lot of other people would also lose. But don't get us wrong: we haven't been fighting just for other people. We've been fighting for ourselves. For our right. For our marriage.

Our marriage—and yes, that's how the story ends—is an expression of our love. So it was our love that was on trial when we went to the federal courts in California in 2009 and 2010 to win the right to marry, and when we went to the Supreme Court in Washington, DC, in 2013 to defend it again. Love is always worth fighting for. What could be worth more?

This is our story, and we tell it ourselves. But it's hard to tell our story with both of us speaking at the same time. So here we take turns telling our story. Each chapter is written by just one of us and tells that part of our story from just her perspective. That makes perfect sense, of course, when we're talking about our lives before we met. Kris is not the best person to tell you about Sandy's childhood on an Iowa farm, or her journey to San Francisco and her first marriage, or falling in love at the tender age of thirty-seven; Sandy is not going to give you the most insightful account of Kris's childhood in the Pink Apartments in scorching Bakersfield, or her first love affair in foggy Santa Cruz, or getting pregnant lesbian-style.

Taking turns made sense to us for a couple of other reasons. After we met, our stories began to overlap more and more, but each of us still saw things from our own perspective and experienced them differently. And some of those things—like having to give a deposition before heading into federal court—looked and felt different to each of us. To give you an idea of how similarly or differently we saw things, some of the chapters in this book overlap to some extent in terms of what they cover. We think that it's like watching a 3-D movie wearing those geeky cardboard glasses: you look through one lens and everything is fuzzy and weirdly blue; you look through the other lens and everything is fuzzy and alarmingly red; but you look through them both at the same time and the picture becomes clear and amazingly real.

The final reason for taking turns is that we are married. Happily married people take turns, even though the taking-turns thing is tricky. And if there's one thing we are, it's that: happily married. How we got there—how we got the right to be able to say that—is the story we're about to tell you.

Just before we get started, though, let us explain a couple of things about how this book works, because it's a little unusual. We've mentioned that we take turns telling our story, and that's true, but it doesn't mean that the chapters alternate with clockwork regularity. Nope. In this book, sometimes there will be two or even three chapters in a row by one of us before the other one says her piece (or, if you prefer, before the other one dashes to center stage, grabs the microphone, and hogs the limelight). It's arranged that way whenever it makes sense in terms of telling our story as clearly as possible. But it's more or less equal overall. If you can be bothered to count them up (and please don't bother, just take our word for it), you'll find that each of us has written about the same number of chapters.

The other thing to point out is that we use different fonts for the chapters, depending on which of us wrote the chapter. When we wrote a chapter together—like this opening chapter and the last chapter in the book—we use this typeface, which is called (for no good reason, according to its creator) Constantia.

When Kris is speaking, she does so in this font. In other words, the chapters by Kris are set in this typeface. (It's called Adobe Garamond, by the way, and is inspired by the typefaces designed by a sixteenth-century Parisian engraver, Claude Garamond.)

The chapters by Sandy are set in this font. If you see this typeface, you'll know you're reading a chapter by Sandy. (This one is called Calibri. It is Sandy's favorite font. And she hopes it is easy on your eyeballs.)

And if you see this typeface, called Consolas (like the fonts used by early typewriters, all the characters are the same width), you'll know you're reading a transcript from one of our court cases.

We use these different fonts to make sure you don't forget which one of us is which. Not that most people do forget. At least, not once they've met us, because . . . well, see for yourself:

That's me, Sandy, on the left. And that's me, Kris, on the right. This is our story.

PART I
An American Story

Kris, age two,
in Bakersfield, California, 1966.

CHAPTER 1

Golden Arches in the Golden State

Kris

My parents left Hinsdale, Illinois, for Bakersfield, California, in 1966, when I was just shy of two years old. My mother was pregnant with my sister, Karin. They packed their belongings into their pale green Volkswagen Beetle and drove off to chase my father's dream of opening a McDonald's. It would be the first McDonald's in the Bakersfield area, and my parents were going to set it up using the last dollars from a small inheritance from my paternal grandmother, Hazel. With its poppies, mountains, and rivers, California seemed as golden to my parents as it must have in 1849 to the prospectors heading west in search of gold and a new life.

We moved into a brand-new house on Harmony Drive. The front yards that gently sloped down to new asphalt had no fences. My best friend, Laurie, and I spent hours riding our tricycles on the driveways, swinging on our swing set, watching our fathers mow their lawns, and occasionally whacking garter snakes on the head. Behind our backyards was an alley we shared with the houses on Christmas Tree Lane. Another block over was Panorama Drive, perched high above a vast open space. A few years later, when our parents trusted us enough to wander across the alley, we'd search the empty fields for the tallest tumbleweeds; sometimes we counted horny toads. Our backdrop was hundreds of oil wells, which to us looked like giant grasshoppers, slowly pulling black sludge out of the ground.

My early years are well documented. My dad was enamored of gizmos, and, thanks to a plethora of photos and home movies, I can see that my mom really wanted a girly girl. There I am as an infant, dressed in an Easter outfit; on another holiday, I am stuffed into shiny patent leather Mary Jane shoes on my way to church. Then, as now, I had round cheeks and short hair. I was frequently scowling at the camera. My mom taped bows to the top of my head to ensure that no one confused me with a boy. (I have rigorously avoided hair ornamentation ever since!)

As I grew older, my wardrobe of choice included Keds, T-shirts, and shorts. I remember how tough I felt in my "uniform." I would challenge the boys to bicycle races, and I would come in, but only reluctantly, at dusk, after a posse of moms called the neighborhood kids home. Those were the years before "real" school. Karin was always trying to tag along, but she was twenty-six months younger than me, which is a lot when you're a little kid, and she couldn't keep up. Our parents would sip wine on the porch with other parents on hot evenings and enjoy parties inside when the weather cooled.

I have a memory of Karin crying in her crib during naptime. It seemed very insensitive of her, so I calmly got up, padded across the hall and into her room, grabbed a toy frying pan, and hit her on the head with it. She stopped crying. At the age of four, I felt all-powerful—until I realized I couldn't keep my dad at home with us.

I was shocked when my parents told me when I was six that they were divorcing. I remember sitting in our living room, glass grapes decorating the midcentury coffee table, our new couch atop lush shag carpeting. My dad was wearing wing tips, white crew socks, and Bermuda shorts. My mom had on cat eye glasses; her blonde hair was slightly teased. I don't remember their words, but I do remember my feelings: disbelief, fear, worry. Dad was moving out that day; Karin and I would stay with Mom at the house. I know now what caused it, but at the time, the decision made no sense. I couldn't remember a single fight or hard day—but then again, four-year-olds tend to focus on themselves.

One night soon after my dad left, I heard a noise I didn't recognize, so I got out of bed. It must have been the middle of the night;

the only light was over the kitchen table. I remember standing just outside my bedroom door at one end of the hallway; at the opposite end, my mom was sitting at the kitchen table, sobbing into her hands. I had a flicker of awareness that my mom needed someone to help her, and I worried that Karin and I couldn't fill that role. I told my mom about that night a few years ago, and she doesn't remember it. It is the most vivid memory of my childhood.

In 1972, when I was eight and Karin was six, we moved to the Pink Apartments with my mom and our new stepfather, Larry. The cheap stucco exterior walls were painted Pepto Bismol pink from the roofline down to the bottom of every front window. From the bottom of each windowsill, gently sloping to the walkway, red lava rocks jutted out unevenly, set in cement and very rough to the touch.

Those rocks were dangerous! Karin was forever crashing into them on her two-wheeler, grazing her towhead on the sharp rocks, her platinum shag turning red with blood. She never seemed to notice the bumps and cuts, and I remember more than once Karin walking into the apartment with blood running down her face, smiling nonetheless. I suspect that lava rock is not used much anymore in the construction of apartment complexes.

We moved to the Pink Apartments after Mom and Larry sold the house on Harmony Drive. My mom was a first-grade teacher, and Larry was a civil engineer. He wanted to go back to college, and we couldn't afford the house while he was in school. The four of us moved into a two-bedroom apartment, where Karin and I shared a room for the first time.

Most of the residents were divorcees, single moms, bachelors, and young families. Our neighbors on Harmony Drive had been better off financially, but the people in the Pink Apartments were infinitely more interesting. Emily Minnig and her son, Steve, lived next door. She was newly divorced and so exotic. She had been a journalist and was an English teacher, and she loved to travel. Steve was obsessed with fire trucks, and he was always up for a playdate with me. In the midseventies, Emily started publishing the *Pink*

Apartment Gazette and hired me as a reporter. I still have copies of it, including the gossipy columns I penned with stories about residents. The parents and kids in that complex were a tight-knit group. The Trovatos cooked mouthwatering Italian meals you could smell from our apartment five doors away; if you timed a visit just right, Linda would let you taste the sauce. Shirley Van Dreal, recently divorced and a high school counselor, lived on the other side of the pool with her two sons. Her boys were too old for me to play with, but she always welcomed Karin and me inside. The Wattenbergers owned a mobile home business and threw great parties. The walkways in the Pink Apartments doubled as bike trails. The flowerbeds were filled with kumquat trees—we ate some of the fruit and threw some at one another. The pool was the hub of activity. In Bakersfield, it was warm enough to swim eight months a year, so many evenings the parents drank white wine around the pool while the kids swam.

My mom became close friends with a woman called Syd(ney) McGinnis soon after we moved in. Like my mother, Syd was also a teacher. Karin formed an instant attachment to Syd's daughter, Nancy. Just eleven months apart in age, Karin and Nancy were in first grade at the same time. Syd, Nancy, and Nancy's eleven-year-old brother Tim lived at the farthest end of the complex, so the laundry room, in the middle, was the perfect spot for play dates. At some point, my mom decided—for reasons I still don't understand—to set Syd up with my dad, and so she suggested that Syd come over one Saturday morning when my dad was coming by to pick us up. As my dad arrived, Larry was at the top of a ladder near the front door working on one of his many weekend projects. We all stood there, in the entryway, talking. The next thing I knew, Syd and my dad were dating.

This was very good news. Syd was the coolest, most beloved teacher at school. I wasn't quite finished with fourth grade, so having the most popular teacher as my dad's girlfriend was a social coup. It was no surprise that, a year later, in 1973, they announced they were engaged to be married. Yet I felt that the decision was a bit ill-timed.

I had hoped to be in Syd's class for sixth grade and to have all the benefits that come from having your teacher married to your dad, but the school policy did not allow students to be placed with their parents. I was shocked to learn that I was assigned to the only other sixth-grade teacher, Mr. Elliott. Damn it. Even so, the fact that half the sixth-graders were in her class gave me quasi-star status. To this day, friends ask me about Mrs. Perry before they ask about any other member of our family.

My dad and Syd moved in together when they got married. Karin and I missed living with our dad, and we longed for the life he led across town with Syd, Tim, and Nancy. They had a two-story house with a two-car garage in which they parked their Cadillac and Fiat. They had cable TV, stereo speakers by the pool, two kinds of ice cream. It seemed so much less stressful than our home in the Pink Apartments. They went on vacations to Hawaii, Florida, and San Diego.

In junior high, my school life became even more complicated. Seventh grade is a tough one for girls, and it was especially hard for me. Three elementary schools fed into the junior high, and I wasn't used to not knowing my way around or to moving from class to class. That year it became obvious that boys were interesting to girls but not to me. It also became obvious that my mom was really mad at my dad. They would fight at the front door or in the driveway when he came to pick us up for the weekend. Karin and I would wait for the fights to end, then ride with our dad across town in silence. When he dropped us off on Sunday nights, the fights would start again. It was also obvious that my mom was increasingly unhappy with Larry.

In 1976, my mom and Larry saved up enough money to move us back to Harmony Drive. Our new home was on a corner, up a slightly inclined driveway. In front was a two-car carport and a two-car garage. Our house was a gathering place for our friends in those years. We used the driveway as a launching pad when we were on bikes, skates, and skateboards. As we got older, we set up a Ping-Pong table in the garage and an above-ground pool in the backyard. On warm nights, my friends and I would hang out on the front lawn. Karin's friends frequently appeared at the front door asking if she was home. My mom's friends would come over on Fridays after work and drink wine, talk, laugh, and sing while listening to my mom's friend Judy Henderson playing guitar.

Larry and I had a special connection: we were the calmest in the family. We both loved softball and puttering in the garage. He taught me how to drive and how to use a power drill. It was no secret that he and my mom weren't compatible, but they tried to make our lives happy. He coached my softball teams and passed me $5 bills so I could go to lunch with my friends.

Despite the troubles in their marriage, Mom and Larry decided to adopt a toddler. After Rodrigo arrived from a Mexican orphanage, the strife seemed to subside. My mom and Larry were focused on the future and the sweet three-year-old who suffered from anemia and malnutrition. I was eleven and Karin was nine. After school, we would pick up Rodrigo from neighborhood sitters, and then we would babysit him ourselves until Mom came home from work. I liked to play soccer with him in the backyard and give him slicked-back hairdos, so he looked like Fonzie on *Happy Days*. Karin read him books and played with him. He put on much-needed weight, learned English, made friends, and tried to fit into our flawed family. Over the years, Rodrigo's name was shortened to Rod, and he chose Rodney John when he became a US citizen during high school. Rodney was the American version of Rodrigo in his mind, and he chose the name John as homage to our Uncle John.

Karin and Rod shared her room for a time; eventually Larry and Mom swapped rooms with Karin and Rod, and Larry built a room divider down the middle of the master bedroom. That left me, the junior high schooler, in an extremely cool room, one with a sofa bed *and* a daybed, an antique trunk, a walnut desk, and bookshelves. The beanbag under the aluminum globe lamp and flocked wallpaper were a dream come true.

Well schooled by my mother in housekeeping, I kept my room immaculate and my music collection perfectly organized. Friends were welcome, but no siblings were allowed. This was my retreat from my family and into myself—the place where I tried to make sense of it all.

*Sandy, age sixteen, cheerleading for the Rockets
in Eddyville, Iowa, 1979.*

Chapter 2

A "Normal Little Girl"

Sandy

The day I told my mother I was gay, she said to me, in bewilderment, "But you were such a normal little girl!" She didn't explain what she meant by "normal," but I knew. Although the whole idea of normal seems to shift with time and place, for my mother, normal meant fitting into small-town America in the 1960s and 1970s.

I was born on a hot August day in 1962 and raised on a family farm in southern Iowa, the same farm that my dad was raised on. We grew corn and soybeans, baled hay, and tended to livestock. Childhood for me was a world away from what it was for girls who grew up in some other parts of the country. They were far more immersed in the pop culture of the 1960s and 1970s than I was. My little-girl world more closely mirrored the kind of America depicted in TV series like *Father Knows Best* and *Little House on the Prairie*—an America where fathers ruled the home and children minded their manners.

I'm a middle kid and the middle girl. The third of four children, I'm five years younger to the day than my brother, five years older than my little sister, Patti, and separated by two years from my older and much more responsible sister, Sharon. I got a pretty sweet deal. Oldest children take the heat: they work their tails off to make their parents happy, seeing few options for escape. Youngest children get away with murder but often end up as the only child when they're teenagers—that's no fun. Middle children tend to fly under the radar. It's awesome.

My dad worked harder than any person I've ever known. Period. And my brother was right behind him. As the oldest and the only boy, David entered adulthood, in terms of farm work, around the age of ten. He was my dad's right-hand man, regardless of whether or not he was interested in claiming that role. In our family, the girls were a distant second, brought into the workforce for the easy jobs. David was up before dawn every school day doing his morning chores. After the school bus made its afternoon trek down the dusty gravel road that led from the highway to our farm, he started his second shift. While he learned how to feed cattle, water hogs, and drive tractors, we girls helped our mom cook, clean, and garden. And by "we," I mean primarily my older sister, Sharon. I learned the art of escape early and could be counted on to be "fast asleep" when it came time to do dishes, mysteriously absent when we had baskets of apples to peel and pies to bake, and high up in a tree with a book when the lawn needed mowing.

Although school days were relatively easy for me and Patti, weekends and summer days had the potential to go south in a nanosecond. Enjoying hot chocolate and buttered toast? Not for long—not when there were cows to round up and orphaned lambs to feed with a Coke bottle full of warm milk. One of my first memories of helping my dad is holding a squealing, squirming pig while my dad sewed up its belly. Yuck. If I winced, I got a swift reprimand. No complaining allowed.

There are few mysteries of life for farm kids. We all knew exactly where babies came from. We regularly witnessed the miracle of birth in the barnyard. And we understood death, especially on butchering day. About twice a year in a cold-weather month, my dad would slaughter a steer (cow) or a hog (grown-up pig). After skinning and gutting it, he would hoist it up to bleed out. Oh, the dubious joy of coming home from school to see a large skinned animal hanging from a pole or a tree. And what, I'd wonder, would my job be this time? Meat wrapping? Paper taping? Writing labels for packages of meat? I learned to spell "roast" early on.

Butchering was a party compared to dressing chickens, however. This activity has nothing to do with dressing in the usual sense. It's more like undressing because first you pluck the feathers, and then you pull the insides out. A day on dressing duty could suck the soul out of you. Because my mom hated chickens, we gave up raising our own fairly early on, and I turned our chicken coop into a playhouse. That didn't stop our grandmother from bringing us flocks of live birds to kill and dress. Few scents compare to the pungent odor of a hot, wet, dead chicken, its soggy feathers ready to be forcefully pulled from its saggy, slippery carcass. "Plucking" doesn't do the job justice; "wrenching" is more accurate.

Although butchering and dressing were unpleasant at best, they were relatively rare occurrences. Not so gardening, which felt like a never-ending task, stretching from spring through the dog days of summer. On summer mornings, while our town friends slept in, our mom would bound up the stairs at the crack of dawn singing "Roll out the barrel, we'll have a barrel of fun!" The irony wasn't lost on us. Getting up at first light to work in the garden, weeding before it got too hot, was not a barrel of fun. Not even half a barrel.

Spring weeding quickly turned into summer harvesting—aka canning. Tomatoes were cooked into vats of tomato juice, beets were pickled by the quart, apples were chopped and stewed into applesauce, and bushel upon bushel of green beans were snapped and steamed in preparation for canning. Our crew consisted of my mom, her mom, us kids, and any unlucky cousins who happened to be visiting. It seemed like canning was done only on the hottest of days, made even hotter as we cranked up the heat on our kitchen and basement stoves to fill dozens of Mason jars with brightly colored vegetables. The boiling beets created a haze of steam—our own violet smog.

As children who couldn't be counted on to not burn down the house or char a limb, our jobs tended to focus on the early stages of the process: picking the produce and preparing it for cooking. Like my sisters, I could snap through a bushel of green beans without thinking long into the evening, until the lightning bugs greeted us with their twinkle.

Much as I complained about it at the time, those canning days are now a fond memory. My tiny grandma, Grandma Johnny (short for Johnston), kept us going with cheerful chatter, intent on keeping us working and in her good graces. On those hot afternoons, sitting in a circle on the lawn in folding chairs surrounded by bushel baskets of green beans, we learned the art of storytelling from her, devouring family history and folklore in the process. Our home was farm to table, without the hip factor.

Barn chores also kept us busy, but less entertained. It was fun to pretend to be a cowboy while perched on the back of a milk cow as a five-year-old; when I was ten and my sister was twelve, it was decidedly less pleasant to round up dozens of huge, sometimes obstinate, cows and bring them into the barn. And then there were the sheep. A baby lamb is adorable and can be turned into a pet fairly easily, but a freshly shorn sheep looks like it came out of a horror movie. One year, I had the job of jumping into bags of fresh wool to pack them tight. This is not a clean or pleasant task. Anywhere a lamb has been, its wool has been. Anything the lamb has done, the wool has been part of. I'll leave it at that. To this day, I avoid lamb on any menu, regardless of the way in which it's been prepared or the pedigree of the restaurant. That's what packing wool does to you.

Wedged between my sisters, I was one of the "girls," as my brother called us. Number two, the one with glasses. The one hiding in a tree, book in hand. Around the age of twelve, I realized that my parents had noticed some of my individual characteristics—perhaps that's when I noticed, too. Although we were a family of readers, I had a more creative bent, creating a portfolio of drawings of girls from around the world, imagining differences in their looks, wanting to explore something other than my own bland culture. My dad brought me a wooden easel from an estate sale. I loved to draw and paint, but I hadn't thought he noticed. I still have that easel.

Around that same time, Dad got me a horse. Ever since I had read *National Velvet* (Enid Bagnold's novel about a girl who trains a horse, The Pie, and rides it to victory in England's biggest horse race), I had been obsessed with the idea of connecting with such a powerful animal and had imagined how it would feel to experience the freedom that only a rider knows. We had grown up with staid, slow-walking ponies—no excitement there! The horse my father gave me was wild, acquired from a neighbor in exchange for grazing privileges. When I balked at the first sight of my bucking, crazy-eyed new friend, Dad told me she was pregnant, and I'd soon have a colt. I named the mare Ginger and the colt Peter. Later, after some rogue horses got into our pastures, Ginger produced a second colt that I named Nan Patch for her pinto spots and in reference to a famous racing horse. I never rode Ginger myself (I valued my life), but I did perch my little sister, Patti, on top of Nan Patch and led her around the farm in my efforts to break the colt.

Not satisfied with my three not-so-well-trained horses, I decided to buy one I could actually ride. That kind of a horse would cost a lot of money, and it was up to me to earn it. With my work experience limited to mowing lawns and jumping in bags of wool, the most promising employment prospect at fourteen was to join a detasseling crew at a local corn seed producer, DeKalb. For a few weeks of several summers, my sister Sharon and I grabbed our homemade lunches at dawn, hopped on the country bus along with a bunch of other tough kids, and hit the cornfields to walk the long rows, pulling tassels from the tops of the tall cornstalks to ensure that the corn would not crossbreed, an early step in the process of seed corn production.

One season of this work at minimum wage netted enough cash to buy Lady. Lady was a rodeo horse, perfectly trained by the cowgirl I bought her from. She could perform like nobody's business. Jump bales of hay? No problem. Turn on a dime at break-neck speed? Sure thing! My life changed with the addition of Lady. I rode every chance I got, destroying our lawn as I galloped up to the front porch. I didn't own a saddle, but with a bareback pad and hackamore (a bitless bridle), I flew around our property, sometimes racing my dad across a field as he drove his tractor at full speed. Lady was my own The Pie.

The real test of my riding ability came when a bunch of wild horses got on our property, and I had to round them up. Normally well-behaved and responsive, Lady turned into a rogue maniac, chasing the horses at top speed, ignoring my commands. Flying over the hilly terrain and under trees, I pulled my body to the side of her neck to avoid getting scraped off her back.

Few things in life compare to the thrill of a good ride. When I was a teenager, that meant galloping on my horse; when I learned to ski as an adult, it meant flying down a mountain as fast as I could manage; in middle age, I confess to earning more than one speeding ticket. The thrill of speed is not to be underestimated. Neither is the thrill of eating.

We did not have soft drinks (aka pop, aka soda) or basically any store-bought drink in my house when I was growing up. We did not have booze. We had sweet iced tea and whole milk. We made the tea, and we milked the cows. The milk was about 10 percent fat; in other words, it was on its way to butter. In the winter, we concocted a thick chocolate syrup from cocoa and the cream that rose to the top and made squiggles in the snow with it for a frozen treat. In the summer, when we had more milk than we could drink, we made vats of vanilla ice cream, taking turns cranking the ice cream mixer. Occasionally, our Grandma Sally would take us to an ice cream social at a local church. That's the *Little House on the Prairie* part of my childhood. They really do have things like that in rural Iowa, and they're fun. Plus, the ice cream is amazing.

We went to Mass every Sunday after dancing to Lawrence Welk in our living room the night before. Who doesn't love a good waltz? High school included marching band, school plays, cheer-leading at Friday night games, and a couple of boyfriends. My one failed attempt at athletics ended in broken glasses on a basketball court during my only sixty seconds playing in a game. Relegated to cheerleading and the arts, living in a bubble of books and horses, the diversity of my world was limited to two categories of peers: farm kids and town kids. My staid and pragmatic parents were the opposite of poetic and romantic. In any case, few things are less romantic than feeding cattle, thawing out pumps, and sowing fields—the primary topics of conversation at the kitchen table.

When I graduated from high school in 1980, I made a beeline to the bright lights of Iowa City and the University of Iowa. At the urging of my recently graduated brother, I joined my older sister's sorority. I loved my first experience in the urban world. Benefiting from generous student aid in the early eighties, I had a full-tuition scholarship, which required that I maintain good grades, supple-mented by grants and student loans. Studying, a necessary evil to stay in school, often got in the way of my role as sorority party orchestrator, which involved me trying—and usually failing—to control the beer-guzzling partygoers smoking joints in the bath-room. My parents were struggling to maintain our family farm in the difficult agricultural economics of the time, and it was a relief to get away from it all at school.

I finished my college education on time, in four years, but I came away with a bachelor's degree in business administration instead of the degree in fine arts that I had really wanted. David and Sharon had advised me to forsake art for admin, and I had listened to them, as I usually did. Although I felt loved by my par-ents, my college life was a different world from that on the farm, and I didn't look to them for guidance during my college years. My siblings had a greater impact on my decisions. On graduation day, my dad asked me what I had gotten my degree in. Sigh. Everyone asked me what was next. I had no idea—the thought of looking for a real job threw me into a panic. My work experience to date included detasseling, waitressing, assisting at a day care center, and tutoring entry-level calculus. I had no idea how to be a grown-up. I did, however, have a few hundred bucks left from my senior-year student loan and a strong desire to explore.

Days after graduation, I boarded an airplane for the first time in my life and flew to Europe with my sorority sister Linda. We visited as many countries as we could squeeze into five weeks on a budget of $800. I returned to Iowa and my parents' farm flat broke. It took me about two minutes to take my sister Sharon up on her offer to move into her apartment in Denver and to look for a job there. My dad had sold my beloved college car, my Saab (or the "Saab story," as my siblings called it), while I was gone, insisting I was lucky to get anything for it because it barely ran, had no heat, and featured a disintegrating interior. I threw my few belongings in my college boyfriend's car, and we headed west.

Denver wasn't for me; I lasted just a few months. I wasn't a mountain girl, and I couldn't find my vibe there. Sharon moved to Chicago a few weeks after I arrived, and I wasn't interested in settling down with the boyfriend I had driven across the plains with. He was about the nicest guy I had known, but when he presented me with a diamond ring for Christmas, I declined. I wasn't even close to being ready to settle down. When I told my parents that I had turned down his proposal, my dad reminded me that "I wasn't getting any younger." I had just turned twenty-two.

My Denver employer, a direct mail advertising company, offered me a transfer, and on Super Bowl Sunday 1985, I drove my recently acquired ten-year-old Pontiac Sunbird to California, U-Haul trailer in tow, radio on the fritz. Having white-knuckled it through three days of snow and bitter cold, I felt like I had landed in paradise when I caught a glimpse of the San Francisco Bay and the Pacific Ocean beyond the Golden Gate.

Before long, I had a bunch of friends and a second-story walk-up flat in San Francisco that I shared with my new friends Mary Jo, Christine, and Melanie. With two jobs, a brand-new Renault Alliance (worst car ever), long braids, blue lipstick, and sturdy

Birkenstocks, life was good, but my family thought I was nuts. They didn't understand why I had quit my "real" job in advertising, relying on a waitressing job to pay the rent. I was looking at graduate programs in art and saving up for another trip to Europe, neither of which made sense to anyone in my family, especially my parents. I finally had the free-spirited life I had longed for, but I was the only one who was happy about it.

When my older siblings came to visit, I could feel their worry. Would I ever grow up? Who was I dating? Was I actually roller-skating? They had adult jobs, working in corporate offices, in suits, from nine to five, with health insurance and investment plans. My sister saw my credit card bill on the kitchen counter and, after lecturing me on how foolish it was to buy a car with a high-interest credit card, paid off the bill for me, made me destroy the card, and put me on a repayment plan to reimburse her. I needed to pull my act together.

I listened to her, but not too closely. It was 1985, and I was twenty-two, having a blast and dating up a storm. I made friends, many of whom I still have and more than one of whom died in the AIDS epidemic, which was rapidly escalating. It was my first experience living among a diverse population: black, brown, gay, straight. I loved the city, the food, the culture, the visible differences in people. I was free but restless, happy but nervous, light-hearted but with a loud inner voice urging me to grow up and settle down. My weekly phone calls with my parents and siblings were full of questions about what was I really doing with my life and suggestions that it was time to go back to being a normal girl.

*Kris, age seventeen, heading out for the night
in Bakersfield, 1981.*

CHAPTER 3

Floating in the Deep End

Kris

It's so hot in Bakersfield that on some days the ground literally cracks open, and so do your lips and feet if you're not careful. We really did fry eggs on the sidewalk. Even though I was born at the Hinsdale Sanitarium (my mom swears that's another word for hospital) in Illinois, I don't remember living in the Midwest—hence my belief that summer is synonymous with dry heat.

Bakersfield is ninety-nine miles north of Los Angeles on Highway 99. When I was growing up, it might as well have been 999 miles. The population was around 400,000, but you wouldn't have called it a city. At best it was a town or maybe a suburb, but a suburb is near a city, which Bakersfield wasn't. The heat combined with the isolation created a paradoxical sense of security and claustrophobia.

My mom and Larry didn't have a swimming pool in the backyard, so I couldn't just open a sliding glass door and jump into the water like I could at my dad's house. Some of my friends had pools, though, and there was the pool we went to for swimming lessons, and the pool at Bakersfield College we could swim in because Laurie Chichester's dad taught botany there, and the hotel pools we accessed by jumping the fence, and the pool we had loved at the Pink Apartments. We needed pools. I loved to swim, absolutely loved it. But sadly, I wasn't a good swimmer. Swimming was easy because I was very buoyant, but that's not the same as being a good swimmer. Always a size or two bigger than my friends and several sizes bigger than my sister, Karin, I bobbed effortlessly in the deep end while others did summersaults, handstands, and cannonballs and raced each other across the length of the pool.

During the eight months of the year that summer lasts in Bakersfield, Karin and I especially enjoyed our time with our dad. A diving board, a slide, and a hot tub! We'd wake up in the morning, put on suits, and stay in the water until dinner. Our stepsiblings, Nancy and Tim, loved swimming almost as much as we did, but they had access seven days a week; we had only four days a month to find bliss in the backyard pool. We played Marco Polo, dove for rings, and held diving contests.

I have fond memories of the years before high school. Swimming was a priority, but so were friends and softball and soccer. We'd stay after school for practice every day, even if it was ninety degrees, and then do our homework. During the summer before eighth grade, it dawned on me that not all my friends were quite so enamored with softball and soccer, and in fact a few had moved on to volleyball or tennis, neither of which was an option for me. As one coach said, "You have no vertical lift."

As someone figuratively, if not quite literally, firmly planted on the ground, I began to notice in middle school two things: my friends were shifting from sports to cheerleading or just quitting altogether, and boys had become the main topic of conversation. "God, how boring," I remember thinking. "When will this ever end? Who cares what he said or how he looked or what he wore?" Boys were irritating and at times intimidating.

By ninth grade, my appearance as an adolescent tomboy made me stick out, and I had learned that some of the boys were mean. In first grade, I had declared I would no longer wear dresses; nothing had changed in the intervening years. My standard uniform was shorts, jeans, or khakis with polo or Oxford shirts. In high school, *The Official Preppy Handbook* was all the rage. I was actually quite stylish for a teenager living in Boston, but in Bakersfield, my choice of clothing was a misstep. I should have told myself to blend in: don't pop your collar, wear plaid, or sport penny loafers without socks. No one else dressed like I did.

I dreaded passing periods at school: too many narrow hallways, too much proximity to students, no adult eyes monitoring the crowds. Those were harrowing years. I knew I was different, but I didn't know why. I kept my eyes down unless I was with a friend. That strategy worked most of the time, but certain groups of boys excelled in humiliating kids, and I was a target because I wore androgynous clothes and kept my hair short. I saw what they did to the students who were bigger outliers than me; those boys could be cruel. Fortunately, I had a core group of friends, and I knew how to divert attention away from myself.

People had been telling me in various ways for years that I should fem it up. When I was young, my mom made matching kaftans for Karin and me to wear with her at Christmas each year. In sixth grade, my mom forced me to quit the boys' football team (I was quarterback) to attend dancing lessons. But nothing forces you to recognize where you are on the masculine-feminine popularity spectrum quite like walking down a hallway in a public high school in Bakersfield, the heat bearing down as brutally as the passing eyes shining with judgment. My lack of awareness was wonderfully protective; my unconscious postponed my understanding of what was really going on until I could handle it.

Twenty years later, Ted Olson asked me under oath when I knew I was gay, and I answered, "I think I always knew." I had different levels of awareness, like when I jumped in the deep end of the pool and then slowly floated to the surface: I focused on the mottled light, then on the palm tree fronds, then on Karin's face smiling down on me from the edge of the pool. It's all there from the moment you hit the water, but you see more details as time goes by. Coming out was like that for me, different depths of awareness, coming into focus over time.

In other parts of California in the first years of the 1980s, things were starting to change. LGBT students, adults, and parents were forming groups like PFLAG, the Stonewall Democratic Club, and the Human Rights Campaign. Stuck in Bakersfield, though, I thought I was the only one of me anywhere. I had glimpses of gayness but no narrative, no context other than jokes and put-downs; gayness was something to be avoided, not acknowledged. I must have known that if I dove into those waters I would drown, that no one would be smiling at me from the edge.

In the fall of 1982, I headed up to the University of California–Santa Cruz, eager to meet my assigned roommate, Anne. I'm sure the housing office staff was relieved to find two girls who appeared to be a perfect match in the stack of freshman dorm applications. We'd both grown up in the rural Central Valley of California, and we had similar tastes in music and a shared liking for orderliness. We both had spent a fair amount of time in high school playing sports, softball and soccer for me, horseback riding and skiing for Anne.

Anne looked exotic to me—loads of curly brown hair, a lean five-foot, ten-inch frame, green eyes. She had a great, deep laugh, and we had an instant rapport. We let our moms help with some of the unpacking while Larry looked quizzically at the coed bathroom in amazement. "Do you share a bathroom with the guys?" "Yep, co-ed floor, every other room, boy, girl. It will be great." "You shower in the same bathroom?" "Yep."

After we shooed away our parents, we made our way out of our dorm rooms in Merrill College to congregate under redwood trees, listening to Jimmy Cliff, Bob Marley, the Clash, and the Cars

---

A 162-Word History of the US Gay Rights Movement: The modern era of gay rights was initiated with the Stonewall Riots of June 1969, when members of New York City's gay community demonstrated en masse after police officers raided the Stonewall Inn, a popular gay bar. With the sexual revolution in full swing, the 1970s saw the emergence of the gay movement into mainstream culture. As the HIV/AIDS crisis intensified in the early to mid-1980s, a sense of more militant activism took hold in the gay community, epitomized by the radical actions of ACT UP, formed in 1987 to advocate for a formal national policy to fight AIDS. In the 1990s, efforts to unite people who identify as gay, lesbian, bisexual, or transgender led to the popular use of the abbreviation LGBT or LGBTQ (Q stands for people who identify as queer or who are questioning their identity). Every June, pride parades are held around the country to commemorate the Stonewall riots and to celebrate the diversity of the LGBTQ community.

while drinking beer and dancing. That first semester was dotted with nights like that. My Merrill friends—Tony, Libby, Karen, Michael, and Ricky—were also up for excursions into town to the boardwalk, the Pacific Garden Mall, Bookshop Santa Cruz, Twin Lakes Beach, Tampico Kitchen, and India Joze, enjoying food we'd never seen in our small towns.

The adventures were greatly enhanced by Anne's presence. I was preoccupied with her but was clueless about why. We'd go our own ways to study and attend class, but otherwise, we were mostly inseparable. My cluelessness became increasingly difficult to sustain as our friendship became more and more affectionate. I started to fall asleep in her bed, and then the day came in February 1983 when, in our room, she kissed me. She left for class and I kept folding my laundry, stunned. When she got back, we continued kissing. We continued until June, when Larry came to take me back to Bakersfield. I knew within a few weeks of that first kiss that I was gay and in love, and I was relieved that I could experience the romantic feelings it seemed like everyone else had already felt.

Unfortunately, an emotional earthquake was in store. Larry drove the Toyota pickup to gather me and my milk crates full of books and records. I don't think he expected to see me distraught—he probably thought I was looking forward to another summer teaching kids how to swim, going to movies, and basking in the Central Valley heat. Nope. Larry watched as I clung desperately to Anne before I stepped into the truck. I don't know what he thought, but he could be forgiven for having winced at life throwing him a curveball. Things hadn't been easy for Larry since I left. Money was tight, Rod was struggling in school, and my mom was stressed with work pressures. Less than a year later, Larry and my mom would get divorced. But Larry was not the kind of person who pries; he was too kind for

---

The Crime of Being Gay: Being gay was illegal in 1964, the year I was born, so I guess it's a good thing I didn't come out as an infant. In fact, being gay was viewed as criminal as late as 1986, when the US Supreme Court upheld the Georgia sodomy case in *Hardwick v. Bowers*, a decision that was not overturned until 2003. In other words, sex between consenting adults of the same sex was punishable as a crime as late as 2003.

that. We spent the first few hours driving home in silence. He kept his eyes firmly on the road ahead, but he wore a sweet half-smile, and he made it clear, without saying so, that there was no pressure on me to talk. By the time we reached Paso Robles, a hundred miles from Bakersfield, I felt like I might be able to cope with a summer in Bakersfield. By the time we pulled into the carport next to the Volkswagen Beetle, I knew for sure I wasn't the same person who had left nine months earlier, but I thought I could fake it for a couple of months. Larry knew I was different, too.

My mom and Karin took a little longer to realize I had changed. Both natural platinum blondes with bright blue eyes (in contrast to my auburn, freckled self), my mom and Karin were wide-eyed and fast-talking. I was a bit more of a tortoise. I liked to take time to interpret feelings and memories. Coming out to them would be painful. I wanted to tell them that I was different from them in ways that were much deeper than just preferring jeans and T-shirts to dresses and purses. As a contemplative, somewhat morose teenager, I had frustrated them with my lengthy stays in my room listening to Bruce Springsteen, Van Morrison, and Joni Mitchell. I wanted privacy, separation, boundaries. They wanted to tell me the details of their day. I decided to wait to come out to them for as long as possible. I figured that I could avoid telling them until just before I left for year two in Santa Cruz. Luckily, I did have confidantes; I spent the early part of the summer hanging out with my pals Joe, Maria, Marta, and Jill.

Maria and Joe had visited me in Santa Cruz, so they already knew. Jill and Marta were compassionate when I told them. Second-string friends heard the news at parties, and by midsummer the only people left to tell were Mom and Karin. One hot July day, sitting on the daybed that Larry had built, my mom calmly said, "It seems like there's something you want to tell me."

"Uh, no, there's nothing I want to tell you."

"Kris?"

"Well . . . OK, there is. I . . . fell in love with Anne and now I know I'm gay."

There was a long pause, and then she began to cry, at first more from the surprise and confusion than from disbelief.

"Mom, it's OK. So much makes sense now."

"But you won't be able to get married, you won't have a wedding or kids."

"I know. I'm sorry."

She paused, and then she said, "I love you no matter what, but now you have to tell your sister."

Sigh.

Later that day, Karin and I slipped into the VW Beetle and headed for Highway 178 and the local mall. Bellowing loudly along with the radio, Karin was laughing, singing, and chirping about the T-shirts and albums she wanted to buy. I knew this was the moment.

As we turned onto the highway on-ramp, I turned down the radio and said, "There's something I want to tell you."

She looked stricken, but I persevered.

"I'm gay."

There was a long pause while she stared through the windshield much the same way that Larry had. Then she whipped around and said, "Just a minute."

She rolled down the window, stuck her head outside, and screamed—just screamed. No words, no tears, just noise. Then she rolled up the window, turned to me with a big, beautiful smile, and said breathlessly, "It's OK, I love you. It's OK."

I catapulted into adulthood that afternoon in Bakersfield. My family and friends accepted me; now I had to do the same.

*   *   *

When I came out to my family and childhood friends the summer after my freshman year at UC Santa Cruz, I thought I could check the box called "coming out" and be done. The reality is that coming out never ends. Three decades later, I come out all the time—heck, I came out this weekend at a party across the street. I still brace myself when I know I need to do it. I worry about bad reactions. I flash back to the years when I was teased without understanding why. If I'm slighted, I still wonder at some level if it's an act of homophobia, even though it's usually more benign.

That day in 1983, I remember thinking my coming out would be the biggest challenge our family would face, but it wasn't even close.

CHAPTER 4

Birth Order

Kris

Every time I inadvertently think about her, it happens. There's a sharp pain in my right side; I put my hand there as if it might alleviate the pain. My throat narrows and my breath moves from my diaphragm to my trachea. Tears leak from my eyes, followed by the familiar voice in my head saying, "Here it comes again." I squeeze my eyes shut until my breathing levels out. I surreptitiously pinch the top of my nose to grab the tears before they fall, hoping it looks like I have allergies and I'm rubbing my eyes. God forbid someone try to talk to me when the wave hits. My voice gets weak, and my lips won't form words the way they're supposed to. The intensity of the physical pain surprises me every time. Decades later, I get the same punch to the gut.

We were born twenty-six months apart. If you want to know how birth order affected me, there are hundreds of books on the subject. What most of them say is that, as the leader of the pack, firstborns often tend to be reliable, cautious, conscientious, controlling, and structured. And they are high achievers. That sounds like a description of me (which, by the way, is what most firstborns think: that it's all about them).

In addition to controlling or wanting to control everything, the firstborn gets a chunk of time with the parents before someone younger steals the limelight. In my case, as my parents' home movies from the time attest, I enjoyed just over two years of being an only child, basking in attention, smiling coyly, entertaining my parents.

I'm sure my parents thought they were going to get another adorable Gerber baby when Karin was born; instead, they got a screamer. The first sign of difference between me and Karin was our birth weights: I was more than nine pounds, and I looked like I was three months old at delivery. Karin had hardly any body fat, and this gave her a slight resemblance to an old lady. We also had different temperaments. I have been described as sedate, focused, and eerily calm. Karin turned colors when she cried or was cold. Her skin was a translucent white, not seen again in our family until my son Elliott was born. Oh, and did I mention that she cried a lot? My life was perfect until December 1966.

I wasn't very impressed by my little sister. I've watched countless siblings wait eagerly for the family's new arrival. Many expectant sisters start practicing their diapering technique, acquire miniature strollers for their dolls, and ask lots of questions about when "their" baby will come home. I was too young to remember this time well, but I do remember my mom being pregnant, and I remember Karin crying in the next room. God, the crying! I was in a crib across the hall, so I couldn't do anything about it, but I'm convinced this was the beginning of my Woody Allen/Larry David internal narration of life: "Really, you need another bottle? You can't figure out a way to take a nap? You're wet? Get over it."

As the years went by, I tried to be a good sister. When we were little, I would "read" to Karin. There's a photo of us on my bed, my arm around Karin's shoulders, our eyes glued to a book, which is upside down. I guess I sounded like I knew what I was doing (firstborn strikes again!). I never wanted to play with dolls or dress up or collect silly trinkets or stuffed animals, which disappointed both my mother and my sister. My childhood bedroom looked like a college dorm room right before the student moves in: hospital corners on the bed, a desk clear of tchotchkes, nothing on the floor. Karin's room looked like the toy box had thrown up. It was fun to visit her there, but I preferred my simple, organized space, decorated in a gender-neutral way—white laminate desk, twin bed, dresser, rocking chair.

As we got older, our differences were reflected in our choice of friends. Karin hung out with the other little sisters and brothers on Harmony Drive. I was friends with the older kids, and we treated everyone else like younger siblings. We spent a lot of time trying to shake the little kids off our tail. We'd hide in alleys, garages, and bushes to keep from having to play with them. We disdained the little kids, including Karin, who cried over the tiniest scrape or spider.

But being younger had some upsides for Karin, not least in the aftermath of birthdays and Christmas. We loved to look forward to receiving new toys and clothes and planning our birthday parties. We were on a fairly austere budget, so gifts from aunts and uncles and grandparents were highly anticipated. Unfortunately, on many occasions, well-meaning relatives sent me gifts I didn't want—I guess they hadn't seen my school photos or noticed my increasingly tomboyish appearance. Barbie dolls, pink patent leather purses, and roller skates arrived from San Diego and New York. Glumly, I would pass them on to Karin. There was one birthday, though, when I was eight or nine, where it started to sink in to the grandparents and a few others that maybe I was a little different. That year I received a G.I. Joe and an erector set. Now we were talking!

When we moved to the Pink Apartments, Karin and I had to share a room, so Mom and Larry gave us the master bedroom, which meant we had our own bathroom—very exciting. But we weren't the most compatible roommates.

Our room was full of furniture, the closets filled with my sister's collections, trinkets, dolls, and clothes. To escape Karin's clutter and to distance myself from Karin's running commentaries on Barbie melodramas, I would jerry-rig a room divider with giant Tinker toys and sheets. One time, the room divider stayed in place for three days! I also took refuge in distractions. For a while, it was an alarm clock that I won from Bobby Sox Softball for selling chocolate bars. I loved it. It was digital, and the numbers were like little black Rolodex cards that were released every minute, revealing the next number. It had a light and a radio. I would stare at the clock while I fell asleep listening to FM radio to tune out Karin's incessant nattering. "Do you like Mrs. Wylie? Mrs. McGee? Mrs. Stramler? I love Mrs. Stramler, she's so nice. I think Mrs. Ludeke is scary, I'm glad she's not my teacher. How could you stand her? I almost went to the principal's office today for not being in line when the bell rang. Cindy wants to know if she can spend the night this weekend. I hope Mom will let her. I'm not tired, not tired at all . . ." Nonetheless, she'd conk out long before I did. I'd stare at my clock, willing myself to stay awake. I loved 11:11, 12:34, 5:55. My obsession with those number combinations lasted for years. I often noted the time out loud in public, and if I wasn't paying attention at home, Karin would yell out a special time from the microwave clock at my dad's house. "3:33!" "4:44!" "12:12!" I'd run over to check for myself.

When I was in high school, although Karin and I no longer shared a room, she would seek out my company. We would hang out in my room and listen to music or talk about our friends. I felt very close to her and yet a bit distant too. The difference between a high school senior and a freshman seemed so big at the time. Not to mention that I was independent and decisive, while she was in no hurry to grow up. Some of the best memories from that time are the nightly dinners our mom insisted we have. Everyone had to take a seat at the table, no TV or excuses. We were expected to be there and to eat everything on our plates. Karin was a very picky eater and would often get in trouble for surreptitiously handing her tuna casserole to the dog under the table or stuffing carrots into her cheeks to spit into the toilet later. Whenever I caught her doing something like that, I would threaten to tell on her, and then she would start either laughing or crying, which always gave it away. Somehow, Karin made almost every dinner entertaining. She would laugh so hard she would cry, or she would cry until she laughed.

Money had always been a struggle for us, but my mom's divorce with Larry in 1983 was a major setback. By then I was at college, and I got an almost-full-time job and moved off campus with my friend Tony Buckman, who was even more broke than I was. I was relieved to be living away from Bakersfield until the day the following year when my mom called me at my new job at the Santa Cruz Garden Center. When I heard my name paged over the loudspeaker, I went to a closed checkout counter and picked up the phone.

I don't remember what she said. I just remember the feeling. My head was swimming, my heart was racing, and I couldn't hear her words. What had Mom said? Karin had had headaches, pain in her eyes, fainting? Karin had gone to the doctor to ask for headache medicine, and she had been sent for a CAT scan. The initial result showed a growth at the top of her brain stem, near the optic nerve. It was too soon to say what kind of growth or what would happen, but she needed an operation immediately. I packed a bag and took a bus to the airport in San Jose. I flew to Bakersfield not knowing if I would get there in time to see Karin before she went into surgery. I was in shock.

After the short flight, I stepped off the plane to see Larry smiling at me in his calming way. Sweet and a little nervous, he always gave me lots of space; he never crowded me or asked me for anything. When I was young, he had made me the rooms that would become my sanctuaries before he took care of the rooms he and my mom needed. When I played softball, he came home early from work to take me to practice in his truck because he knew how much I loved the truck. That afternoon, he waited for me at the airport to take me to Karin.

We rushed inside Mercy Hospital, where I had been a candy striper before going to college. I knew exactly where Karin would be. She was draped in white sheets, her head wrapped in gauze and her skin alabaster. She was already partially anesthetized—enough that her filters were off. As she screamed "Kissy Face!" I wrapped my arms around her. I climbed up on the gurney and stayed there until it was time to roll her down the linoleum hallway. Then I walked beside her, holding her hand all the way to the doors of the operating room. Then I let go. I let go.

We waited for hours. The doctors told us the tumor was in a challenging location. The brain stem is very dense, with bundles of nerves that carry signals from the brain to the rest of the body. Both voluntary and involuntary organ control, as well as sight and speech, could be affected by the surgery. Finally, after many hours, the surgeon walked into the waiting room. His face said everything, and my mom began to weep before he opened his mouth. He held out his hands to hold hers. She fell to her knees, and Larry and my dad came over to help her up. I was across the room watching these men try desperately to help my mom. The surgeon said it was a glioblastoma: the worst kind of tumor in the worst place. He had taken out what he could, but it wasn't enough. They would send it to pathology; maybe it was slow growing or even benign, but it was clear he wasn't hopeful. Before he finished his spiel, I ran out of the room. I rushed outside and down Truxtun Avenue. I made it a few blocks before I realized I didn't want to be alone. I needed the people in that waiting room. I went back; everyone was sitting there in silence, in shock. I sat by my mom. I had to figure out how to tell Karin, who would be awake soon.

A little while later, the nurses led us to Karin's post-op bed. I'm sure she knew when she saw us, just like we knew when we saw the surgeon. Before we could tell her what the doctor had said, she flatly stated, "I don't want to know, I don't want to know." We sighed in relief. We could get through this day if we followed her lead. She reached for me, and I got in the bed and stayed there all night. Tubes were in both arms, her head was bandaged, monitors were everywhere. My mom and dad and Larry eventually went home. We were devastated; none of us could help each other, but others could help our parents, and I could help Karin.

Karin was eventually discharged, and the next phase of treatment began. She underwent radiation five days a week. She would miss some school, but she would still be able to graduate at the end of the year. When she started chemotherapy, she was so sick and weak that my mom would call me in Santa Cruz to say, "I don't know if I can do this by myself." Karin lived with my dad and Syd for a while because she couldn't navigate the stairs at my mom's. Finally, the treatments ended, and Karin rebounded.

My mom found a pediatric neuro-oncologist in San Francisco, Dr. Spanos, who specialized in this type of tumor and new treatments. We were filled with hope. Karin loved him—we all did. He and his team were so kind to her; they laughed at her jokes and didn't shy away from our ragtag family. For a while, the CAT scans showed that the tumor had shrunk and was barely detectable. I would drive the Toyota Camry wagon my mom had given me to meet Karin and my mom in the city. Sometimes, Karin would fly up alone, and I would pick her up at the airport and accompany her. She was only eighteen, but she already had had surgery, radiation, and chemo.

On one of the trips to San Francisco, Karin and I went to Stow Lake in Golden Gate Park for a picnic. We rented a paddleboat and ate pink popcorn. Desperate for comic relief, we laughed at the ducks and turtles. Before it got dark, I wanted to show her my most recent discovery. We drove over the Golden Gate Bridge on Highway 101, north toward Sausalito. As we came off the bridge, we could see a tunnel with a rainbow outlining the entrance. Karin rolled down her window, her face puffy from steroids, her short hair growing back from the chemo, and she screamed, "Hold your breath and make a wish." I hit the gas because this was a long tunnel. As we emerged, we both exhaled loudly and laughed. "What did you wish for?" Karin asked. "You getting better."

Karin graduated from high school a few months later, having been accepted to the University of California–Santa Barbara. She moved into the dorms in the fall of 1985. It seemed as though my wish, and all the wishes from our friends and parents, had worked. Karin loved UCSB and the freedom she had there. She worked in the campus childcare center and met a guy named John who loved her. He was there the night she had a stroke in the hallway of their dorm. He called an ambulance and carried her to her room to wait for it. After that, my mom moved Karin to a rehabilitation center in Los Angeles, and then, at the start of the summer of 1986, back home to Bakersfield.

I was still in Santa Cruz, having just graduated, and was working two jobs to save money for graduate school. I went home as often as I could that summer, but in late July, my mom called and said, "I think you should come home. I want you to come home now." I knew my mom was scared and that something had shifted. Karin was back in the hospital, she wasn't breathing well, she was weak, and her balance was so off that even walking to the bathroom was challenging. We knew these were signs that her organs were failing as the tumor wrapped around the nerves that controlled her breathing and heart. We spent the days with her at the hospital, and at night would head home for a late dinner and a beer or a glass of wine.

My mom's phone rang incessantly; her mother, her brothers, her teacher friends, and my dad and Larry were constantly checking in to see how Karin was. Every time the phone rang, we were struck with fear that it was the hospital with bad news. Judy Henderson's youngest, Katie, lived in the same complex as my mom, and she volunteered to take calls at her place. After we told everyone to call Katie, my mom and I enjoyed peace and quiet in the evenings, a welcome break from our clamorous days at the hospital.

On August 6, there was a knock on our door. It was Katie, who softly said, "The hospital called, and they want you to come now." My mom and I drove there in silence. We had left Karin just a few hours earlier, and we retraced our steps to her room. Karin's door was closed, and the nurses we had come to know well were all standing by it. One put her hand on my mom's shoulder. She opened the door. Karin was draped in white, her hair shiny and clean, her hands folded on her chest, her eyes closed. My dad had been with her since we had left a few hours before; now his face was drawn, and his eyes were wet with tears. As I looked past him, I noticed how bright the lights were and how quiet it was in the room. My parents knew that I needed some time on my own with Karin. I got in her bed, held her hand, and stroked her cheek.

Karin's funeral was beautiful: the grass was Kelly green, the sky was bright blue, choir friends sang songs, and the white chairs held more than a hundred friends and teachers and family. We buried her ashes in the hills outside of Bakersfield, and we embarked on the lifelong effort of letting her go. Yet, my body still won't let her go. I still have that involuntary reaction when I think about her. All these years later, I feel less frustrated by it and almost relieved that after almost four decades of trying to get beyond those feelings, I can still experience her presence so acutely. I can still conjure her laugh and her smile, which makes me happy but also reminds me how much I miss her.

The gift of being a firstborn is really the gift of having a sibling. I assumed that Karin would be in my life forever. It never occurred to me when I built that room divider or hid from her in the backyard that I would do anything for her to find me later. I still think I see her in crowds, and I dream of riding in the car with her. I miss her in the big moments as much as in the small moments of joy that come from simply living.

Karin and Kris celebrating Karin's nineteenth birthday,
Bakersfield, 1985.

Beach day! Sandy with Frank (left) and Tom,
in Carmel, California, 1991.

CHAPTER 5

A Grown-Up Life

Sandy

While waiting tables and trying to figure out what to do with my life, I met Matt, the man I would marry in a matter of months. A late-night regular, he was inquisitive and intelligent, funny and dashing, and a few years older than I was. I still thought of myself as immature in some ways, and he seemed to me like a bona fide adult. A Bay Area native, he had just taken over his father's pharmacy and was working long hours, coming into the restaurant after the dinner rush, always ordering the same thing and engaging me in conversation. We both were down-to-earth, liked to explore, loved family, and had been raised Catholic. His mother was from Nebraska; I was from its neighbor, Iowa. He owned a small business; I grew up on one. He had four siblings and a small army of cousins; I had three siblings and my own army.

We also had our differences. He loved sports; I loved the arts. I lived a fairly carefree existence; he had just bought his father's business and was considering buying a house. I had gone to a public university on a scholarship; he had attended an Ivy League university. I was a Democrat; he was a Republican. We put these differences aside, but over time they wouldn't stay there. Deeper divides lay ahead.

Our families were thrilled by our engagement, throwing parties for us and enthusiastically helping us prepare for a traditional wedding. On a beautiful fall day in 1987, they joined us at Saint Philip Neri Church in the quaint bayside suburb of Alameda for a full Mass and wedding ceremony performed by my husband's cousin, Father Tim, followed by another cousin singing

Ave Maria. I wore a simple ivory-colored satin dress with a veil over my long hair. My siblings, their spouses, and my one young nephew were in attendance; my sisters, both pregnant, stood beside me as my bridesmaids. My parents beamed with happiness. My dad told me he loved me. It was the first time I remembered him saying that to me. My parents were proud of me. Their little girl had reached the seemingly elusive goal of marriage.

Returning from our Yosemite honeymoon to our modest duplex in the bustling Latino neighborhood of Fruitvale in East Oakland, I went to work at a grown-up job at a real estate title and escrow firm, and my husband went back to the pharmacy. That Christmas, we announced the happy news that we were expecting. We had assumed it would take months, not days, to conceive, but I loved the idea of being pregnant at the same time as my sisters.

Our first son, Tom, arrived three weeks after we moved to a narrow Victorian house in Alameda. On Tom's fifth day of life, I turned twenty-six. I wasn't sure what lay ahead, but I was optimistic. After a few days back at work, and just two months into motherhood, I quit my full-time job. I couldn't bear to be separated from Tom all day, and I was certain we could make ends meet by tightening our belts while I tried to launch a career in real estate. The housing market was heating up, and the time seemed right for a change. We were also looking to the future; we wanted another child and a bigger home.

We bought a big, dilapidated, rambling bungalow in the summer of 1989, just before Tom's first birthday. I was determined to make this our "forever" home. The house had plenty of space and lots of elegant period details; we ignored the sagging roof, crumbling foundation, and rotting kitchen. The Loma Prieta earthquake hit a few weeks later, killing sixty-three people, disrupting Game 3 of the World Series that was being played in San Francisco, knocking chunks of stucco off our house and our chimney off the roof. We could barely distinguish the damage that the earthquake caused from the years of neglect.

After we repaired the foundation, roof, and stucco and got the kitchen under control, I took on the tasks of redoing the landscaping and redecorating the interior. I had spent my childhood watching my parents make repairs to the farm and our home, and so I tackled some of the rehab myself. I learned what not to do as well as what to do. The not-to-do list included tiling anything, putting up sheet rock, and replastering ceilings. But I was good at cleaning, painting, and planting. Two weeks before our second child, Frank, was born, I was trimming our new kitchen counters with a jigsaw.

Frank came into the world on a sunny October day in 1990. My two blonde-haired monkeys were rough and tumble, full of life and adventure, and very entertaining. I was smitten. My husband and I settled into the hard work of raising a family. With adoring grandparents just blocks away, a bunch of local cousins, and plenty of friends, life was good. Still, I struggled to fit in with my politically conservative in-laws, and I missed my own family. Once a year, I took the boys to Iowa to see my folks and spend time with my rapidly growing extended family.

Those early years of the 1990s were a busy blur. I made friends with the moms at the local park and worked part-time, dabbling in real estate and doing accounting for the pharmacy. The retail pharmacy and medical supply business was slowing down, but we managed to pay the bills each month. We lived in a great neighborhood with plenty of kids and big backyards, and a park and beach right across the street. I joined a babysitting co-op, and more often than not there were several kids in our yard, digging for worms, making "potions," or jumping off the swing set.

Our financial situation became increasingly precarious, however. I couldn't convince my husband to do much about the failing pharmacy, and I started to panic. Real estate wasn't a reliable industry, and I needed stability. When a friend asked me to work for her at a local social services office through a temporary staffing agency, I jumped at the chance. In this new role, I would provide technical support to first-time computer users. I, too, would be a first-time computer user (close to one, anyway), but my friend assured me that I could learn on the job. I would work while Tom was at kindergarten and Frank was at preschool.

Determined to move up the ranks, I soon increased my hours, and within months I was working full time, leaving the temp agency to become a county employee with a reliable salary, health insurance, and paid time off. I fit well into this environment of left-leaning social workers, dominated by women. I felt like I had found my tribe, and my analytical skills were well suited to working with computers. And it was a relief to have better control over our financial situation, particularly because the pharmacy was declining rapidly. As was my husband.

The pharmacy was a 1950s business in a 1990s world. With a potbelly stove and a rocking chair where my father-in-law spent much of the day listening to Rush Limbaugh's version of social and political commentary, the shop was no match for Walgreens and other modern drugstores. My husband wasn't on top of the business or his own health. He spent most of his time at the store, working Monday through Saturday, and often on Sunday too, but that investment paid no dividends in terms of modernizing the store and left me alone with the boys much of the time. I abandoned my role as bookkeeper when it became clear that it was causing too great a strain on our marriage; angry exchanges were provoked by my critical voice combined with his insistence that the business—and by extension, he—was fine. I became overwhelmed by the full-time job; the big, old house; and our two very active children. He spent less and less time at home and more time drinking.

The drinking took me by surprise, although it increased over many months, years even. I could count on one hand the times I had seen my parents so much as sip a drink. I didn't see the early signs in Matt, nor did I want to, but I soon learned firsthand just how devastating alcoholism is. It steals lives and futures, and it stole my boys' father. I resented the drinking, and I resented Matt even more for bailing on adulthood, for leaving it up to me to maintain our family's life. The respect and love I had felt for him in the beginning were replaced by anger and detachment. He had always been a good dad, and he was a loving father to the boys. He took them to baseball games, hoisting them on his shoulders to give them the best view. He coached their Catholic school sports teams, cheering loudly at every basket the boys dunked and every home run they hit. Matt was a great swimmer and made sure the boys were, too, insisting they join the local swim team before the first day of kindergarten and attending every swim meet. He gave them the athletic confidence I never had. He loved the boys fiercely, and he told them so frequently, but his problems were taking a toll on our family.

Although motherhood and my career agreed with me, my marriage did not. By the mid-1990s, our early political differences had been dwarfed by other, much larger, problems. We were not working as a team or as a couple. Caught up in the daily grind of work and managing the boys, I focused on those things and tried not to think about the disappointment and emptiness I felt. I stopped trying to make the marriage work, and eventually I stopped caring whether it worked or not. I was grown up, but I was fed up, too.

Kris, a week into motherhood, with Spencer (left)
and Elliott, San Francisco, 1994.

CHAPTER 6

Baby Steps

Kris

My mom was devastated when I left Bakersfield after Karin died, and so was I. I didn't have to go—I could have asked San Francisco State University, where I was about to start the master's in social work program, for a deferral and stayed in Bakersfield to recover from the grief that kept grabbing me and shaking me. The truth is, I wanted to leave. I didn't feel at home in Bakersfield, and I wanted to escape the conservative, dusty town. Being anonymous in San Francisco was a relief compared to feeling like everyone in Bakersfield knew my sister had died. Plus, San Francisco was the opposite of scorching, homogeneous Bakersfield: it was diverse, foggy, hilly, old, and surrounded by water.

So, in August 1986, I drove a beat-up Toyota Corolla wagon to Santa Cruz to pick up my belongings. I knocked on my friend Gail's door. I was lonely, lost, and deeply wounded by so much loss.

The door flew open, and Gail grabbed me. She pulled me into her studio. Her hair was blue and her Doc Martens were red, her homey place painted bright yellow and festooned with weird art and flowers. We sat down on the bed to talk. As I told her everything, she held me, and I cried until I fell asleep.

The next morning, Gail and I loaded up my car with boxes, and I made the two-hour drive to San Francisco. While I was still in Bakersfield, I had answered an ad for a roommate in the city; after a brief phone call, the deal was done. I was moving to Twenty-Fourth Street and Noe—I had no idea where that was, but it turned out to be in a part of San Francisco that was referred to as Baja Noe. It was a sweet, transitional few blocks between the more affluent Noe Valley, dotted with bagel shops, cafes, bars, shoe stores, and boutiques, and the Mission District. The Mission in those days was vibrant and filled with a mix of young families and struggling artists and people streaming off BART heading into bodegas and bars. My new roommate, Kathryn, was an attorney who wanted to save money by sharing her apartment. For $300 a month, I would take over the single, light-filled bedroom with hardwood floors and a closet. Kathryn would sleep on a futon in the living room. I laughed for the first time in days when I saw that she had converted her five-drawer filing cabinet into a dresser. She had a great smile and twinkling eyes.

Because Kathryn was working full time, I had the place to myself most days. I eventually got the hang of the antique gas stove and the French press coffee pot. Our paths sometimes crossed in the evenings, and she would give me tips on where to buy burritos, bagels, and wine. Kathryn loved wine, and she loved people. We spent several weeks getting to know each other, but I didn't tell her about Karin. I felt like crying 90 percent of the time, but I only cried in my room or on the bus on my way to class. In fact, I had a routine: I'd cry when in the shower and while getting dressed, but not again until I was on the bus to San Francisco State University. Yet, at other times, I would be overcome with a deep sadness that welled up in my eyes with no warning. Judy Burkhart, an ex-girlfriend from Santa Cruz, also lived in San Francisco, and I hung out with her and her fiancé on weekends. Eventually, I confided in Kathryn, and she came to understand that I couldn't talk about Karin without falling apart.

One day, Kathryn suggested I go with her to watch a softball game in the outer Mission District. Softball, yes! I had played since the age of eight. It was my favorite activity at UC Santa Cruz, where I had played on the same coed intramural softball team all four years, the perfect Friday afternoon precursor to drinking beer at the Whole Earth restaurant, with its sprawling redwood deck overlooking the Bay Tree Bookstore. The thought of playing softball—and reliving the memories of those days—sounded great. When we arrived at the field, I could see the women on the team were right up my alley. Slightly older, lesbians, with varying softball skill levels. They were all lawyers, with one exception. Lynne Parenti was an ichthyologist at the California Academy of Sciences. She had named the team the Amazon Mollies after the only breed of fish that is solely female except when it needs to reproduce, at which point some transform (I'm sure there's a scientific word for this) into a male long enough to mate. These fish live in the Amazon River and are called mollies, hence the name of the San Francisco Parks and Recreation Level C Women's Softball team for which I would eventually play first base.

I was making incremental progress dealing with my grief over Karin. Practices and games were three or four times a week; therapy was twice a week; classes and internships were every weekday. Around the time that Kathryn started dating a new woman, I developed a fondness for the left fielder of the Mollies, AA. AA (no one called her Adria-Ann!) was an immigration attorney some years older than I and seemed to be friends with everyone on the team. She offered me rides home from games and team pizza outings. She had salt-and-pepper hair, green eyes, and a great swing. We went to see a movie at the Castro Theater one weekend; another night, she invited me over to watch *Cagney and Lacey*. Her apartment in Hayes Valley seemed so grown-up—artifacts from trips to Latin America, fancy kitchen gadgets, comfortable furniture. Our friendship developed into a relationship. She was steady, kind, and sweet, supportive of my starving-student status and my struggle to find solid ground. The impact of her love was enormous. I felt safe and protected with her. She was thirty-nine to my twenty-two. The Mollies were happy for us but a bit incredulous. We thought they were pessimistic.

I became lifelong friends with many of the Mollies. I played with them for eight years. I am still close to teammates Nancy Tavernit and her partner, Olivia. I see Tina Ramoy and Lynne Parenti in Washington, DC, where they have lived for almost twenty years. I miss the women I don't see regularly, so many of whom were there year after year, playing softball and poker, caring for each other.

Eventually Kathryn moved out of the apartment, and I convinced my childhood friend Leslie Sullenger to move in. We had been friends since I was in third grade and she was in fourth. We had bonded over divorced parents and their new spouses, had spent years being the slowest but funniest defenders on our soccer teams, and we understood each other in a way that felt unconditional.

After a few years of living with Leslie and dating AA, I moved out of the apartment on Twenty-Fourth Street and moved with AA into a flat on Collingwood Street. We loved it there. Our new home was almost as close to the center of the Castro as you could get without living in a bar.

Most of those who lived in or visited the Castro were gay men; as a lesbian couple, AA and I were outnumbered and somewhat invisible. The HIV/AIDS crisis was slowing down, but the intensity of the loss was still palpable. The Castro Theater was a hub of nightly activity, films, and socializing. Bars and cafes were full every night, and music streamed out of them most afternoons. Bookstores, coffee shops, and clothing stores were popping up; they drew eclectic customers and contributed to a "never a dull moment" feeling that the neighborhood still has. Rainbow flags hung from lampposts, homes, and businesses; petitioners were always outside Bank of America collecting signatures; and you could *never* find a place to park!

The Castro District: In the wake of World War II, San Francisco became known for being hospitable to people seeking alternative lifestyles. The emergence of the Beat movement reinforced this impression, and more and more gay men moved to the city. In 1964, *Life* magazine declared San Francisco the gay capital of America; the Castro District, the cultural center of the capital, became known as the gay mecca. Gay bars proliferated; lesbian bars soon followed. Castro resident Harvey Milk was elected as the first openly gay city supervisor in 1977. When he and Mayor George Moscone were gunned down at City Hall in 1978, the city erupted into riots. Attention soon turned to even more pressing matters, as the gay community was decimated by HIV/AIDS in the 1980s and early 1990s, infusing the once-vibrant community with a sense of tragedy and vulnerability. As advances in treatments for HIV/AIDS slowed death rates in the 1990s, the Castro began to reassert itself as a colorful hub of gay life.

I graduated with a master's from San Francisco State University and took a job in Oakland at the Alameda County Social Services Agency as a child abuse investigator. As I became more secure in my relationship with AA, and with myself, I started to want to get pregnant and have kids. At first I didn't say anything about it because it seemed impossible. But as time went on, I noticed that more and more acquaintances were beginning to talk about starting families and that, increasingly, lesbians were getting pregnant too. I convinced AA that it was a good idea for us. The age difference was her biggest reservation, but I wanted to get pregnant as soon as possible. I was about to turn twenty-eight.

In hindsight, I think my desire to have a family came from my longing for a biological connection—for a network of such connections. My parents had moved to Bakersfield and away from all their blood relatives in Chicago. I knew my paternal relatives a bit, but my mother's brothers lived hours away, and we had met my dad's half-siblings only a few times. I longed for the ease and familiarity my extended stepfamilies in Bakersfield had with each other and for gatherings free of travel. I envied my friends who saw their aunts and uncles, cousins, and grandparents often. When my biological parents divorced, my sense of biological connection frayed even more, and when Karin died, it grew very thin indeed.

With AA's reservations overcome by my enthusiasm, we visited a local fertility specialist and learned what we needed to know to get started. I've heard that today you can see childhood photos of sperm donors and in some cases current photos. Not in the nineties. In those days, you weren't given extensive information about donors, just basic characteristics such as height, weight, hair color, age, race, religion, education level, and profession. Some records included short notes from the nurses describing the donor's appearance, such as "nice smile" or "very handsome."

We bought enough sperm for several months. We'd check my cycle religiously, and when it seemed that I was ovulating, we'd go in for a quick test for confirmation and bring home the sperm, packed in dry ice in an Igloo cooler. By the end of the fourth cycle of trying, I still wasn't pregnant, and the staff at the clinic suggested I undergo some tests. After a number of scopes and needle sticks, the most anyone could say was that I had "unspecific infertility"—whatever that means. Yet, even though they couldn't specify what was causing my infertility, they could specify a remedy. I started taking a pill to push my hormonal system a little harder. The pills made me moody. Very moody. After three more months of trying and being very moody, I took the next step: an injectable medication called Clomid, which carried the risk of multiple births in the same pregnancy.

In the daily grind of trying to get pregnant, it was hard to focus on the aspects of being a parent that had seemed so appealing in the first place. AA and I decided fairly early on to tell my parents we were trying. They were very happy and a little confused.

Highly motivated to get pregnant, and then highly motivated to stay pregnant, I said yes to everything. Pills to increase fertility? Sure. Shots to increase fertility? Why not? We approached each new level of treatment with modulated optimism; we were fortunate that it took only about eighteen months to conceive.

I first used Clomid in March 1994. After the insemination, we waited. The pregnancy test a few weeks later came back negative. I was discouraged, but the doctors told me not to be concerned—I had just started. I should go home and rest up for the next cycle. A few days later, I flew to Scottsdale, Arizona, with my stepsister to meet my dad and stepmother at the San Francisco Giants' and Chicago Cubs' spring training. Within a day, I was exceptionally tired. All I wanted to do was nap. We'd sit in the hot sun cheering, and all I could think about was going back to the hotel to sleep. I chalked it up to fertility stress. I still felt tired when I got back home. A few weeks went by, and I still hadn't started my period, so I couldn't start another cycle of Clomid. The doctors were worried about a possible ectopic pregnancy and had us come in. Sure enough, I was pregnant—and, thanks to the miracle of ultrasound, we could see it was with twins! It seemed that the test a few weeks earlier had returned a false negative. AA and I zoomed home, called my parents, and sunk into blissful relief at being pregnant.

Until the final trimester, I stayed busy doing what I needed to do and what I thought I should do before the twins were born, in case I could never do it again. Despite a series of weird but temporary ailments, like rashes and tendons that stopped working, the pregnancy was uneventful until the end of September. I was put on bed rest in early October. My extremely large midsection made lying in bed unbelievably uncomfortable. No position was tolerable for more than five minutes. I was constantly starving—not from lack of eating but from the production of two humans, and I was *bored.*

So many women had told me their stories of blissful, profound, and magical pregnancies. They would say things like, "My favorite experience ever was being pregnant." Or, "I wish I could be pregnant all the time." Now, granted, the touchy-feely New Age movement was in full swing in San Francisco in the 1990s, but really—"Loved being pregnant"?

I was thus delighted when Twin A, whom we named Elliott, and Twin B, whom we called Spencer, came into the world on October 30, 1994. Elliott beat his brother by two minutes. They did not rush in, however. After Elliott had been in respiratory distress in utero for several hours, the doctor delivered the twins by C-section. AA and I had arrived at the hospital two days earlier, thrilled by the prospect of finally meeting our babies; almost thirty-six hours later, Elliott's laissez-faire attitude about joining us on planet Earth forced the issue.

From a baby's perspective, birth involves some form of having your skull squeezed, which is a cue to hurry up and be born. Oblivious to the drama unfolding outside my abdominal wall, Elliott was having none of that. We peered in on the twins via ultrasound; Spencer seemed to be patiently waiting for things to happen, while Elliott was doing his best backstroke in a failed attempt to emerge after any of many contractions. The C-section was a success, but leading the way out of the womb had proven a bit traumatic for Elliott. With low heart and respiration rates, he simply couldn't cry, and he was wheeled off to the NICU. Spencer, relaxed and wide-eyed, was whisked into my room for lots of one-on-one time.

A few hours later, when I was able to get up, I shuffled down the hall to visit Elliott. He caught my eye from across the room—the largest baby in there by several pounds, translucently white, sleeping serenely in a layette, needles poking into his forehead and wrists, but no sign of trauma. He was calm in the midst of chaos. Walking into the room, I reached down to touch his tiny blueish-white fingers, and he immediately grasped mine. Within hours, he was wheeled into my room to join Spencer, and my crash course in breastfeeding began in earnest.

CHAPTER 7

My Brown-Eyed Girl

Sandy

In 1996, I was teaching wary social workers in Oakland how to use computers when I met Kris. She was a student in my classroom, sans reverence for the instructor. Required to attend my Introduction to the Computer class, she clearly didn't take it seriously. While I was busy describing for the third time how to log on to an application and launch a window, she was flashing her dimples, her big twinkling eyes under dramatically arched brows catching mine. Sitting in the back of the class, she was quick to laugh at my off-the-cuff banter. I was intrigued and couldn't peel my eyes away from her. When the class ended, she lingered to chat, and we took note of our respective office locations.

Working in relative proximity, we seemed to "accidentally" run into each other frequently over the next few months. Just short of stalking, I managed to swing by her cubicle on a regular basis, interrupting her work with impunity. Soon, we began our workdays with joint coffee runs, escaping from our drab government building to grab java at the sweet little lesbian-owned coffee bar down the street. Hours later, I would be back in Kris's office to share lunch. Swiveling her chair toward me, she would lean back, head cocked, dimples deep, welcoming my intrusion. I soon learned her sandwich of choice, followed by her favorite restaurants, her travel stories, her music tastes, and funny parenting moments.

Taller and broader than I am, Kris is a powerhouse. With wide square shoulders, she holds herself with an air of confidence that, combined with her infectious laugh, makes her stand out.

Her short-cropped, wavy brown hair was swept to the side over bold eyeglass frames, giving her the look of a lawyer or professor, unique in the sea of social workers. Wearing preppy button-downs, dark jackets, and glossy loafers, she was atypical of her peers in both dress and in attitude. She was a perfectionist in a sea of average—a type A outlier.

Laughter has always fueled my life. I love to laugh and to make other people laugh. I was voted class clown in my senior year of high school, and humor comes easily to me—it is the language I understand better than any other. Kris not only made me laugh; she laughed at my every caustic comment and sarcastic side-note, irony being her stock in trade. We found humor in the same things, especially the irreverent. Surrounded by lovers of bureaucracy and left-leaning social workers, we spoke the same language, and in her presence, I felt known and understood.

Kris embraced life with a gusto that blew my mind; always on the hunt for the latest and greatest, she was the office go-to person for entertainment recommendations. Want to hear new music? She's your gal. Interested in talking politics? Yes, please! I wanted to talk music and politics, entertainment and parenting, current events and philosophy; I wanted to talk about anything just to hear her voice and to keep her eyes on me. There wasn't a day she wasn't on my mind. I couldn't be around her without wanting more, and I couldn't see her without catching my breath. As my marriage failed, our friendship grew; she increasingly became a focal point of my energy, my thoughts, and, eventually, my desires.

My heart aflutter 90 percent of the time, I became a functional teenager. I chopped off my long blonde hair, ditched my dresses and skirts, and dropped twenty pounds because I forgot to eat. I listened over and over again to the mixed tapes she gave me; the romantic tunes of Sarah McLachlan, Natalie Merchant, and Jewel running through my mind at all hours. These kinds of feelings were new to me—I couldn't explain them even to myself. Almost subconsciously, I acted on them.

When I slipped my hand into hers one evening in the dark of a movie theater and felt her warm squeeze in response, I knew my affection was returned, and our romance began in earnest. Turning our heads toward each other, we gently kissed as my heart raced. Time stood still. I had never kissed a woman before, and I hadn't been pining to do so until I met Kris. She's a game changer.

Workday lunches, funny e-mails, and cups of coffee gave way to phone calls late into the night, love notes, and spending as much time together as possible. I wrote poetry, a once-in-a-lifetime phase. These feelings, and my responses to them, were puzzling. I hadn't been looking for a lesbian romance; I had generally waved off most descriptions of "falling in love," certain that they were overly dramatic. I mean, really? Suddenly, I was the one in love, and all the drama made sense.

Time with Kris on a weekend was a rare delight. I remember driving down the Pacific Highway one sunny afternoon in her red Saab. Van Morrison pounding in the background and the sun gleaming on the ocean, Kris was vibrant and beautiful, head bobbing to the music, golden-brown curls whipping in the wind. Her olive-green shirt was the perfect complement to her sun-kissed, freckled face. As she turned to smile at me, she grasped my hand. Her touch was electrifying; I felt swept away. I stared at her on that drive, realizing that I couldn't imagine not having her in my life and wanting to hold onto that moment forever.

Falling in love with Kris was a transformative experience. As much as I surprised my friends and family, I surprised myself. When I fell in love with Kris, I had to choose to accept it. I had to trust myself more than I'd trusted anyone. I had to let go of the need for approval. I had to shed my skin and start anew.

I'm not the gay adult who was a gay kid. I'm the gay adult who was just a kid, who didn't know what she might become and who figured it out along the way. My life growing up was pretty easy. I was a white kid in a white place; a girl comfortably sandwiched between sisters. I worked hard, laughed hard, and generally stayed under the radar. I knew that my parents loved me, and I followed the rules . . . until I didn't. At the not-so-tender age of thirty-seven, I fell in love with a brown-eyed girl.

Some days Kris's eyes look brown; other days they don't. In the sun, they flicker with gold; on a foggy day, they're green. I call them hazel. Hazel. What a beautiful word. When we toyed with the idea of having a child together in the early days of our romance, we enthusiastically embraced the name Hazel as an option, although more in homage to Kris's grandmother than to Kris's eyes. Hazel Alice, the girl we never had.

Van Morrison's brown-eyed girl doesn't have a thing on mine.

CHAPTER 8

Every Time She Smiles

Kris

Sandy and I met in the spring of 1996, when I was attending mandatory computer training to learn how to file court reports for the Alameda County Department of Social Services. That first class included an unruly group of child abuse investigators who were dubious of this new plan to have us type our own court reports. How could we be expected to visit homes to care for traumatized children and be expected to use a computer too? I walked into that classroom, listened to the instructor, and decided that I really did want to learn all about keyboards and mouses and WordPerfect. I *really* did.

Love at first sight sounds so trite, so cliché. But I started falling in love with Sandy that first day. She was wearing an orange-and-white checked blouse and a navy skirt; her blonde hair rested on her shoulders; her ID badge dangled around her neck. She spotted me in the last row, and she smiled at me. I made a joke after she made a dozen to let her know I was funny, too. I had to get to know her. Everyone else thought they needed to get back to their desks, and all I could think about was how to get to Sandy's desk. Where was it?

I looked her up in the office directory and saw that she was on the third floor; I was on the second. Now I had to figure out a reason to go to her desk. Ah, I needed to borrow the manual she mentioned in class. Perfect. I waited a few days, so she wouldn't think I was too enthusiastic. When I finally drummed up the courage, I silently stood in front of her until she looked up at me and smiled. That smile . . .

* * *

One day in March 1999, Sandy and I went to the Presidio in San Francisco for a picnic. Sandy packed a basket full of delicious treats and put it in the trunk of her old, gray Mercedes, beside a blanket usually reserved for watching Little League games. We carried our supplies to a hill overlooking Baker Beach; as we settled in, as if on cue, the sun began to shine. It seems like most days, when you plan something like this in San Francisco, you're smacked with hair-whipping wind, damp fog, no parking. Not this time. It was like walking onto a Hollywood set for two people infatuated with each other, so they could gaze into each other's eyes while the Golden Gate Bridge radiated orange in the midst of an indigo-blue bay.

Our desert island of bliss was a grassy spot on a hill overlooking the ocean. Our kids were safely on playdates, and the day stretched out before us. The liberation we felt wasn't due only to being kid free; it was also the sensation that we were about to pull a Thelma and Louise. Hands locked, deep stares that said "we can do this," knowing we could jump—but without the tragic ending of the film.

Three years had passed since we had met in the Introduction to the Computer class, and it had been months since we had kissed in the movie theater. That day, I had the sensation of looking down a road I'd been traveling on for miles and seeing the road ahead, with Sandy's head on my shoulder and her hand clutching mine. I knew this was a defining moment.

We gazed into each other's eyes for what seemed like hours, and I said, "I love you." No interruptions, no one yelling "Mom!" No to-do lists, no gas tank to fill, no cooking or laundry to take care of. I was in a semi-delirious state, knowing that moving forward with Sandy in my life was essential.

I'm not one prone to exaggeration, unlike Sandy. If I love a movie, I will say it was well done; Sandy will assert that it was the greatest film of all time. If I drink a great IPA, I will say, "There is a master at work in this place"; Sandy will say, "I've never had beer this good, ever." So for me to say that I was euphoric that day is not an exaggeration. Even today, when I hold her hand, my heart slows down to a manageable rate, which for a highly anxious person is heaven. When I see her bare shoulders, I know that I'm looking at the most beautiful woman in the world. Eighteen years later, when I catch a glimpse of her neck after she puts her hair up, or her silhouette in the right light, I sigh. No one else has ever had such an effect on me.

Being in a relationship with Sandy was nonnegotiable, a must-have. She is, simply, the right person for me.

But right doesn't mean perfect—that's not possible; right for me means we fit together. We complement each other in subtle and not-so-subtle ways. On the obvious side is laughter. A major prerequisite. Her sweet, loving tenderness is the perfect antidote to my acerbic, grumpy sarcasm. With Sandy I can be vulnerable; her shoulder is my favorite place to land after feeling disappointed, her kisses goodbye and hello are highlights of each day. She smells divine. Her eyes still twinkle like they did the day we met, but they're framed by laughter lines now.

All this compatibility offsets the spaces where we don't fit so well. I long for privacy and space, quiet, and unstructured time. She thrives on overlapping social engagements and spontaneous visits in-between. Crowds exhaust me, and preparation for hosting guests makes me grouchy. Sandy begs to have friends over and shop and cook for them. Our fights stem from these kinds of differences, but they also lead to deeper, older issues we each brought to the relationship. Who tries harder, who cares more, who is getting what she needs. We spin the record, hoping the other will answer "you." We fight with ourselves and with each other for fundamental reassurance and validation that we're still important enough to each other to put each other first. And then we do just that. We put each other first.

That day in San Francisco, staring into each other's eyes and feeling swept away, gave us the running start we needed to move forward and start a life together. It's complicated and it works, and if it's not always happily ever after, it's definitely happier than I ever would have been without Sandy or her smile.

Celebrating Kris's birthday in San Francisco.

CHAPTER 9

Rearview Mirror

Sandy

As I was delighting in my newfound love, I was embarking on a gut-wrenching divorce. It was bizarre and unsettling to live with such joy and pain. I was consumed with guilt at my role in the failure of my marriage, fury at my soon-to-be ex-husband for his accelerated decline, and worry about my boys—yet I was full of hope for the future. I didn't know what that future would hold, or whether it would include Kris, who had her own choices to make. I did know I felt that I could be in control of my future. I knew I could fall in love. I knew I could be a single parent. I knew I could choose to be happy. And I was sure that my happiness would eventually lead to a better life for the boys.

I left my first marriage in a messy way. By the time I filed for divorce in May 1999, my husband and I were not only not a romantic couple; we weren't even friends anymore. I wanted out. My feelings for Kris fueled a fire that had been kindled years before.

Few things are harder than telling your kids their parents are divorcing. You know that their lives will change dramatically, and you know that in that moment, you will take something away from them they will never regain. When Matt and I told the boys that we were getting a divorce, the boys were angry, mostly at me and understandably so. They didn't want the divorce, and, on so many levels, I didn't want it for them. I just couldn't see a different way. I couldn't sacrifice my own happiness anymore.

The boys were in third and fifth grade when, in October 1999, their dad moved out of our house and back to his parents' home across town. I rented the master bedroom to a tenant, taking one of the boys' rooms while the boys bunked together.

The ensuing months gave Kris and me some space and time to explore our relationship. By then I had been promoted to a different agency, so I no longer saw Kris at work. We started going on formal dates, meeting each other's friends, and making new ones together. I was living alone for the first time in my life. My kids were enduring their split-custody life between our house and their grandparents' home.

Kris and I got to really know each other and our respective kids. Frank and Tom were entertained by the preschool antics of Spencer and Elliott. When we took them swimming, the big boys put the little boys on their backs, racing in the pool, the little ones laughing hysterically. Two moms, four boys. Not exactly the standard arrangement, but it had its appeal. Kris and I started to talk about eventually living together.

I had to sell my house, a particularly painful by-product of my divorce. I wanted to move away from Alameda, though. The island made me claustrophobic, and I felt like I couldn't breathe there. I spent months preparing the house to sell, making it as beautiful as possible to get top dollar, borrowing money from my folks for big-ticket items. The day we signed the documents to transfer title to the buyers, I cried on the shoulder of my friend and real estate agent, Maureen. She said over and over again, "You don't have to do this if you don't want to." But I did. I had to.

We had to be out of the house one month after the papers were signed. During that month, I packed what I could, and I gave away furniture and most of my collection of random artwork, vintage teapots, mismatched china, classic hardbound books, and stained glass. I cleaned out my small art studio full of half-finished projects and jars of paint, but I carefully saved the easel that had been with me since my childhood in Iowa. I sent the boys to friends' houses as often as possible so they wouldn't be there as I dismantled our home; this was no celebratory affair.

We were all sad. This had been our forever house. I had transformed the family room into a jungle of brightly painted furniture and palm trees. I had planted flowers and trees in the garden, ripped out concrete, made patios from old bricks, and transformed every square inch at least once. Mannequins were entwined in vines in the yard, and a red polka-dot television was a focal point of the kitchen. I loved the crazy colors, the painted clouds on the ceiling, my estate-sale collections of items thoughtfully displayed throughout. I loved being at home in my home.

The last day in our house was also my favorite holiday: Halloween. What's not to love about a day devoted to dressing up, acting out, and eating candy? The fact that it has no connection to religion (at least in my world) and that there are no gift obligations makes it serious fun. That year, however, the fun was tempered as I walked through the empty rooms in tears, whispering goodbye to the claw-foot tub in the bathroom, the sleeping porch that had held my art supplies, the balcony where I had so often retreated, the garden I never got to finish. The life I couldn't finish.

While the boys joined their friends trick-or-treating, I drove a borrowed pickup truck with a few belongings to Kris's house to begin our new life. Driving through the tunnel under the Oakland Estuary, through Oakland, then to Berkeley and over to Albany, I felt the weight lighten on my shoulders. I felt like I could finally breathe. I had passed a tipping point that I hadn't even known existed. There are some things you can do until you just can't. I just couldn't stay married. I just couldn't stay in Alameda. I barely looked in the rearview mirror as I sped away from the family pharmacy, the Catholic schools, and the eyes that judged me. I was heading for my new life—and toward the love of my life.

CHAPTER 10

What Is Normal, Anyway?

Kris

I was in the relationship with AA for twelve years before I left. We had made the decision to have kids after being together for seven years. AA grew her already burgeoning solo law practice to make sure we had the resources to get pregnant and so I could stay home with the boys until they were six months old (the only time I ever stopped working full time). One of AA's biggest challenges was to open her her law practice, which gave her the flexibility and freedom to work and to be a parent. We both tried to provide the boys with a happy life. We moved to a house near Glen Park, a neighborhood perched in the hills of San Francisco, but as the boys got bigger and more rambunctious, we all wanted more space (and sun). We bought a tiny bungalow across the San Francisco Bay in Albany and moved there when the twins were two.

As exhausted and happy as I was at being a new mom and as close as I felt to the boys, my feelings for AA were subtly changing. We had met at a time in my life when I desperately wanted to feel calm, secure, and settled. I did feel those things with AA, but the boys opened a door to a different me: a part of me that was happier and more joyful—feelings that had felt too big and too risky to handle in my twenties. In retrospect, the intense feelings of abandonment I had felt after Karin died could only be cured by the attachment I felt as a mother to Spencer and Elliott. The feelings of connectedness and belonging that parenthood gave me shook something loose inside me that had been dormant for a decade. I wasn't conscious of the emotional shifts beyond what I felt for the boys until I met Sandy and felt what I imagined I couldn't feel for another person.

In 1998, when the kids were in preschool, AA and I told the boys we were separating. We all wept. They hugged us tightly and asked questions. My heart broke for them, knowing what living between two homes would do to our family bond and how much we would all have to sacrifice to make it work. Elliott wrapped his arms around my neck and wouldn't let go. Spencer sat on AA's lap, rocking and clinging to her. This was their first significant loss; I still feel the pain of that conversation.

Although we all rallied and followed our routines, from morning crepes to bedtime stories, the impact of the separation was felt in many ways, some subtle—like the boys not eating or sleeping well— and some not so subtle, including struggles around school pickups and drop-offs. For months, we all suffered from the loss, but everyone made the best of it. I'm still a little in awe of how resilient and flexible the boys were. The biggest hiccup I remember came later that year. AA and I took turns picking up the boys from preschool, but after a few weeks I noticed something different about Elliott. Rather than playing with the other kids in the sandbox, he would be in the classroom, quietly drawing with Spencer and their beloved teacher Gigi, or playing basketball with his buddy Jacob. He didn't greet me with exuberance, and it took us longer to get to the car. Before the separation, the boys and I had a ritual of stopping at Indian Rock, a giant outcropping about a mile away from our home, climbing to the top, and having a snack. Now, Elliott and Spencer were not interested; they just wanted to go home. AA and I navigated the separation and two-family waters carefully, assuring our boys that we loved them, that they still had both their moms, and that we would always be a family.

By the end of 1999, our transition to two households was complete. At my house, a mile away from AA's, Elliott, Spencer, and I settled into days that included playdates after school, art projects, baking banana bread, sleepovers, and school activities.

Slowly, I introduced Sandy and her sons to my sons, and throughout the winter, spring, and summer of 2000, we gradually embarked on the process of blending the two households into one. We had not been prepared for this—indeed, nothing about the end of my relationship with AA or my new life with Sandy was planned. But if we had no blueprints for what we were doing, Sandy and I had an abundance of hope and commitment.

*   *   *

My boys now had two families, and neither family was the most conventional, but Elliott and Spencer embraced the fact that they belonged to, and were loved by, both—a fact confirmed in the fall of 2000, when the boys were six and had just started first grade. Elliott's teacher, Monica Grycz, shared her policy for volunteering. Parents who wanted to volunteer in the classroom had to commit to one day a week. That kind of a commitment was impossible for me, because I had a full-time job seventy-five miles away in Sacramento, and AA was working just as much but with a far shorter commute. AA and I agreed to share the gig if Mrs. Grycz would go along with the plan, and she did.

AA was the first to take her turn. Her experience turned out to be quite amazing, as she quickly relayed to me. Mrs. Grycz was organized and funny; she pushed each kid at his or her own level; she gave a wink to parents whenever their child did something darling. I couldn't wait for my turn. The following week, I headed into class as the morning bell rang. Elliott excitedly lined up with friends while Mrs. Grycz promptly opened the door and greeted each student by name. She directed me to the back of the room to wait for activities to start after morning circle time.

The first learning activity was preceded by officially welcoming a new student. Jacob had joined the class at the end of the previous week, but now Mrs. Grycz was taking the time to help the kids get to know him better. Jacob shared with the class, in a pronounced

Southern accent, that he had just moved from Atlanta and had never been to California before.

The questions flew: "Where is Atlanta?" "How did you get here?" "Do you have sisters or brothers?" "Which street do you live on?"

After these questions were answered, Mrs. Grycz refocused the class on the activities for the day. At the end of the instructions, she said, "Elliott's mom will run the math table, so if you want to start with math, please raise your hand."

Jacob's hand shot up. "Teacher, that ain't Elliott's mom. His mom was here last week."

Elliott looked at me with big eyes. I smiled back at him.

"Yes, Jacob, that is Elliott's mom."

Elliott's eyes got bigger. I smiled and winked at Mrs. Grycz.

"Jacob, this is Elliott's mom Kris; she volunteers in our class. So does his other mom."

Jacob declared, "What do you mean he's got two moms? That ain't normal!"

There are lesson plans and there are lessons. At that moment, every bit of training, experience, and wisdom guided Mrs. Grycz's response. I held my breath, not knowing her or how she would handle this in front of me.

"Jacob, Elliott has two moms, you have one mom. Sasha lives with her grandparents. Bobby lives in two houses, one with his mom and one with his dad. We all have different families; they're all still families, and they love each other. I know your mom loves you, and Elliott's moms love him."

Elliott had the faintest smile. I was relieved and proud of Mrs. Grycz for such a perfect response. Jacob accepted it. We went on with the activities for that morning but not before Elliott ran over to hug my waist for everyone to see.

Chapter 11

A Proposal

Kris

I proposed to Sandy on Christmas Eve 2000. We'd been a couple for a while, our new family seemed happy, and I was ready to seal the deal. It was a warm, sunny day, and I suggested we walk to Indian Rock in the Berkeley hills, one of our favorite spots. When we took the kids, as we often did, they would climb the rock while we perched on top and watched the sun set over the bay. I'm not romantic, but I figured Indian Rock might be the right place for a proposal.

This time, however, I didn't invite the kids. We hiked to the rock and took our usual seat, a spot worn smooth from years of people sitting there. My hand in my pocket clutching a tiny velvet box, I asked Sandy to marry me. She looked delighted and quizzical at the same time. I'd never proposed to anyone before, and I wasn't sure if her response was normal. Actually, it seemed a little restrained for her.

Finally, she said, "Yes."

Then she said, "But how would we do that?"

"I don't know . . . we will figure it out together."

I placed the diamond ring on her finger; it was a size too big, but she insisted on wearing it home. We shared the news with the kids—ages six, ten, and twelve—over dinner. It was one of the happiest holidays I'd had. The next morning, we woke early, enjoying the boys' excitement about gifts over homemade cinnamon rolls and coffee. Later in the day, Sandy and I sat down together, starting the process of figuring out how to get married in California, a state that banned same-sex marriage.

When the kids went to bed that night, I asked Sandy if I could look at the ring. She looked down in horror; it was gone. We scoured the house and then ran to the curb, bringing the trash bags back inside. Since the last garbage pickup, we had celebrated my mom's birthday, enjoyed Christmas festivities (which with four boys entails considerable cardboard, plastic, and wrapping paper), and prepared many meals; there were at least half a dozen garbage bags on the curb. As we carried them into our living room, I could feel myself starting to panic; as we went through bag after bag, Sandy slowly seemed to freeze with fear. The ring could be at the bottom of the kitchen drain or resting between blades of grass in the front lawn. Just as we both lost hope, the ring appeared at the bottom of the last full bag. Before either of us said a word, I gave Sandy a look that said "Don't move." I ran to our room, grabbed the velvet box, and put the ring gently back inside. When I came back into the living room, Sandy was slumped on the couch, exhausted and traumatized. I knew we couldn't go to bed feeling this way after such a great day, so I sat down next to her and said, "This is actually a good omen; just think, if we can find a diamond ring in the garbage, we can do anything." Even though it was midnight, we laughed (somewhat hysterically) and resolved to take the ring the next day to a jeweler to get it fitted.

CHAPTER 12

Renovations and Explanations

Sandy

With my Alameda house sold, my sons and I moved in with Kris and her sons into their modest two-bedroom in Albany—a sweet little town, full of bungalows and college professors, nestled between the San Francisco Bay and the Berkeley hills. When the owner decided to sell the house, Kris and I pooled our money and bought it. It was a short-lived but financially wise investment. We gave the kitchen a face-lift and painted the walls, making it cheerful and homey.

Although the quarters were tight, we made it work. My boys had been stressed by the move, and although they wouldn't have chosen this situation, they were adjusting. I felt calm and steady, and I loved seeing Kris every day. I also loved the anonymity I felt in this new community, just ten miles from Alameda but worlds apart in other ways. The air felt lighter, and I felt a sense of freedom away from the conservative and religious world I had come to resent. I embraced my new liberal community, found a great yoga studio and organic grocer, and got to know the many hiking trails of the Berkeley hills.

By Christmas Eve 2000, our first as a cohabitating, Santa Claus–faking couple, the four boys were being pretty good sports about sharing one room. Shiny new bikes were hidden in the garage, waiting to be placed next to an ornament-covered tree. I was desperately trying to make up for having moved my sons from their beautiful, spacious childhood home to a tiny abode in a new town.

That afternoon, Kris and I had the house to ourselves, a rare opportunity to finish holiday wrapping sans kids. We were relishing our newly formed household; despite the cramped quarters, we were happy. Kris asked me to go on a quick outing in the hills to our favorite spot, Indian Rock. We scrambled up the side of the enormous boulder using the chiseled steps, careful not to tumble down the steep face. Making our way to the top, we nestled into the smooth groove, perfect for two, with a full view of the bay.

I love that rocky perch; it is where I feel at peace with myself and with the world. We talked about the boys, the holiday, our hopes, and our dreams for the future. We contemplated our options for something more comfortable and practical than the tiny bungalow.

On this foggy Christmas Eve, we watched the cloaked sun slip toward the sea, the Golden Gate Bridge a shadowy silhouette against the sky. Kris reached into her pocket, pulling out a small, black velvet box. She turned to me, opening the box to reveal a diamond ring, and, with tears in her eyes, asked me to marry her.

Ever the pragmatist, I said, "Yes. But . . . how?"

But my doubt was quickly overshadowed by the excitement of this turn of events. We were going to get married! But really . . . how? There were no legal options for us. We could have a domestic partnership celebration, but that didn't feel the same as a real wedding. Our kids were still adjusting to our blended family, so we would need to wait a while. We weren't exactly awash in money, my divorce wasn't final, and our most pressing problem was that we needed a bigger house.

Still, we were thrilled to be engaged and happy to stay engaged for the time being. We also knew that although a wedding would be significant and meaningful to us, it would provide no legal protections for us or for our kids. We had already filed as domestic partners in Berkeley to buy our house, in Alameda County to receive health benefits, and in the state of California for everything else. We had drawn up legal documents to spell out the terms and protections of our domestic partnership—hardly the stuff of romance.

We started the hunt for a roomier house. I wanted a traditional home with stairs and hardwood floors and plenty of room for our loud, growing boys; Kris wanted to stay in Elliott and Spencer's school district. I wanted to be within walking distance to Indian Rock, a bus stop, and good coffee. Kris wanted to be near good beer and her boys' other home. We found almost everything when we saw a two-story colonial in a beautiful neighborhood in North Berkeley, just blocks from the twins' school, on a tree-lined street. It had four bedrooms upstairs, a den, a sunroom, and a deck overlooking a creek. It also had the world's tiniest kitchen and a basement you could film a horror movie in.

We weren't deterred by the deficiencies of the kitchen, the hazard tape draped on the deck, or the "Do Not Cross" signs on the bridge over a creek we crossed to get to the crumbling patio. All we could see was space.

Many months and dollars later, we were settled in and loving our new home. Those first months were a blur of contractors, concrete, and steel beams as we installed a new foundation, roof, deck, and patio. Later, we would paint the interior and have the house remodeled to create another bedroom, a rumpus room, and an art studio.

Although my relationship with Kris was strong and the ties between our children continued to grow, my relationships with my siblings were strained. My older sister and brother were far from impressed with my new life, and my younger sister was simply disbelieving, certain I was trying to get attention by being gay. My ex had told my sibs early on about my relationship with Kris, before I was ready to do so myself. They were angry with me for ending my marriage while starting a new relationship, and I was certain that their feelings were affected by the fact that my new relationship was with a woman. In my family, "love" was almost a forbidden word, "in love" was a foolish phrase, and divorce was equivalent to failure. The words "lesbian" and "gay" were nonexistent. We simply didn't talk about love. We talked about family and future. Houses and jobs. Politics and the economy. Safe topics. I had spent my life trying to please my siblings, looking to them for approval, even more than to my parents. Dealing with their disappointment was agonizing.

At the same time, I was in the process of separating myself from dependence on familial approval. I couldn't live the lives my siblings chose. I didn't want to. I didn't need them, my parents, or my friends to understand or support my decisions in the way I had when I was younger. As my friend Rafael said, "You're a grown-ass woman, you make your own decisions." I was a grown-ass woman, and I chose Kris.

Even so, I felt the pressure that my brother and sisters gradually amped up to tell my parents what was going on. I put the moment off over and over again. "What's the rush?" I thought. I would have happily waited a few more years to break the news, but that was impossible. My parents wanted to visit me—at my home. In California. There was no getting out of telling them the truth. Honesty can be a drag, it really can. It sounds great until you have to do it. With my parents. Then it's awful.

So there I was, one weekend morning in 2001, at the tender age of thirty-nine, sitting on our bed, dreading the conversation as I dialed their number. After a few minutes of chitchat, I said, "Mom . . . I'm seeing someone."

This was obviously a chickenshit way to start, but it was the best I could muster.

"You are? What's his name?"

She sounded pleased, not a surprise because she was constantly reminding me that I was young enough to remarry and have more children. She didn't seem to realize that I was more than busy with the two I already had. More? Uh . . . no.

"K-K-Kris," I stuttered. "But . . . Kris isn't a man. She's a woman."

There was silence for about an hour. Or maybe a few seconds.

"What do you mean? I don't understand."

Oh joy. This was going swimmingly. I considered throwing up, but my imaginary housekeeper was off that day, so I plunged ahead.

"Mom, I'm seeing a woman, and *her* name is Kris. We've been seeing each other for a while."

Seeing each other was something of an understatement. We had been living together for over a year. And we were now living in a second house we had bought together. But why go into details?

Her breath came rapidly. "You mean you're romantically involved with a woman?"

She spoke with such agony that I felt like dying.

Then, after another long and painful silence, came the question I was not expecting.

"Is she at least Catholic?"

Wow. I mean WOW! This was actually a good sign; she was bypassing the obvious problem of being gay and going straight to religion. I was shocked. I knew religion was important to her, but I was blown away that this was her first response.

"No, she's . . . Methodist."

This was a bald-faced lie. Kris, my darling atheist, was in our room and looked at me with a "WTF?" face. I shushed her, hissing "I have to!"

Atheists are unacceptable in my mom's world, and I couldn't give her a lesbian and an atheist in the same sitting. It would be cruel and crazy; two words that didn't need to be together on that day, in that moment. And Methodist seemed like a safe bet. Do Methodists have rules? Who knows? I didn't. If you're going to lie about religion to your Catholic mom, be strategic. Choose a religion that fits the "not going to hell" bill and one she probably doesn't know much about.

Having secured a satisfactory response to the religion question, my mother decided that I should tell my father. Right then. This made telling my mom seem like a day at the beach. I did not want to tell my dad a thing about my love life. Not ever. My dad bore a significant resemblance to the man in *American Gothic*, the Grant Wood painting of a somber farm couple, the man holding a pitchfork. In fact, the setting for that painting was a thirty-minute drive from my parents' home. My dad's entire life had been focused on one thing—work. Our conversations usually revolved around the weather and the crops. It was a safe space, and it was the only way I knew to talk to him, especially on the phone. He was gruff, quiet, and introspective. He had never raised a hand to us, never needed to. A stern look was far more effective, and a simple "Stop acting so silly" worked wonders when my antics weren't appreciated.

"Here, talk to your father," my mom said as I stopped breathing.

"Hi, Dad," I stammered, knowing I would not be asking about the rainfall or the harvest today. "I just told Mom, and now I'm telling you, that I am involved with a woman, and her name is Kris."

You know those really long days? This was a really long few minutes. My body shriveled into a shadow of my normal, robust self.

Dad finally responded gruffly, "Do you need help getting out of this thing?"

Gay Rights in Berkeley: Widely known as one of the most progressive communities in the country, Berkeley was the first city jurisdiction to recognize same-sex unions of any type (then in the form of domestic partnership health benefits for city employees). Before Kris and I bought our first home in 2001, we registered as domestic partners with the city, county, and state to access the favorable tax rules and other benefits that married couples enjoyed. Ironically, we were so worried that the elderly sellers of our home wouldn't want to sell to a gay family that we insisted that the offer be presented in a gender-neutral way, taking advantage of our gender-neutral names—Kris and Sandy—in the "Please sell your house to us" letter that accompanied our offer. Kris and Sandy could have been two men, two women, or one of each!

His response was also a surprise; I thought he'd be disbelieving or even angry—and I certainly thought he had more confidence in my ability to cope.

"No, Dad, I don't need help, and I don't want out of the relationship. I am with her because I want to be, and I'm happy. I just wanted to tell you and Mom about it."

Of course, I didn't really want to tell them, I had to. Yet it was a relief to have it out in the open. The rest of that call is a blur. I do remember that it didn't go on much longer, and it ended with my mom back on the line, voice full of teary disbelief and confusion. "But you were such a normal little girl . . ."

Over time, my parents got to know Kris and her boys, my dad winning them over with his ear-wiggling trick, my mom quietly chatting with Kris at the dining room table when she came to visit us. Over the next few years, as my dad slowly declined into Alzheimer's, understanding my relationship with Kris was the least of our family's many concerns. My mom accepted Kris into the family in spite of her bewilderment at the path that I had chosen. When my dad passed away, the day after my forty-eighth birthday, the local obituary included Kris's name as a member of the family.

Still, Mom will occasionally look at me quizzically and ask, "Are you sure you're happy?"

She asks from a place of love, and I'm thankful that this is her main concern.

Yes, Mom, I'm happy.

*Our first legal marriage, San Francisco City Hall,
February 2004. From top to bottom, and left to right:
Frank, Laura, Tom, Kris, Sandy, Elliott, and Spencer.*

Chapter 13

A Weekday Wedding

Sandy

Settling into a new home with a newish blended family is no small feat. All the boys were with us half of the time, per our joint custody schedules, and we generally had some kids at home. The little boys were in school nearby, near both their homes. The big boys finished grammar school at the Catholic school they had attended since kindergarten, St. Joseph's in Alameda. They had chosen to continue to go to school there, enduring the thirty-minute drive in traffic every morning and afternoon and forced conversation with me, the driver, to be with their friends. Their school embodied the "it takes a village" approach to parenting and learning, and I was happy for that village in that regard. And I was grateful for the liberal priest, Father Rich, who patiently heard me out when I beseeched him to teach religion as a critical thinking course and to stop referring to being gay as soemthing that should be forgiven.

Although Kris had a congenial relationship with her ex, mine was troubled. Matt had continued to decline, and the boys and I struggled in our relationships with him. As his health and ability to parent deteriorated, custody shifted to me. Now well into adolescence, the boys were angry at their dad for being an alcoholic, angry at me for taking them away from their life in Alameda, and rejecting Kris's efforts to help parent them. It was hard on all of us. Yet, a brotherly bond grew between the four boys, and we had good days and bad days, just like any family. Slowly, my boys migrated their lives to Berkeley, with Tom choosing to attend Berkeley High, a choice Frank would make two years later. They loved the freedom they had in Berkeley, the diversity of the city and the school, and their growing group of friends. I was relieved.

Meanwhile, Kris and I were building a life of new friends and new responsibilities as we got involved in the kids' school activities. I took my boys skiing and tried desperately to teach Kris and the twins to ski, a brief effort that led to lessons. We made crepes on Sunday mornings and negotiated movies on Saturday nights. We bought a huge used hot tub for the back patio. Life was rolling along as we were all finding things to love about our new home and our family of four boys, two moms, and a wandering cat named Murphy.

We got to really know each other's kids, and eventually parents and siblings. Our boys became brothers. Our families became each other's families. We worked on our house and turned it into a home. My dad built a skateboard ramp for Tom, and we built a tree fort for the twins. Frank racked up baseball trophies; Spencer racked up musical instruments. Elliott and I played peacemaker more than once, and we all learned to appreciate Nirvana, and eventually Eminem, as Tom blasted music from his poster-covered room.

As soon as our bank account recovered from the drain of house repairs, we were ready to make it official. In 2003, we began to plan our wedding in earnest. We decided that, although the ceremony would not be legal in the eyes of the law, we were going to have not just a wedding but a fabulous wedding, complete with lots of guests, solemn vows, and a glorious setting.

Kris and I are good party planners, and by late that year, we had a solid plan. We wanted the boys to give us away. Approaching, or perhaps in the midst of, middle age, we were beyond having our fathers participate in this way, nor did we imagine that they would be enthusiastic participants. Having the boys play that role made sense. We knew we wanted to have the wedding in Berkeley. We secured the historic Brazilian Room for August 1, 2004. Not far from Indian Rock, this beautiful building designed by architect Julia Morgan (she also designed Hearst Castle for the real-life Citizen Kane) is nestled in the rolling green hills of Tilden Park. With a high, beamed ceiling, thick stucco walls, and patios overlooking rolling green hills, this California classic was the perfect setting to celebrate our union with family and friends.

While we were consumed with planning our August wedding celebration, something electrifying was brewing. People had been talking about gay marriage in earnest when, on February 12, 2004, Gavin Newsom, the progressive heartthrob of a mayor in San Francisco, announced that San Francisco would begin issuing marriage licenses to same-sex couples. In other words, San Francisco was about to let same-sex couples get married *legally*. Couples like us! Stunned when we heard the news, Kris quickly called to get us an appointment at City Hall. Suddenly, we were going to get married! For real! We couldn't obtain a coveted Valentine's Day slot, but we did get a romantic Tuesday morning appointment. That day we packed the boys into our Volvo wagon, the twins excited to miss school for an adventure, Frank worried about his Catholic school knowing why he was missing class (and begging me to make up a medical appointment excuse . . . which I did), and high school freshman Tom begrudgingly joining us.

As we drove across the bay, the older boys implored us to avoid the media. They had seen the coverage and had no interest in being a part of the circus. We assured them we would stay under the radar, but unbeknownst to us, our appointment was right after Rosie O'Donnell's. Oh yes, there was media. Walking up the granite steps of San Francisco City Hall, we were joined by Laura, Kris's energetic and supportive mother. Her platinum hair blowing in the breeze, Laura gave each of us tight hugs, the longest saved for her oldest and now only daughter, her eyes misty with love.

We met with one of the many volunteers performing marriages at City Hall. He ushered us through the standard phrases of commitment, our vows echoing along with those of other couples in the cavernous marble space, our gaggle of boys as our witnesses. We took each other as lawfully wedded spouses, in sickness and in health, and sealed our marriage with a kiss. Wearing nice-enough but hardly wedding-worthy outfits, we reveled in the intimacy of the moment, the seriousness of our promise, and the hopes we shared for our future together. Our joy was quickly interrupted by the cameras and journalists who lingered after Rosie's wedding and decided that our boy-heavy family, complete with grandma, was newsworthy. We were on television that night; more than one of the boys was charmed by his moment of fame.

Within hours of standing on the steps of City Hall, we had deposited the boys on the steps of their respective schools, and we were back to planning our wedding celebration. We had rings to buy and a cake to order, invitations to design, and boys to convince to wear tuxedos. But now, instead of planning a celebration of our commitment to each other, we were also planning a celebration of the fact that we were legally married. We'd tied the knot in San Francisco City Hall, no less! The summer celebration was going to be even more of a celebration than we had dared hope!

CHAPTER 14

City Hall, Boys and All

Kris

As Sandy and I shared the news of our engagement with our parents, friends, and coworkers, most of whom seemed happy and less confused than we were. They all seemed to assume we would have a wedding just like any other wedding. We decided to follow their positive outlook: we picked a date in August 2004 and booked the Julia Morgan-designed Brazilian Room in Tilden Park, not too far from Indian Rock.

In February 2004, as we were drafting the "Save the Date" note, news broke that San Francisco mayor Gavin Newsom had directed the city clerk to marry all couples, gay and straight. At first, I was dubious. How could he do that? Did the mayor and the city clerk even have the authority to declare that same-sex couples could be married? Yet, suddenly, the possibility existed that Sandy and I could be married legally. The evening news showed streams of happy couples getting married at San Francisco City Hall while reporters warned that this window of opportunity might not stay open long.

Sandy and I felt a sense of urgency to make our impending marriage legal, so I made an appointment at City Hall for Tuesday, February 17; we kept the kids home from school so they could accompany us. Luckily, my mom could come, too. Since the twins had been born, my mom, who now lived a few miles south of San Francisco, had come to our house every week to help with them. We'd come home from work to find dinner waiting, kids' homework done, and cookies in Tupperware. We would laugh sometimes about her exuberance in doing chores at our house, such as folding our underwear into little balls, reorganizing the cupboards, or throwing away things she didn't think we needed anymore. On February 17, she met us in the City Hall parking lot, where news trucks lined the curbs.

As we approached the steps to City Hall, Frank asked if we were going to be on the news. "Of course not!" we replied. Once we were inside, however, we discovered that Rosie O'Donnell was just ahead of us on the schedule, there to marry Kelli Carpenter. When the camera crews got a glimpse of our contingent in line behind Rosie and Kelli, we became the focus of their attention. Two moms, four boys, and a grandmother—this particular configuration hadn't been seen yet! We were on the local news that night, and a few weeks later, a *60 Minutes* segment included a shot of us getting married. This would not be the first time we underestimated the media!

When we arrived home that afternoon, we were greeted by a bouquet of flowers and a huge card signed by every teacher at Spencer and Elliott's elementary school. I had assumed our marriage would be met with the same indifference that our relationship had evoked over the past few years, so the outpouring of excitement and joy was astounding. I had not experienced this kind of public support before. Is this what happens to all couples when they get married?

I accepted the good wishes warily. I tend to be superstitious, and I didn't want to sabotage our happiness. The tension between wanting to share our joy with friends and family and the dread that something would interfere with it was based on years of experience; good things don't often happen to lesbians in love.

Although we had been planning our wedding for months, we had actually been planning for a celebration of our commitment—we hadn't expected to be celebrating our legal marriage. But on August 1, 2004, Sandy and I celebrated our legal marriage in front of a hundred loved ones. A string quartet played *Head over Feet* as I walked down the aisle with Spencer and Elliott. Sandy followed, Frank and Tom on each arm. She was radiant as she came toward me. The boys were beaming in tuxedos with tails—at their insistence—and black

Converse high-tops. We were so happy to declare our love and commitment to each other in front of our parents, siblings, and friends.

However, when we returned from our romantic honeymoon, a very nasty surprise was waiting for us. Among the unopened mail that had arrived while we'd been in Italy was a letter from the San Francisco city clerk. The form letter informed us that the February marriage had been voided. To add insult to injury, the letter asked if we would prefer that our $32 marriage license fee be refunded or donated to charity. We couldn't blame the city, though. The Supreme Court of California had ordered a halt to these marriages just one month after they started as a response to several groups that had sued the City and County of San Francisco. On August 12, the court voided all the licenses that had been issued during that month.

How could it be that we'd been married and unmarried in the space of six months? We were reeling from the emotional impact, and we felt a responsibility to all the teachers, friends, and family members who had supported our marriage, who had sent flowers, cards, gifts, and good cheer. Should we return the wedding gifts? Send everyone a note saying, "I know you thought we were married, now it turns out we're not." No etiquette book has a chapter on how to handle this kind of situation.

We were not legally married, but we had already owned two homes together, we had joined our finances, we filed and paid our taxes as domestic partners, we participated in each other's family functions, we laughed and we cried together. We often felt forced to downplay our status as a same-sex couple, such as when we attended school functions. In situations like those, we feared that the consequences of being legally unmarried could cause someone to discriminate against us or against the kids. We couldn't legally call ourselves married, but "being married" was the only phrase that described our relationship. Being the rule followers we are, we never said we were married. That was a long time to live a double life, imposed on us by a discriminatory law.

*First dance at our wedding in Tilden Park,
Berkeley, 2004.*

CHAPTER 15

Married in Every Way But One

Sandy

August 1, 2004, was the happiest of days, but it was preceded by the saddest.

My ex-husband and father of my beautiful boys had died ten days earlier. The call came late at night. One of his brothers was on the phone, saying, "You need to bring the boys to the hospital, Matt is alive but unconscious." He had fallen and hurt himself badly and had been taken by ambulance to the hospital, unidentified for hours, until a nurse who had known him from his swim team days identified him and called family. A loving but eventually very sick father, he lost his battle with alcohol addiction, dying of kidney and heart failure at the age of forty-seven. We made it to the hospital before he passed, but my boys were heartbroken. I was too. In the minivan on the way home from the hospital, the silence was deafening, punctuated by the quiet sobs of Frank, thirteen. Tom, fifteen, stared out the window with glazed eyes. How do you comfort your child in the wake of such a loss? The next day we talked about the wedding ceremony and whether we should postpone it. The boys' wishes would dictate the outcome. They numbly agreed that we should go ahead with the plan. We were all exhausted, but we chose as a family to move forward, to celebrate our marriage and embrace the future.

Ten days is not long enough to recover from losing your father. A lifetime is not long enough. The Friday before the wedding, the boys and I attended their father's funeral. It was held at the Catholic church that flanked the school they had attended since kindergarten. The church was packed with the families of many of those students, as well as their father's large extended family. Their dad's cousin performed the Mass, acknowledging the struggles Matt had faced, and the beautiful parts of him, too. At the luncheon that followed, Matt's Uncle Victor squeezed my hand, saying, "It sure is good to see you, even though I'm not talking to you." We were ragged with sorrow, but surrounded by so much love. I marveled at how grown-up Tom and Frank looked, so tall and slim in their dark suits and ties, wishing their dad could see how beautiful they were. We hugged old friends, some of whom we would see two days later at the wedding.

*   *   *

On Sunday, we woke up to a beautiful August morning, white clouds billowing against a bright blue sky. My sister and brother had arrived the night before, and Kris's father and stepmother had also made their way up to the Bay Area. Kris was beautiful in a simple combination of black pants and a white jacket; I wore a two-piece strapless white dress. We walked down the aisle, each flanked by our own sons clad in black tuxedos with tails (their choice) and matching black high-top Converse sneakers (ditto). The boys took their roles seriously. The setting was elegant and romantic, violins playing Alanis Morissette tunes while the fog rolled in. Our lesbian Buddhist friend Padmadharani married us as my "something borrowed" pale blue silk wrap billowed in the breeze, my "something old" engagement ring waited for its "something new" wedding band, and Kris beamed at my side.

Kris placed the ring, a simple platinum band with square diamonds, on my finger, and I placed a wider version of the same on hers. We had designed our rings and had them made by a local jeweler. My eyes were damp with tears as I said "I do."

While our guests dined on Mediterranean food, we walked around to the tables, chatting with family and friends. Kris's parents were in attendance, as were her stepsister and her adorable little daughter Georgie. Sharon and David, my two older siblings, had come from the Midwest, but my parents, younger sister, and other relatives had declined our invitation. Although my family attendance was sparse, our circle of friends wasn't, and I was happy. We danced our first dance to our favorite Damien Rice song, *The Blower's Daughter*: "and so it is, just like you said it would be . . . I can't take my eyes off of you."

Our sons joined us for the second dance. They had been strongly encouraged to dance with us. You might say forced. In fact, we told them they had to dance with us just once, during the second song. We had all taken a boxstep dance lesson from our friend Patricia. Her clear and authoritative instruction buoyed our attempts to make the boys comply, and they took turns dancing with us, counting quietly as they "led" us, saying, "I'm done, right?" at the end of the song. A proud moment for us, but it couldn't end fast enough for the boys. Sigh. That is the stuff of parenting.

There was dancing, more dancing, toasts. Spencer, age eight, was the one boy to give a speech. He embodied our hope and enthusiasm, quipping, "Everything worked out just perfect!" Perfection was hardly how we would have described our lives, but we had pulled it off. We had been married in the eyes of the law and in front of friends and family.

The day after the celebration, Sharon flew back to Chicago, taking my boys with her. Still reeling from the loss of their dad, they needed family, and hers was what the doctor ordered. A week with their cousins Katie, Laura, and Annie, all around the same age, would be a welcome change of scenery and a chance to practice driving on the quiet roads of Michigan, where they would be vacationing. The little boys went back to their other mother's home; a few days later, Kris and I went on a weeklong honeymoon.

After a lovely trip driving through the bucolic hills of Tuscany to the jagged coast of the Cinque Terre and then south to the chaos of Rome, we returned home to find an ominous envelope awaiting us. On August 12, the Supreme Court of California voided all the same-sex weddings that had occurred the previous winter. The form letter was brutal, offering to compensate us for our marriage license fee. We tried to absorb the stunning news.

In the eyes of anyone who looked at my ring finger, our marriage seemed legitimate. In the eyes of the law, however, it was not.

Even though we didn't have legal status, Kris and I felt married, our friends regarded us as married, and we behaved like a married couple. We had the trappings of an American family: a rambling home, four kids (in three different schools in three different cities), demanding careers, scattered families, lots of pizza. But legally, we were not a family with married parents. The fact that we did not have the same legal rights as married heterosexual couples continued to grate on us.

But life went on, as it does. The next few years were a whirlwind of school events, homework, and kids' sports. Our lives revolved around the boys' schedules and appetites. We joined Costco and cooked in volume. Our cat chose to move out of our hectic home to the local bookstore. We didn't blame him for leaving—in fact, we were surprised our neighbors weren't evacuating their homes, too. Every day, Tom practiced his skateboard moves on the patio, each crash louder than the last. When he wasn't flying into the concrete, he was blasting Nirvana out of his bedroom window. Frank joined the water polo team and found his tribe in the pool. Spencer and Elliott ran in packs of boys, bouncing soccer balls and scraping knees and elbows, hosting sleepovers in their tree fort by the creek.

Just to keep life interesting, Kris surprised me with a Chihuahua puppy on my birthday. I was surprised, all right. Never in my

---

Annullment: Although we and the rest of the gay community were thrilled by Gavin Newsom's decision to issue marriage licenses to same-sex couples, his action contravened what was then state law. For that reason, in August 2004 the Supreme Court of California annulled the marriages that Newsom had authorized. Nonetheless, Newsom had brought national attention to same-sex marriage and propelled the debate forward.

adult life had I uttered the words "I want a puppy." Or "I want a four-pound, hyperactive, jumping, peeing pet." I'm pretty sure I've gazed longingly at diamond earrings and sassy convertibles, but puppies? Not so much. Nevertheless, there he was on my big day, his big eyes dwarfing his tiny, quivering body. We named him Pablo, after Pablo Picasso. Kris had to convince me that naming him Jesus wasn't funny enough to make up for the flack I would get from my mom. Pablo was wildly adorable and wildly out of control. The boys loved him, even though he snatched food right out of their hands and nipped at their toes. He followed me everywhere, dogging me every single step I took. Every single one.

We had Pablo for several years before he was hit by a car. Never an intellectual, he had a penchant for racing out the front door whenever the door opened. It's a miracle he lived as long as he did. But when he died, a part of us died, too. Frank was despondent in his room, the little boys were in tears, and I was also inconsolable. Tom was in Mexico on a school trip, but he got the sad news from his brother. On the third day of our grieving, Elliott suggested that maybe if I sat on Kris's lap I would feel better. Kids have great ideas sometimes.

Tom went to college. The little boys moved through middle school. The shoes by the front door got bigger, and Kris and I lost our height advantage. The kids got hip to the fact that if they hung out in the hot tub with us, we would turn the conversation to school or girls, and they informed us that they wouldn't join us if we were going to pepper them with questions. Doors were slammed as independence kicked in, and we were kicked out of bedrooms. I became a sleuth, trying to unlock the mystery of what these boys were up to. Joining the parent governance council at Berkeley High seemed like a straight shot to the inside track of how the school ran and what daily life was like.

We were all growing older. Well into our forties, Kris and I were focused on our careers during the day and running the household the rest of the time. I joined the county health department as director of technology, and Kris became the executive director of a state agency to oversee the distribution of tobacco taxes designated to support early childhood health and education, under the administration of Governor Arnold Schwarzenegger. Having endured years of an onerous commute to San Mateo, she traded heavy traffic for distance, commuting nearly three hours each day to Sacramento and back.

I made yearly trips to Iowa with whoever could join me. Kris and I had stopped focusing on marriage. We had a living trust in our lockbox and life insurance in case something terrible happened. That was the best we could do. The boys referred to each other as stepbrothers. And I was a stepmom. But was I a wife?

PART II

Fighting for Our Rights

Protesters demonstrate against Prop 8 in front of the California State Capitol in Sacramento, 2008.

CHAPTER 16

The Ballot Box

Sandy

After Gavin Newsom briefly opened the window in 2004, the push for marriage equality started taking hold in fits and spurts. Canada. Massachusetts. Iowa. IOWA! It blew my mind and made me proud. Gay couples in Iowa were getting married! Iowa was becoming a gay destination-wedding state! It was a "pigs are flying" time in a state with a healthy population of pigs. My mom started joking about Iowa being ahead of California in her frequent "Are you sure you don't want to move back?" conversations. I consider my mom a pretty accurate bellwether as to how quickly the average American can adapt to change. So things were looking up.

While Iowa and Massachusetts were leading the way, California was trying to catch up. The group of cases known as *In re Marriage* wound its way through the courts, the lawyers arguing with eventual success that the state of California could not discriminate against same-sex couples in the issuance of marriage licenses. Kris and I were cautiously optimistic that progress was on the horizon.

On June 16, 2008, the Supreme Court of California ruled that same-sex marriage was legal in California. It was a celebratory time. In a period that became known as the "second window," loving couples lined up to get married throughout the state. However, a cloud hung over the otherwise festive atmosphere. It was an election year, with a charged electoral environment. Barack Obama was the Democratic Party's presidential candidate, with enthusiastic support from our household, and hope was not only in the air, but also on signs everywhere in our progressive Bay

Area neighborhood. The hope was tempered by the hateful rhetoric on lawn signs elsewhere and in the media from a campaign supporting a ballot measure, Proposition 8, that, if passed, would change the California Constitution to deny same-sex couples the right to marry.

Kris and I couldn't believe that our rights were being put to a vote and that the state constitution was at risk of being changed to enforce discrimination. The situation was surreal—I simply didn't believe Prop 8 had a chance of passing, while Kris was hopeful that Prop 8 would not pass but less optimistic than I was. The vile media campaign cast a pall over the joy that should have been as couples poured into San Francisco in the wake of the *In re Marriage* decision. We celebrated the marriages of friends with fervor, but we decided against going to City Hall for our own legal union. We still had a bad taste from the revocation of our marriage certificate in 2004, and we questioned whether the 2008 marriages would remain legal in the event that Prop 8 passed. I was also struggling to parent my younger son, Frank. Eighteen and a senior in high school, he had distanced himself from me, and indeed from all of us, and Kris and I felt the timing wasn't right to walk down the aisle again. We decided to wait out the election and plan our final marriage when we knew it would be a sure thing—a secure marriage that couldn't be taken away and wouldn't take away anything from our boys.

As the election approached, the propaganda was increasingly offensive: ads portrayed gay couples as harmful to children, a

---

The Turning Tide: By 2008, the cultural tide was firmly turning in support of marriage equality. In May of that year, the California Supreme Court ruled in the *In re Marriage* cases that the right of same-sex couples to marry was a constitutional right, opening a second window of opportunity for same-sex marriages. Even before the ruling came in, however, proponents of what would become Prop 8 started raising funds and collecting signatures for a ballot measure to deny this right. Prop 8—formally titled "Proposition 8: Eliminates the Right of Same-Sex Couples to Marry Initiative Constitutional Amendment"—was a response to the cultural shift. The November passage of Prop 8 by a narrow majority stopped us and tens of thousands of couples from being able to legally marry despite the fact that we were fully engaged (no pun intended), tax-paying California residents. But there was no turning back the clock on progress. LGBT couples in California had tasted equality in 2004 and again in 2008, and they were ready to fight for it.

menace to society. We were hurt and angry. I went with my friend Jennifer to wave "No on Prop 8" signs in front of the Grand Lake Theatre in Oakland, laughing with disbelief when an angry man in a passing car yelled out the window, "Why don't you marry a dog?" When I joined protesters on Telegraph Avenue in Berkeley, Frank called me to say a water polo teammate had driven by and seen me, Frank's "radical" mother. An outspoken kid himself, Frank seemed more amused than anything. Full of opinions, he followed current events and the political process closely; as a newly minted adult, he would be voting for the first time.

On November 4, 2008, we hit the polling station. I followed Frank to the voting booth, camera in hand, taking pictures as he entered it. He told me that if I didn't put the camera down, he wouldn't vote. I put it down. A meddling and possibly invasive mother, I asked how he voted when he emerged. He said he voted for Obama and against Prop 8. He was quick to add that he didn't vote that way for me, but did so because it was the right thing to do. I was cool with that, and in fact admired him for it.

That night was a tough one. Kris and I were glued to the television as the numbers scrolled across the screen. We were joyful as the results for Obama came in, the electoral count increasing as state after state weighed in. As the night wore on, though, it became clear that our optimism as far as our rights were concerned had been ill placed. The majority of our fellow Californians voted against equality.

Obama was in, and our rights were out. Obama had won comfortably. Prop 8 had a narrower margin of victory, but it had passed. The California Constitution would be changed to exclude us.

What a bittersweet moment. Kris and I cried, our tears a combination of joy and sorrow. Weeks later, we stayed home to watch the inauguration. I wore my nicest dress as Kris and I stood in our living room, saying the Pledge of Allegiance out loud and saluting our new president as second-class citizens.

Rob Reiner (left) and Chad Griffin.

CHAPTER 17

Can You Hold?

Kris

To continue our story, I need to turn back a few years. In 2000, I started working as the head of First 5 San Mateo County, entrusted with investing tobacco tax dollars to improve the lives of young children. For five years, I enjoyed one of the best professional experiences of my life. San Mateo County is in the heart of Silicon Valley, the hub of America's high-tech industry, which lies between San Jose and San Francisco, seventy-five miles to the north. Tech companies, local government, philanthropic organizations, and the local schools worked together to create a high quality of life for county residents, and First 5 funds were icing on the cake. During my tenure in San Mateo County, First 5 distributed more than $20 million for access to health and education services for the county's youngest residents.

The chair of the First 5 California Commission, which was funded by California's Proposition 10, was Rob Reiner, better known as the director of such Hollywood movies as *When Harry Met Sally, A Few Good Men,* and *The Princess Bride.* Prop 10 had passed in 1998 thanks to Rob's efforts, as well as those of political consultants Chad Griffin and Kristina Schake. Chad had met Rob and Michele Reiner in the mid-1990s, when Chad was a White House staffer for President Clinton. He had been tasked with helping Rob tour the White House to scout locations for an upcoming movie, *The American President.* A few years later, Chad left the White House to launch a consulting business in Los Angeles and lead the philanthropic and political work of the Reiners. Kristina had worked with the Reiners on a variety of causes, and she eventually joined Chad in the business, which became Griffin|Schake. Chad subsequently served as executive director of First 5 California, and Kristina was its communications director in the early days.

In 2005, I made the leap to state government when I was appointed executive director of First 5 California. I was ready for a change, and the downside of my new commute to Sacramento from Berkeley paled in comparison to the excitement of working with Rob and the commission. In June 2005, I took the helm of a state agency with more than one hundred employees, seven commissioners, and fifty-eight county commission partners, working with a legislature with a Democratic majority and, for most of my time there, a Republican governor. I was dismayed to realize that my experience in San Mateo had prepared me for policy and program challenges, but not for the reality of politics in the state capitol or the financial crises California was about to face (compliments of the dot-com bust).

I spent the next few years engaged in an annual struggle to protect First 5 California funds for their intended purpose; political forces kept trying to redirect dollars to fill holes in the state budget. Starting in 2005, transfers of as much as $50 million a year were made from First 5 California to the state. Many times during funding cycles, I would ask Chad and Rob to help me navigate the treacherous waters and salvage as much of its revenues as possible. Given their history with First 5, their relationships with political leaders, and their ongoing commitment to protect First 5, they could be counted on to step in when necessary.

By March 2009, California, like the rest of the country, was in a deep recession. I called Chad to ask for help. Could he or Rob ask Governor Schwarzenegger to please stop pilfering First 5 money before First 5's entire reserve was gone?

As always, Chad was a sympathetic interlocutor: responsive, inquisitive, and ready to act. I reminded him about the hundreds of millions of dollars that had been moved from the First 5 account to the state budget to fill holes in health programs that were the responsibility of the state during my tenure as executive director. I cited the impact on the programs Rob had launched and the need for the shell games to stop.

As Chad and I were ending our conversation, I mentioned that Sandy and I had seen the documentary *Outrage* the night before. Chad was listed as an executive producer. (What couldn't he do?) I told him how much we had enjoyed the film.

He said wanted to tell me about a new project Griffin|Schake was working on with the Reiners to launch a public education campaign to raise awareness of the importance of marriage equality in the wake of the passage of Prop 8.

Chad asked me, "Did you and Sandy get married during the window?"

I knew he meant did we get married in 2008, before the election. I replied, "No, we couldn't go through it again." We couldn't bear the thought of getting married again only to have it reversed by the courts or the voters.

He paused then, and he asked, "Can you hold?"

I waited on hold for several minutes—very unlike Chad to leave someone hanging like this! Normally calls with him were quick and to the point; this was out of character.

Finally, Chad came back on the line. He apologized for the hold and said he'd gone to talk to Kristina, and they had agreed they wanted to share a little more with me about their marriage equality campaign plan. In addition to the public awareness aspects he'd already told me about, they were close to finalizing a plan to pursue a legal remedy.

Chad started talking faster in his faint Southern accent, and I realized I needed to take some notes to keep track of what he was saying. Chad explained that in early 2009 he had met with Ted Olson—a conservative attorney with an illustrious career arguing in front of the US Supreme Court—who had expressed interest in challenging Prop 8. Olson said he would join the legal team under one condition. He insisted on inviting David Boies—a liberal attorney with an impressive career who had been Olson's opponent in *Bush v. Gore*—to act as co-counsel. (In that case, on which nothing less than the outcome of the 2000 presidential election hinged, Boies had represented Al Gore, and Olson had represented George W. Bush. Bush subsequently appointed Olson US solicitor general.)

With Boies on board, the Reiners were starting a round of fundraising to launch the case, and Chad and Kristina were going to form a new nonprofit to coordinate all the above. But there was a problem: they couldn't find plaintiffs. They wanted to enlist a few "regular" couples to meet with reporters, to give interviews, and to share their stories of wanting to wed. But this was proving more difficult than they had anticipated. There were plenty of outstanding examples of committed, loving relationships, but when confronted with the time commitment and exposure of their personal lives, those couples had declined to join the case. By now, Chad told me, time was running out on the self-imposed deadline to take legal action in the spring. The team knew that other advocates and attorneys were likely looking at the constitutionality of Prop 8 and were considering a federal challenge as well. Ted and David were pushing Chad to complete the search; they knew that it would be helpful to be the first to file, to ensure that the full force of the strength of David's firm combined with Ted's firm would be supported by fundraising led by Rob and Michele and the brilliant strategies of Chad and Kristina. It would take the efforts of many to win not only in court but also in the court of public opinion.

The entire case sounded like a long shot to me. How could they pull off what Chad was saying? How could the courts fix the fallout from Prop 8? How could two straight attorneys from opposite political parties make sure that gay people had the right to marry?

I told Chad that I also wanted Prop 8 undone. I wished him well, and I was about to hang up when he said, "I have a question. Would you and Sandy consider joining the team? Would you be willing to be plaintiffs in this case?"

"Plaintiffs, in a case challenging Prop 8?"

How do you answer a question like that?

After a pause, all I could think to say was, "I have to talk to Sandy."

We hung up, and I stared at my computer screen. It was only lunchtime, but I called Sandy and asked her to come home early that afternoon. Sandy knew well the problems First 5 faced. I think she thought I had yet more bad news on that front and couldn't talk about it from the office.

As I drove back to Berkeley from Sacramento, seventy-five long miles, I turned the idea around in my head. How would being plaintiffs in a case like this reflect on our kids, on our parents, on our careers? Would we be able to juggle yet one more thing in our very busy lives? With each turn of the prism, I would come back to the team Chad had assembled and the possibility of undoing Prop 8.

When Sandy arrived home, I was waiting in the dining room. It was one of those rare afternoons when none of the boys was home. The sun shone through the window onto the hardwood floors. I sat in the chair that faced my grandfather's painting; Sandy sat across from me. She looked nervous, almost scared.

We spent the afternoon trying to absorb the question and consider the possible answers. What if we could restore the right to be married and then get married once and for all? If we could be a part of that solution, that vision, I wanted to help. I had wanted to be married on Indian Rock, I had wanted to be married at San Francisco City Hall, and I had wanted to be married in Tilden Park in Berkeley. Now I wanted to be married because not being married was intolerable.

Sandy concluded, "Yes, we can do this. It's the right thing to do."

I smiled at her. "The boys have to agree, too, or we can't go forward; there might be some attention on them."

We both knew why that would be hard. Frank was at the end of his senior year in high school. The high school years hadn't been easy. Tom had moved to Santa Barbara for college two years earlier, and Frank was biding his time at home. The twins were in eighth grade, not really little boys anymore. We had our work cut out for us—tracking down all four boys to talk to each one individually as they ran in and out on their way to school, water polo, soccer, fencing, and friends. I thought convincing Sandy would be the hard part!

I called Chad the next day and gave him a qualified yes. We needed to talk to the boys, and he needed to run thorough background checks on us. I gave him our social security numbers, address, dates of birth, and Sandy's maiden name. He said the process would take several days. I said I needed at least that long too, and we both laughed.

It took us two weeks to talk with the boys. One by one, each agreed we should do it. By the time I called Chad to tell him the six of us were on board, he had the background reports in hand. We had passed the vetting process.

I was standing on our back deck, looking at the redwood tree in our neighbor's yard and our picnic table decorated with the clay heads the boys had made in art class—what Sandy calls "patio art." The sun was shining when Kristina came on the line and said, "We'd be so happy if you and Sandy would be plaintiffs in the case."

Nothing has been the same since. Our relationships to each other, to our kids, to our family, and to our friends all have been affected by our decision in ways we never could have anticipated. What mattered that day was that we had a chance to change the lives of Californians denied the right to marry—and that we might finally be legally wed for good.

We were about to tackle the California Constitution. Bring it on. I was tired of holding.

*Ted Olson announces the legal challenge to Prop 8
at a press conference, San Francisco, 2009.*

CHAPTER 18

The Dream Team

Sandy

We agreed to say yes to being plaintiffs pending the unanimous agreement of all four boys. Frank's response was quick and positive; he had a heightened awareness of the issue, having voted for the first time the prior November. Tom, immersed in his second year of college life, gave a thumbs-up during a rushed phone call. I was almost surprised, not that they said yes to fighting Prop 8 in court, but that they said yes so quickly. My boys' debate skills had been honed on me. I was exhausted from raising teenagers and relieved that they were so supportive. The little boys, not so little anymore, were more of the same, enthusiastic and inquisitive, relating the issue to *Brown v. Board of Education*, which they had learned about that spring. We didn't ask our parents or siblings; only the boys would have a voice. And that voice was clear: Sure!

To effectively challenge Prop 8, however, it wasn't enough for us to tell the lawyers we wanted to be married. We had to apply for a marriage license and be turned down. So it was that on a quiet day in May 2009 we met Enrique Monagas, the youngest of our lawyers, at a café near the Alameda County Clerk-Recorder's Office, where marriage licenses are issued. One of the few gay attorneys at the firm and newly married himself, Enrique was as bright eyed and bushy tailed as they come. Over coffee, we bonded over our new adventure and then headed in to apply for a marriage license, knowing the clerk would have no choice but to deny it. The building was familiar to both Kris and me; we had both worked there years before.

Walking into the lobby, we waited our turn and then approached the friendly clerk, asking her to issue a marriage license as we presented our identification. A sweet, middle-aged African American woman with curly henna-tipped hair, she said she was very sorry that she couldn't issue a license to us and that she wanted her manager to come and tell us why. Moments later, her manager approached, nervously apologizing for the fact that the law had changed; he asked us to return some day when they could issue marriage licenses to same-sex couples. We felt badly for them. Clearly, this was a very uncomfortable part of their job. It's hard to feel good about discrimination.

Late that Friday afternoon, the last business day before Memorial Day, Enrique quietly filed suit in the district court challenging Prop 8. Our legal team knew it was only a matter of time before someone challenged Prop 8 in federal court, and they wanted to make sure they would be the first, knowing the advantage that would bring. It would be months before we realized that Kris's surname was in fact part of the case name: *Perry v. Schwarzenegger*.

The following week, we flew to Los Angeles to meet our coplaintiffs and the legal team. A handsome couple a decade younger than us, Jeff and Paul were youthful and freewheeling. We would come to regard them as family, but at this moment, we were fumbling strangers. We met in a hotel lobby, and the four of us were photographed together, in couples and individually, as the media team prepared to announce the case. Photos complete, we headed to the Los Angeles office of Gibson, Dunn & Crutcher to meet our lawyers.

When Kris first told me about the invitation to become plaintiffs, and about the legal team that would be leading the fight, I

Our Coplaintiffs Jeff Zarrillo and Paul Katami: Homeowners in their thirties, Jeff and Paul lived in Burbank, a dozen miles northwest of downtown Los Angeles, with their darling little pugs. Jeff was a manager for AMC Movies, while Paul was in the fitness industry. They looked every bit as Hollywood as they sound. Fit and handsome, they were also fun and friendly. I had to continually resist the urge to behave maternally toward them, feeling our differences in age acutely.

didn't have the foggiest idea who Ted Olson or David Boies was, but I certainly knew about *Bush v. Gore*. I was intimidated by the prospect of our famous duo, particularly the conservative Olson. A quick Google search turned up article after article about legal victories and political engagements and a history of supporting causes and leaders that I was opposed to. I found it curious that he was on the right side of marriage equality and had publicly supported it. Even more curious was the prospect of Ted Olson teaming up with David Boies, who had been the opposing counsel in *Bush v. Gore*. We were intrigued by the combination, but we had faith in Chad and Rob's belief that this strategic partnership was critical to winning. Over the years, Ted and David had managed to obtain many Supreme Court rulings in their favor. Surely this was a good sign.

So as we entered the elegant suite that June day, we were intrigued but also shy. Ted and David were seated at a large conference table. Stately in appearance, they greeted us warmly and got down to business quickly. They explained why they took the case, the case strategy, and what they hoped to achieve for us, for California, and for the country. Fierce advocates of civil rights, with a resolute dedication to justice and the US Constitution, they were no strangers to each other or to the high court. A former solicitor general of the United States, Ted had argued more than sixty cases before the Supreme Court, including *Bush v. Gore*, winning the majority of them. David's progressive political leanings were more aligned with our own. He had also seen his fair share of Supreme Court victories, and he was known for his razor-sharp mind and incisive skill in the courtroom.

We were wowed by the legal team and more than a bit intimidated. Actually a huge bit, though "huge" and "bit" don't go well together. The combination of Ted and David and the full support of a prestigious legal firm, coupled with the pending media blitz, felt momentous. My normally chatty self faded into a softer and more somber persona. We had been asked not to share anything about the case prior to the announcement to the media, and I felt sneaky complying. Within minutes of the press release, our phones were ringing with calls from reporters. Per the instructions of the team, we forwarded all inquiries to the media staff at the newly formed American Foundation for Equal Rights, relieved to do so.

After an initial flurry of media activity, things quieted down. Spencer and Elliott, now fourteen and taller than Kris and me, graduated from middle school; the next week, Frank, the family athlete and fearless leader of the Berkeley High barbeque club, graduated from high school. We were a family in transition, busy with ceremonies and parties, packing and reorganizing, and always work, work, work. Kris was commuting three hours a day to her Sacramento job during a state budget crisis. I was spending my free time at Berkeley High attending graduation planning and school governance meetings.

We often managed to get a few days at a family friend's vacation home at the beach, and that summer was no exception. In Bolinas, perched on the edge of the world, we invited friends out to share the view and the rambling beach house with Adirondack chairs perfectly positioned to see the twinkling lights of San Francisco on rare fogless evenings. One night, our friends Nancy and Olivia joined us. Champagne and Tomales Bay oysters were first, second, and third courses for us, the boys opting for pasta and ending the evening with s'mores. I interrogated Nancy, a lawyer for the city of San Francisco, about how the Ninth Circuit operates.

Where is the court? How big is it? How is it laid out? What happens in a hearing, and how long does it take? What is the judge like?

Nancy patiently answered my questions until Kris implored me to stop. Relieved that our role in this case would be limited to sitting quietly and listening, we approached our first court date with excitement.

CHAPTER 19

Toughening Up for Trial

Kris

When Sandy and I agreed to be plaintiffs, we had jobs that were more than full time, four boys, a big old house that cried out for attention as much as the kids did, and friends and family we loved to spend time with. We did have some flexibility in our schedules. Our vacation balances had grown with our seniority at our jobs, and the boys had grown too. Tom had already left the nest, Frank was a senior in high school, and Spencer and Elliott were finishing eighth grade. We finally had some free time in our lives—but not much.

Given the limited amount of time we had, we based our decision to be plaintiffs on the premise that we would be plaintiffs primarily in name only. The plaintiffs in previous marriage cases in California and in other states had shared their stories of love and discrimination with lawyers and a few reporters, providing authentic examples of lives lived as second-class citizens to balance out the dry legal arguments necessary to argue for equality. Chad wanted help influencing the public to be more supportive of same-sex couples while the legal team fought the case in court. We would lend our names to the legal briefs prepared by Ted and David, but other than that we would be able to maintain our lives, albeit with periodic interruptions for court dates and press interviews.

By 2009, many of the marriage cases across the country had focused on challenging whether a state could amend its constitution to ban same-sex marriage. We were doing that too, but we were also challenging a more fundamental legal issue: can laws passed directly by voters or state legislatures be challenged in federal court based on the argument that they violate the constitutional rights of some citizens? For almost one hundred years, Californians had supported "direct democracy," where voters file propositions that become law if the majority of voters pass them. This process can lead to a majority discriminating against a minority who then require protection from their own state; hence the need for more than one branch of government. In lieu of a costly political campaign, the legal challenge was launched. The argument in our case would be that we had had a constitutional right for a brief time, and then it had been taken away. The briefs Ted and David planned to file would rely on other marriage cases, such as *Loving v. Virginia,* to argue that marriage is a fundamental right of the individual and that a state does *not* have a right to marry only those the state approves of. Our lawyers would also rely on the Fourteenth Amendment of the US Constitution, which states: "No State shall make or enforce any law which shall abridge the privileges or immunities of citizens of the United States; nor shall any State deprive any person of life, liberty, or property, without due process of law; nor deny to any person within its jurisdiction the equal protection of the laws."

Around the same time that we began working with the legal team, the nonprofit American Foundation for Equal Rights (AFER) was formed to coordinate the litigation, public education, and fundraising to cover the legal costs associated with the case. Ted's and David's law firms would contribute considerable pro bono efforts, but their support alone could not cover the cost of the trial. AFER would drive a full-scale, national public education campaign to grow support in favor of same-sex marriage by emphasizing the ordinariness of same-sex couples. This campaign would create the backdrop for the legal arguments showing that we deserved protection under the Fourteenth Amendment for equal access to life, liberty, and the pursuit of happiness.

Loving v. Virginia: This 1967 landmark civil rights case invalidated laws that prohibited interracial marriage.

As the legal gears were set in motion, Sandy and I waited for an invitation from AFER to share our story with the press. Waging a public education campaign at the same time as the legal battle was unusual for same-sex marriage cases. AFER modeled its approach on political campaigns and an election-style strategy to win over the public and the judges as a way of guarding against a bad outcome in court. If we didn't win in federal court, then maybe we could win in the court of public opinion. This was a very different approach from the one employed in the *In re Marriage* cases, where the court ruled that state statutes limiting marriage to opposite-sex applicants violated the California Constitution. To win those cases, Therese Stewart and Dennis Herrera, from the San Francisco City Attorney's Office, along with the National Center for Lesbian Rights and plaintiff Karen Strauss, fought the ban on same-sex marriage in California by focusing on changing the minds of the judges with legal arguments. With limited resources, however, it was difficult to wage a campaign to influence public opinion at the same time.

While we were getting a crash course in the American legal process and the role we would be playing, other issues were unfolding. California's attorney general, Democrat Jerry Brown, chose not to defend the lawsuit; he agreed that Prop 8 violated the due process and equal protection clauses of the Fourteenth Amendment and therefore should be struck down. Republican governor Arnold Schwarzenegger also declined to participate in the defense of Prop 8, while encouraging the court to resolve the matter quickly. A few years later, Brown was elected governor and Kamala Harris was elected attorney general. Both ran on platforms promising not to defend the proposition, although it had been passed by a majority of the voters, and the state continued to decline to defend Prop 8 in court.

With the state unwilling to defend the proposition, two groups decided to take on the task themselves: the official proponents of Prop 8, ProtectMarriage.com and the Campaign for California's Children. We referred to them collectively as "the other side."

As if it wasn't odd enough that the top elected officials in the state wouldn't defend a law passed by a majority, my anxiety was enhanced by my role as executive director of First 5 California, a state agency directly connected to Governor Schwarzenegger (and then later to Governor Brown), an agency whose employees were mostly civil servants who had spent their careers working in state government. Up to that point, I had lived a bifurcated life, working in Sacramento and living in Berkeley, two cities separated by seventy-five miles and vastly different lifestyles. To say that I felt like a fish out of water in Sacramento is an understatement. Although I was open at the office about my relationship with Sandy and our life in Berkeley, my focus there was on navigating the political currents that swept up the legislators and the governor's office. It was *not* advantageous for First 5 California or for me to draw attention to my sexual orientation or to *Perry v. Schwarzenegger*. In fact, I'm certain that a handful of First 5 staff were unhappy with and unsupportive of my role as a plaintiff, and I think some found positions in other agencies or resigned rather than be associated with me at that time. On the flip side, far more staff members and commissioners were very supportive of me personally during that time and went to great lengths to let me know. My appreciation for them is immense. Unfortunately, my desire to not make others uncomfortable was ultimately upended by our very public role in the case and by the fact that the case, named *Perry v. Schwarzenegger*, pitted me directly against my employer, the state of California.

Chapter 20

Perry v. Schwarzenegger

Sandy

On June 30, 2009, Kris and I drove across the San Francisco–Oakland Bay Bridge for our initial court date at the US District Court for the Northern District of California in San Francisco. We had some apprehension about how the public and the media would treat us, but that was second to our curiosity about what would happen in the courtroom.

We first went to the Mission Street offices of our lawyers so we could all drive to court together. We had dined with our team, including board members and public relations staff from AFER, our lawyers, and Jeff and Paul, the night before. Once we were in the courtroom, Kris and I were ushered into the second row, behind the lawyers; Jeff and Paul were nearest the aisle on our left; and Chad was on our right. Like at a wedding, our team and our supporters were on one side of the courtroom while the proponents of Prop 8 and their smaller band of enthusiasts were on the other side. The courtroom came to a hush as the stately Chief Judge Vaughn Walker (hereafter referred to as Judge Walker) entered the courtroom. Judge Walker was widely respected by the court and the public. His political views didn't exactly square with our own, but we had been assured by our counsel that he was deeply principled and fair.

The court was brought to order at precisely ten o'clock, with all rising as the judge entered the courtroom and sitting after he had seated himself. After a warm but perfunctory welcome, there were introductions all around. Lawyer after lawyer introduced himself or herself by name and announced whom he or she was representing; it was a formal affair in a very imposing room. After the lawyers stated the basic tenets of their arguments, Judge Walker addressed the lawyers.

The first order of business was who would be representing whom in the case. Although the case was filed as *Perry v. Schwarzenegger*, it was really all four of us (Kris and me, Jeff and Paul) against the state of California. The state of California declined to argue the case, Attorney General Brown firmly on the side of equal rights and Governor Schwarzenegger right there with him, but the state supported the court in hearing the case. That left the court in an awkward position, one that was remedied when lawyers for those who had funded the massive media campaign and fought for the passage of Prop 8—and whom we referred to as the "proponents" of Prop 8—requested that the court allow them to intervene and represent the people because the state of California had declined to do so. Judge Walker heard the argument to intervene but clarified the context in which it would occur. He addressed counsel and said that he felt that a full presentation of the facts would be necessary for the court to come to a judgment. A full presentation of the facts—in other words, a trial.

We stopped breathing for just a moment. A trial? Who had said anything about a trial?

I wasn't the only one shocked by this turn of events. I turned to Theane Evangelis, one of the few women on the team, and whispered, "Will we have to testify?"

Wide-eyed, but without skipping a beat, she nodded her head and whispered that she thought so.

Until that moment, we had expected and had been advised that our role would be passive. The lawyers would present their respective statements of facts and a ruling would be made. I had relied on our friend Nancy Tavernit, San Francisco City Attorney, for an explanation of that scenario, embarrassed to ask our own lawyers too many questions. We were stunned by the notion of a trial, but the lawyers were thrilled. There would be an opportunity to bring facts and evidence into the courtroom to prove that harm was being done to thousands of same-sex couples and individuals. There had been campaigns and plenty of rhetoric up to now, but the facts? Not so much.

We returned to court two days later, on July 2, for a hearing for preliminary injunction (to temporarily lift the ban on same-sex marriage), the motions to intervene (who would be allowed to defend Prop 8), and case management (the timeline of the case). Judge Walker granted the motion to intervene, which meant that we officially had an "other" side. On the issue of the trial, he provided additional context for his earlier decision:

JUDGE WALKER: And in that connection, there are, as indicated in the June 30 order, a lot of factual questions, a lot of factual assertions have been made. Now, this is a trial court, this is not the Supreme Court of the United States where we deal with these boxcar philosophical issues. We deal with facts; we deal with evidence; we deal with testimony of witnesses. And to the extent there are factual issues, I think we need to proceed in the way in which a trial court proceeds to deal with those issues, to present the facts, to present the evidence, and to make what determinations are necessary.

. . .

I say all of this because I'm reasonably sure, given the issues involved and given the personnel that are in the courtroom, that this case is only touching down in this court, that it will have a life after and what happens here, in many ways, is only a prelude to what is going to happen later.

So I am inclined to think that how we do things here is more important than what we do, that our job in this case, at this point, is to make a record. And I want to give the plaintiffs, the defendants, and the intervenors the opportunity to make the record that they think is appropriate for the decision. And so I think we've got our work cut out for us. But, I'd like to invite counsel to tell me how they wish to proceed.

First, I should turn to the plaintiffs with respect to the motion for preliminary injunction; anything further that you wish to say in support of that?

Mr. Olson?

MR. OLSON: Your Honor, thank you.

Let me say, preliminarily, that we understand and appreciate, respect the wisdom of your Honor's June 30th order as you have articulated it again today. We accept it, and we are prepared to go forward on that basis.

We, or rather our counsel, had our marching orders. It was game on; we had opposing counsel and a trial to prepare for.

During the summer, the media focused on the legal action and the players, particularly the unlikely duo of Ted and David, the bipartisan team fighting for gay rights. The media loved the story, and our lawyers loved the media right back, happy to explain to reporters how and why they supported marriage equality for all. After June graduations, July summer fun, and "Fogust" (August in the Bay Area) transitions back to school and college, we got back to the business of the case.

On October 13, 2009, we drove to San Francisco for the motion for a summary judgment hearing that the proponents had requested. The summary judgment hearing would allow the lawyers on both sides to present their case to the judge and get a ruling immediately (unless the judge thought all the arguments needed to be heard in a full trial before he could come to a decision). It promised a quick resolution to our lawsuit, if everything went as planned.

As the court came to order, Judge Walker invited opposing counsel to state why it was seeking a summary judgment, why a full trial was unnecessary. Chuck Cooper, impeccably dressed and with slicked-back gray hair parted in the middle, represented the proponents. Speaking in a slow Southern drawl, he addressed the court:

MR. COOPER: We say that the central and defining purpose of marriage is to channel naturally procreative sexual activity between men and women into stable, enduring unions for the sake of begetting, nurturing, and raising the next generation.

Plaintiffs say that the central and the constitutionally mandated purpose of marriage is simply to provide formal government recognition to loving, committed relationships. And, in keeping with that purpose, the plaintiffs say that they have a fundamental constitutional right to marry the person of their choice; to marry the person that they love.

I thought Mr. Cooper was on target. We did indeed believe we had a constitutional right to marry the person we loved. I thought that his argument was a tad simplified, though, and I was pretty sure that "they" didn't marry for the sole purpose of procreation. Apparently, the judge didn't either:

THE COURT [in other words, Judge Walker]: Well, the last marriage that I performed, Mr. Cooper, involved a groom who was 95 and the bride was 83. I did not demand that they prove that they intended to engage in procreative activity.

Now, was I missing something?

MR. COOPER: No, your Honor, you weren't. Of course, you didn't.

THE COURT: And I might say it was a very happy relationship.

MR. COOPER: I'm very—I rejoice to hear that, your Honor.

I was filled with joy. Not only because the truth was right there but also because our judge had a sense of humor. We got a funny judge! Who knew that was even possible? Despite his austere appearance, with his regal carriage and silver hair, Judge

Walker knew how to make the business of law amusing. In a federal courtroom. A judge after my own heart!

Mr. Cooper continued:

Our point is the institution of marriage, like other in-
stitutions that states establish, that governments establish and they bring into being to serve certain important
societal interests—

THE COURT: Well, apropos that, what is the difference,
from the point of view of the state, between an opposite-
sex marriage and a same-sex marriage? From the state's
point of view, how are they different?

MR. COOPER: Your Honor, they're different in one fundamental respect, with respect to this purpose, this—the
central purposes that we cite to you for the institution
of marriage: it's simple biological reality that same-sex
couples do not naturally procreate. Opposite-sex couples—that is the—the natural outcome of sexual activity
between opposite-sex couples.

THE COURT: Well, fair enough; but procreation doesn't
require marriage.

MR. COOPER: No. No, your Honor, it doesn't; but the
state's purpose—

I'm no lawyer, but I was pretty sure that procreation wasn't going to be the winning argument in this case. Kris and I were solid proof that you don't have to be a straight couple to be a family. And it seemed unlikely that Mr. Cooper was in the actively procreating class of married people; his wife of many years was seated in the audience alongside one of their adult children. His argument was keeping the onlookers engaged, however. What's not to love about a discussion of procreation?

Minutes later, Judge Walker chastised Mr. Cooper to "come down off the mountain for a moment, and talk about a little law," referring to a 1987 Supreme Court decision that allowed incarcerated individuals access to marriage. Judge Walker quoted Justice Sandra O'Connor in that decision:

Justice O'Connor wrote,

The right to marry, like many other rights, is subject to substantial restrictions as a result of incarceration. Many important attributes of marriage remain, however, after taking into account the limitations imposed by prison life. First, inmate marriages, like others, are expressions of emotional support and public commitment. These elements are an important and significant aspect of the marital relationship. In addition, many religions recognize marriage as having spiritual significance for some inmates and their spouses. Therefore, the commitment of marriage may be an exercise of religious faith as well as an expression of personal dedication. Third, most inmates eventually will be released by parole or commutation, and therefore, most inmate marriages are formed in the expectation that they will ultimately be fully consummated. Finally, marital status often is a precondition to the receipt of government benefits, and so forth.

Buoyed by the hope that Kris and I might someday have access to the same rights as our incarcerated brothers and sisters, we kept a watchful eye on both Judge Walker and Mr. Cooper. A civilized debate for sure, but Mr. Cooper didn't appear to be on the winning end. He stumbled in response:

MR. COOPER: And—and, your Honor, there's no—and this does get back to my earlier point. There is no purpose of marriage—there is no definition of marriage that would—that would offer clear and dividing lines between those people who enter into it, and—and its purposes; even this purpose that the—and maybe I should say especially this purpose that the plaintiffs cite as being the central purpose of marriage: to recognize loving, committed relationships. Even that can't possibly be restricted to only those couples who can fulfill that purpose or who intend to fulfill that purpose.

I began to wonder if Mr. Cooper was going to provide more support for our argument than his own, a theme we would see over and over again on this day and much later.

THE COURT: I'm asking you to tell me how it [same-sex marriage] would harm opposite-sex marriages.

MR. COOPER: All right.

THE COURT: All right. Let's play on the same playing field for once. Okay.

MR. COOPER: Your Honor, my answer is: I don't know. I don't know.

THE COURT: Does that mean—does that mean if this is not determined to be subject to rational basis review, you lose?

MR. COOPER: No, your Honor.

THE COURT: Okay.

MR. COOPER: I don't believe it—it does.

THE COURT: Just haven't figured out how you're going to win on that basis yet?

The words "I don't know. I don't know" would haunt Mr. Cooper. They would be repeated back to him time and time again, and he would rue the day he spoke them. When he uttered them, we were shocked. You could hear the collective gasp in the courtroom as we all realized that the proponents had no argument. No real argument for how giving equal access to marriage to couples

---

Rational Basis: In US constitutional law, rational basis review refers to the default standard of review that courts apply when considering constitutional questions, including due process and equal protection questions under the Fifth Amendment or the Fourteenth Amendment.

like us would harm their own marriages. Chuck Cooper himself couldn't articulate this argument. Wow!

Kris and I went from wide-eyed shock to ear-to-ear grins, squeezing each other's hands from our second-row bench seats. We shared furtive glances with our extended AFER family.

The exchange between Mr. Cooper and Judge Walker continued, Mr. Cooper insisting he could prove that "sexual orientation is not immutable, and gays and lesbians are not politically powerless."

Hmmm. I begged to differ, as would our counsel in no short order. Mr. Cooper was out of step with the real world on this one—not only Mr. Cooper but also his Alliance Defense Fund colleagues, conservatives among conservatives. They were an angry-looking bunch, clearly annoyed by the pushback Mr. Cooper's arguments had received from the court. It made me smile. Oh, the joy of being on the winning team!

Finally, Judge Walker thanked Mr. Cooper for his remarks and invited Ted to speak. Ted dove right into the issues and cases that had just been discussed: interracial marriage, a prisoner's right to marriage, the Defense of Marriage Act (DOMA), and domestic partnership. Judge Walker debated Ted as vigorously as he had Mr. Cooper, challenging him on his assertion that the case belonged in federal court and prompting Ted to refer to the similarity between our case and *Loving v. Virginia*:

JUDGE WALKER:That gets to the point that Mr. Cooper made repeatedly and very ably; and that is, with all of the changes that are going on in the states that are, one by one, recognizing same-sex marriage, and the expansion of domestic-partnership rights, and so forth, aren't you just getting ahead of yourself by asserting this claim under the federal constitutional provisions?

MR. OLSON: Well, that would be exactly the same argument that was made and was rejected in *Loving versus Virginia*.

THE COURT: Well, but at that time, if I remember correctly, only about a third of the states prohibited interracial marriage at that time. Is that not correct?

MR. OLSON: That's correct, but there was a trend in the direction of states eliminating those prohibitions that were—the US Supreme Court held to be unconstitutional.

THE COURT: Right.

MR. OLSON: We don't say to the people in this country, "Wait until the population agrees that your constitutional rights can be recognized."

THE COURT: But what makes a single Federal District judge in San Francisco able to recognize these profound constitutional principles that 52 or 53 percent of the people of the State of California could not?

MR. OLSON: That is why you are there. And that is why we have a federal Constitution. That is why we have a federal judiciary. And that is the obligation that's given to you when you took the oath of office.

Ted noted that even arch-conservative Justice Scalia had pointed out that procreation had nothing to do with the right to marry in his dissent in *Lawrence v. Texas,* the case in which the Supreme Court struck down the sodomy law in Texas:

MR. OLSON: That exhaustive presentation of arguments and the arguments that Mr. Cooper, as you said, very articulately made today are virtually identical to the very same points made by Justice Scalia in his opinions in Romer and Lawrence, but those were dissenting opinions. [. . .] And at the end of his dissenting opinion, Justice Scalia said [. . .], "What justification could there possibly be for denying the benefit of marriage to homosexual couples exercising the liberty protected by the Constitution? Surely not the encouragement of procreation," he added, "since the sterile and the elderly are allowed to marry."

JUDGE WALKER: Perhaps it shows why dissenters shouldn't always write an opinion?

MR. OLSON: It hasn't discouraged Justice Scalia.

As much as I respect him, he was outvoted in those two cases, but he was right about that point. What is the justification?

We do have a difference—Mr. Cooper and I—with respect to this right of marriage that the Supreme Court has mentioned over and over again, and has said is among the most fundamental rights, if not the most fundamental right. It is a right of the individual. It is not a right granted by the state. It's a right of an individual.

Judge Walker allowed Ted to continue this argument for a short time before interrupting to inquire about rational basis and the decades-old public sentiment and argument for tradition over change. Ted responded to the concept of tradition over change by insisting that "the state has to establish a rational basis for the exclusion of those individuals."

Ted continued to undermine Mr. Cooper's argument by calling out its ludicrousness:

MR. OLSON: The other part of what Mr. Cooper says is that if you can envision any conceivable argument at all, then—then the prohibition on same-sex marriage must stand. That's not the test.[. . .] California doesn't want its citizens to have rights in California, and then be denied those rights in other states.

I could go through the various points that were made by our opponents in their brief about what the rational basis would be. They don't make any sense.

What does—what—the reason why they keep coming back to procreation and the raising of children is that that might be a rational basis, but it doesn't work in terms of excluding individuals who wish to marry someone of the same sex, because procreation doesn't require marriage, as your question pointed out. Marriage doesn't yield pro-creation.

Same-sex marriage does not dilute, diminish, inhibit, or deter opposite-sex persons from getting marriage.

And the prohibition of same-sex marriage doesn't mean that individuals who would prefer to be married to some-one of the same sex is going to go out and marry someone of the opposite sex, produce children, and raise them in a happy relationship. . . . You asked the point: if you had to prove that there was a harm by allowing same-sex marriages to exist alongside heterosexual marriages, what would that harm be?

And I think I heard Mr. Cooper say he didn't know.

Now, he's spent a lot of time on this case. And I don't know, either, what the harm could be to heterosexual mar-riages by allowing same-sex marriage. What it comes back to is the phrase that you see over and over again in the briefs of my opponents: the traditional definition of mar-riage.

JUDGE WALKER: Tradition is not an unimportant consider-ation when it comes to interpreting constitutional prin-ciples.

MR. OLSON: It is not.

Ted ended his opening statements clearly delineating the fun-damental problem he hoped the court would address:

What California has done is created a classification—individuals who are gay or lesbian—and put them in a different status with respect to rights accorded by the state of California: recognition of the fundamental right of marriage.

That is constitutionally impermissible. It violates the Due Process clause, and it violates the Equal Protec-tion clause.

If anything, the motion by the proponents for summary judgment has illustrated the fact that judgment, in fact, should be entered in favor of the plaintiffs, and that injunction that we seek, which we hope we will have an opportunity to talk to you about again on January 11th, should be granted.

After a lengthy rebuttal from Mr. Cooper followed by a lunch break, Judge Walker brought the court back to order. He delivered a detailed oral review of the complaints, arguments, and rebuttals that had been presented that morning, and then he denied the motion for summary judgment, insisting that resolving the issue of the amendment's validity would require hearing testimony at trial.

Try as they might, opposing counsel had failed to convince the court that we could avoid a trial. Their desire to avoid bringing testimony into play was evident. What facts would support their argument? What experts could they rely on to prove that discrimination was justifiable? We had a dream team of lawyers and a slew of experts to tap into. It was time to kick into high gear.

Due Process and Equal Protection: Due process deals with the administration of justice and thus the due process clause acts as a safeguard from arbitrary denial of life, liberty, or property by the government outside the sanction of law.

The equal protection clause, which took effect in 1868, is part of the Fourteenth Amendment of the US Constiution. It provides that no state shall deny to any person within its jurisdiction "the equal protection of the laws."

Kris preparing for trial, San Francisco, 2009.

CHAPTER 21

Perry v. Raum

Kris

The courtroom drama would never have happened had Judge Walker not unexpectedly declared that he would like to set the case for trial. When he made the announcement, Sandy and I, Jeff and Paul, and Chad and Kristina were sitting very close to each other, in the front of the room just behind the short divider that separated us from the lawyers and the judge. Little did we know that day that we would spend dozens of hours on that bench, knees pressed together, anxiety transmitted through fidgety legs, tapping toes, and clenched fists. On this, the first "real" day of court, it was so quiet in the wake of Judge Walker's words that Sandy's gasp was audible. Chad immediately tensed and moved to the edge of the bench. Ted Olson and his Gibson, Dunn & Crutcher colleagues Matt McGill, Ted Boutrous, and Chris Dusseault shook their heads like they had water in their ears but then almost instantly seemed to relish the idea. The judge must have expected this kind of response, so without missing a beat, he said, "Shall we take our calendars out and see when we can get started?" Years of experience had prepared Ted Olson and Chuck Cooper to put on their game faces and oblige.

Once the date was set, dozens of attorneys from both Ted's firm and David's firm flew into action, prepping for multiple scenarios. Several members of the team were tasked with focusing on us by seeking in-depth explanations of how Sandy and I met and how we felt when Prop 8 passed, while others conducted a worldwide search for experts who could testify to the court about evidence that would support the argument that Prop 8 was harmful to us and our family.

We prepared off and on for weeks, with Ted Olson and attorneys Chris Dusseault, Ethan Dettmer, Enrique Monagas, and Sarah Piepmeier. They pushed and prodded me to reveal long-hidden aches and pains of growing up and being different. I couldn't figure out why they were so focused on that when the point of the trial was to win the right to marry. Revisiting my life in Bakersfield seemed irrelevant. The lawyers worked with me for hours to prepare for my deposition. Some days, Sandy and I would travel to the law office early in the morning and not return until after dinner. Other days, we'd answer detailed emails or join conference calls from home or work and then go to the law office to answer questions "mock deposition" style, fielding numerous questions from multiple attorneys. In addition to trial prep, our days were full of media interviews as well as the usual work duties and family obligations.

Depositions, which precede trials, are interviews with witnesses and plaintiffs who intend to give testimony, conducted with both sides present and documented by a court reporter and video. As in court, you take an oath to tell the truth, the whole truth, and nothing but the truth. To practice my deposition, our lawyers asked probing questions about my childhood and my identity. Until my deposition prep, I had been able to protect my privacy. Questions up to that point in the process had centered around falling in love with Sandy, raising our kids, and the kind of work I did. As the attorneys dug deeper into how I felt about being gay, I had to give more and more examples of discrimination. I started to feel vulnerable. The team was sweet and supportive but relentless. They had a good sense of what the other side might ask, and they didn't want us to be surprised.

For me, the hardest day we spent at the Gibson Dunn offices was the first day Sandy and I worked directly with Ted. Predictably, he had a yellow legal pad and several No. 2 pencils. He wore a soft brown cashmere sweater and a sweet smile. He never rushed or lectured us; he listened, gently steering the conversation to our early years. We talked about what it felt like to be different, and I revisited feelings from the hallways in middle school and the dread of high school dances. Although many of my friends have suffered so much more over the years for being gay—from family rejection and bullying to verbal abuse—I still wince when I think about those years and how "other" I felt.

After we had meandered around the core question for hours, Ted asked me, "How does it feel to be different?" I burst into tears. All that heartache was closer to the surface than I had thought. I'd tried to put distance between myself and Bakersfield and how I felt there, but it hadn't worked. I told Ted that "I knew who I was, and it had made me stronger," but I didn't like that I had been forced into being strong by building walls or hiding my feelings. Hiding was a necessity, and it had changed me, permanently.

Nothing makes me feel more self-protective than coming out to a new person. I wish I could say the only hard years were the ones in Bakersfield, but that's not true. Cars full of men have leaned out windows and yelled "dyke" at me many times. Cashiers call me "sir" as much as they call me "ma'am," and I know that my dad struggled introducing me to colleagues in Bakersfield because when he did, he would have to come out as someone with a gay kid. Bakersfield doesn't reward difference; it punishes it. Everyone in my family knows that, and in their own way, each expressed concern to me about how hard being out to the world would be there.

During my deposition prep, I told the team about falling in love with my college roommate and coming out to my parents. I shared my anxiety about my family rejecting me. We talked about my long-term relationship with my former partner and how our relationship ended. The best part of deposition prep was talking about falling in love with Sandy. Our team must have known at some point that I had done enough reflecting to speak directly and honestly on the stand about my experiences. When the time finally came, I felt like I was being handed over to the enemy, who offered nothing but disdain and judgment.

The day of my deposition, I stepped into the conference room where the video camera was already on its tripod, the court stenographer was seated at her stenotype, and the lawyers for both sides, Ethan Dettmer and Brian Raum, awaited. Mr. Raum was an attorney for the Alliance Defense Fund and was on Chuck Cooper's team, part of the effort to shore up the religious arguments against marriage equality. Just as my attorneys had predicted, he started with questions about my profession, my childhood, my hometown, and my family. He pivoted to when I moved to college and came out. He was puzzled by my statement that I wasn't able to understand my sexual orientation until I was eighteen. He wanted to know how many people I had slept with, and if they were men or women. Had I ever fallen in love with a man? I told him that I had had boyfriends and we had been intimate, but I had never fallen in love with a man. I had only fallen in love with women. That of course took us to the topic of Sandy and the whole point of the deposition: Why did I want to be married?

It became obvious that Mr. Raum wanted to clarify a couple of issues. One, was I really, really sure I was gay. Two, was I really, really sure I had been discriminated against. He reminded me that I did, after all, have a job, and in high school I had had a boyfriend. Could I really give an example of being discriminated against? Well, let's start with why we were there that day. I couldn't marry the person I loved. I told him that, during my annual physical each year, I filled out a form that had no box to check for "Domestic Partnered" but had questions about my relationship and birth control. I pointed out that I couldn't visit Sandy in a hospital if she fell ill. This last statement seemed to enrage him. How did I know I would be refused visitation? I calmly replied that Sandy and I had spent thousands of dollars creating an estate plan that included medical power of attorney; our lawyer had advised us that if we didn't take that step, Sandy's parents, siblings, or children would be the only ones who could visit her in the hospital or make health decisions if she were sick or injured. Mr. Raum asked the same questions several times, hoping I would relent and say, "Never mind, I'm not worried about being separated from Sandy in an emergency or losing control of her care." At one point, Ethan had to ask for a short break to help Mr. Raum regain his composure.

Looking back at that moment, I wonder if Mr. Raum intuitively knew we could win on the issue of basic fairness, dramatically illustrated through the example of one spouse being vulnerable and the other prohibited from protecting his or her dignity. That issue goes against the American belief that self-determination is a unique right of the individual that is not to be denied or blocked, especially during a crisis. The law in California was very clear. Unmarried couples, even those who were "domestic partnered" like Sandy and I, had limited rights, especially in matters of great significance such as health decisions and jointly owned property. Fortunately, Sandy and I had the means to protect ourselves, but even still, we were deprived of more than 1,100 federal and state rights to protect each other and our family in situations involving health providers, employers, and the state and federal government. During my deposition, Mr. Raum seemed to understand that he did not have a winning line of questioning.

The deposition gave me confidence for the next round—the trial. I was convinced I was gay, and I was convinced I had been discriminated against; now I had to convince the judge. The other side seemed to have little evidence and little confidence in its ability to win on merit. Instead, it seemed they wanted me to say, "Oh, right, what am I doing here? I'm not gay, I actually feel like a first-class citizen. Never mind, let's all go home."

As the trial approached, though, my anxiety was palpable. We prepared for it in a way that did not include memorizing answers to questions. Ted knew that if he pushed for memorized answers in the courtroom, we wouldn't have a natural exchange. The process felt like peeling an onion. How did I meet Sandy? When did we fall in love? When did we start living together? The easy questions were followed by tougher ones, focused on personal experiences of discrimination and my worries that my children would be negatively impacted by me.

Sandy preparing for deposition,
San Francisco, 2009.

CHAPTER 22

Baseball Analogies

Sandy

You can take the man out of baseball, but you can't take baseball out of the man. Said by no one, ever. Not that I know of.

In the wake of Judge Walker's decision to go to trial, our team went into high gear. Kris and I attended weekly briefings with the AFER people and a slew of lawyers. We learned more about the strategy they would employ, the arguments they would make, and the experts they would engage. We also learned that we would be deposed well in advance of the trial.

Over the course of several days and grueling sessions of questioning, Ethan Dettmer, Sarah Piepmeier, and Enrique Monagas, lawyers from the San Francisco offices of Gibson Dunn, asked increasingly personal questions about me and Kris, our lives, and our love. Nothing was off limits; it felt like a deep dive into a one-way, intimate friendship that became much less friendly as they prepared me for the most invasive and offensive questions. An intensely private person, I found the process excruciating. I tried to steer the conversation to humor to escape the inquisition, peeling into laughter as I exaggerated or ad-libbed absurd responses to break the tension.

The day of my deposition, I met Sarah and Ethan in their offices. No Kris to act as a buffer. Coached to keep my responses succinct and focused, I felt prepared. Sarah and Ethan knew that I could go off on tangents a little too readily, but on this day, I was determined that nary a joke or a story would be told. I was in a rare somber state, eager to get the process over with.

Wearing a camel jacket, plaid skirt, and boots, I followed my lawyers into the deposition room, where the court reporter was readying her equipment to record the proceeding. We were joined by Brian Raum and his colleagues from the conservative Alliance Defense Fund. Mr. Raum took the lead on questions. We all settled in as he started with easy, general questions. Where was I from? Where did I go to school?

I am from Iowa. I grew up on a family farm, and I am the third of four children in a church-going family. I was a cheerleader in high school. I went to the University of Iowa, where I was in a sorority. I had long hair and all the trappings of mainstream motherhood. I was not the lesbian he expected to see.

Then came the real questions, and Mr. Raum's face hardened as he began. When did I start dating? Who did I go out with? What was the nature of those relationships? Exactly what happened in them? Mr. Raum turned a deep red as he hammered for specific answers.

I answered truthfully. I performed well under oath, and, frankly, I have nothing to hide. Yes, I dated men, or rather, boys, in high school and college. Wonderful guys. Yes, I cared about them. Yes, I married a man in my midtwenties. Yes, I had loved him. All true. The other thing that was true was that I now loved a woman, and I wanted to marry her; I was in love with Kris.

I could feel Mr. Raum's blood pressure rising. He wanted to know more about those relationships with men. He wanted to know the nature of those relationships. When I said they were romantic relationships, he was unsatisfied. He wanted intimate details. I thought romantic was detail enough. In an effort to get me to disclose more information, he employed baseball terminology. What "base" was reached in each of those relationships?

We have more of our parents in us than we may realize. I gave him my best Iowa deadpan stare and restated that the relationships had been romantic. And I stopped there. My people don't talk about "bases" to lawyers. It's not dignified.

I wasn't the only one squirming. Ethan, my preppy, straight-laced lawyer, nervously objected to the invasive questions. Sarah and I exchanged looks that contained a thousand words. Later, when we broke for lunch, we laughed about the awkwardness of it all. Sarah was the only lesbian on our legal team, and Kris and I felt a particular alliance with her. Ethan, ever the gentleman in his tiny spectacles, was mortified. I think I felt sorrier for him than for myself. I have pretty thick skin and a high tolerance for awkward.

Redirected by Ethan's objections, an increasingly agitated Mr. Raum had asked one question over and over: "Could I fall in love with a man again?"

"I don't know if I could. What I do know is that I'm in love with a woman, with Kris, and I want to marry her."

Mr. Raum's skin flushed as he reworked the question, asking me to consider what might happen if Kris were not in my life for some reason. If there were no Kris, could I fall in love with a man? Again, I repeated truthfully that I didn't know. The only thing I knew for certain was that I loved Kris and wanted to marry her. I had no interest in imagining my life without Kris in it.

Immutability was the issue he was hammering on. Is being gay an immutable characteristic or a choice? As the only plaintiff in the case who had been in a heterosexual marriage, I was the target for creating a case against immutability. My deposition lasted a full day, in contrast to the shorter stints endured by Kris, Jeff, and Paul. Although I understand that immutability was an important argument for our lawyers to pursue, and certainly for many people it rings true and deep, the concept bothers me. I don't like it. The hair on the back of my neck stands up when I hear someone say, "No one would choose to be gay," or "They can't help being gay." Such phrases are deeply offensive, as if being gay is morally wrong or harmful to society. Being gay is not wrong and it's not bad. It's not. Love is not harmful; hate is. Rejection is. Growing up immersed in religion and spending most of my career in the field of human services, nothing could be clearer. Love and acceptance are what matters and are worth fighting for.

I stared back at Mr. Raum, silently daring him to ask me one more time if I was certain that I loved Kris. Oh yes, I was certain.

My deposition stretched on for hours, tedious and redundant hours. Mr. Raum seemed thoroughly pissed off by the end of it. The angrier he looked, the more satisfied I felt. I imagined how repulsed he must have been by me. He didn't like my answers, and he didn't like me or "my people." And he certainly didn't want "us" to have the same rights he had.

*   *   *

My deposition had been grueling, as had the preparation. But that was nothing compared with getting ready for the witness stand in federal trial court.

CHAPTER 23

Full Disclosure

Sandy

I have rarely felt more vulnerable than I did when I was preparing for and testifying about who I was and why I believed I had the right to marry the love of my life. I could entertain a crowd with off-the-cuff jokes and quips, but I could barely tolerate being exposed on a personal level.

Ted Olson joined our Gibson Dunn team for trial prep. Ted's job was to peel back the layers of self-protection and help Kris and me tell our stories clearly and authentically in our own voices. We met with Ted and our San Francisco team over the course of several days, each time exploring another strand of our story, another layer of background. The process was intimidating. Ted's approach was different than during the deposition prep, and I felt the weight of our responsibility more acutely. He was serious and somber, delving into issues of family, love, shame, and desire.

Ted asked me about my prior marriage, the substance of it, and how it ended. Questions delved into my other relationships, the nature of those, how Kris and I met and fell in love, and why we wanted to marry. The benign questions about my childhood were a cakewalk. The questions about my prior marriage were more loaded. I felt protective of my sons and the privacy of my deceased ex-husband. I wanted to avoid the topic entirely, not wishing to expose my sons or the pain of that loss. But full disclosure was necessary.

Nothing seemed off limits. None of my joking antics worked to shift the questioning or conversation away from the intimate details of my life and my heart. Ted did his best to draw me out, asking more nuanced questions about my responses to get to the most salient points. I felt connected to Ted; his warm and steady way put me at ease. I wanted to provide the best testimony possible, so I tried to follow his directions and be thorough and concise. Like Sarah and Ethan, Ted played devil's advocate, preparing us for a hostile cross-examination. The sobering moments were always followed by warm words of encouragement and validation.

Cycling back and forth between me and Kris every thirty minutes or so, Ted would go over similar questions with Kris; he dug into her childhood more deeply, helping her find her voice to explore and describe the process of realizing that she was gay and how she came out to herself and eventually to others. It was beautiful and painful to watch. Kris is remarkably stoic, rarely showing emotional pain. In those hours, though, she opened up to Ted and gave voice to her story. The story she had never told—the story that needed telling. Hearing Kris talk about feeling different as a child, her struggle to fit in, and the defense mechanisms she developed to ward off criticism and unwanted harassment gave me a deeper appreciation of her strength.

By the end of our trial prep, we felt close to Ted. Not only had we been the recipients of many warm hugs, he had assured us that our stories were critical to presenting the facts in court. He knew half of our secrets and many of the intimate details of our lives normally reserved for close friends or kept to ourselves.

We also got to know our coplaintiffs, Jeff and Paul, better. They had taken up residence with AFER staff members at a house in San Francisco for several weeks. With greater access to them, we began to bond over our shared experience of baring our souls to relative strangers in the conference rooms of Gibson Dunn. While we were preparing for trial with Ted, they were doing the same with David.

The law offices were lively and packed the day before the trial. The AFER team was there, as were various members of the AFER board, including the Reiners (Rob and Michele); film producer Bruce Cohen and his adorable husband, Gabe; gay activist Cleve Jones; and hunky screenwriter Dustin Lance Black (who had won an Oscar the previous year for *Milk*). And we had media. Chad had invited *New York Times* journalist Jo Becker to chronicle the case and photojournalist Diana Walker to capture images. They were joined by a small but mighty documentary film crew—Ben Cotner, Ryan White, and Rebekah Ferguson—who quietly skirted the crowd, camera in hand, capturing interesting conversations and furtive glances.

We got punchy, or rather I got punchy, as the day went on. Relieved to not be talking about discrimination or the history of my life, I launched into a spoof of my testimony, pretending to be a mail-order bride, to entertain Kris and the guys. Chad popped into the conference room to give me a "Seriously?" look. Evidently, they were filming in the adjacent room and my voice carried a little too loudly. Marriage, after all, is serious stuff.

On January 11, 2010, the morning of the first day of the trial, Kris and I woke early, staring into the dark quietly for some time until I broke the silence.

"Fuck."

Kris responded, "I know."

We were anxious not only about our own testimony but also about the prospect of cross-examination. We were prepared to field almost any question, but we knew the questions could get unpleasant quickly. Our anxiety was amplified by the prospect of the trial being televised. Our lawyers had petitioned the court to allow cameras in the courtroom to make the proceedings available to the public. Although we supported the idea in principle, on a personal level it was intimidating, and I secretly hoped that cameras wouldn't be allowed. We knew it would an amazing way to bring our case into the living rooms of millions of Americans, but I worried that I would somehow humiliate someone: my mom, my kids, myself.

A car picked us up; we held hands in silence as we rode across the Bay Bridge. We met Jeff, Paul, and the AFER team at their house. Arriving as the sun began to rise, we joined the guys and Kristina for coffee, bagels, and a group session about anxiety. Jeff was rehearsing the statement he would make to the press on the front steps while Paul fussed with their ties. We teased them about their unmade bed and cluttered kitchen. Chad, Adam, and Kristina had been up for hours, managing logistics and media. I asked Kristina if my pink-and-black suit was suitable, having also brought a more somber alternative. She responded sweetly, "It's perfect."

As we approached the court, we saw the crowds that had gathered. Many people had come to rally on the steps of the courthouse in support of marriage equality, while others filed inside in an attempt to get a seat in the courtroom. Across the street, some bizarrely decorated trucks with speakers boomed hateful condemnations of gays. It was a bizarre juxtaposition of love and hate, albeit with love clearly winning.

We made our way through security through the back door of the building, passing a large sign that read *"Perry v. Schwarzenegger,"* and headed up to the courtroom, our home away from home for the next couple of weeks. We were ushered into a room adjacent to the court to meet with security, where we learned that precautions had been put into place for our trial "just in case." This meant that when we went to the ladies room, we had a new friend walking with us. And our new friend wore a badge and carried a gun. Yippee.

After a series of hugs, squeezed hands, and "Can you believe we're here?" smiles, we took our seats. Our counsel sat directly in front of us, and the opposing counsel and supporters were on the opposite side of the aisle. The atmosphere was far more charged than before. Brian Raum, the Alliance Defense Fund lawyer who had deposed me, was seated alongside Chuck Cooper and several other colleagues. I wondered how they felt about the trial, and if they really believed that their position had integrity. I wondered if their kids were embarrassed or had tried to dissuade them from affiliating with the wrong side of the issue.

As Judge Walker brought the court to order, the crowd hushed. Although the case name had been shortened to "Perry," our names were all read aloud, along with the long list of individuals we were suing, including the governor and the attorney general of California and the clerk-recorders for Alameda and Los Angeles counties. Our list of names paled in comparison to the long list of lawyers who were introduced, including lawyers representing the city of San Francisco who had successfully intervened to join us in the suit.

The first course of business was cameras in the courtroom. This issue had made its way to the Supreme Court, our side advocating for full public access to the proceedings, the proponents insisting that such access would impede and possibly harm their witnesses. The ruling, announced by Judge Walker, allowed for the presence of cameras in the courtroom to capture the trial on film, but only for the purpose of sharing it with other federal courtrooms. Access to the public was denied, but the footage would exist. Judge Walker drew chuckles from the crowd as he explained how the Supreme Court had come to this decision. Kris and I squeezed hands, letting out a barely audible sigh of relief at the announcement, oblivious to the fact that every word uttered in front of the judge would be tweeted or otherwise shared outside the courtroom throughout the proceedings.

With the preliminary issues out of the way, Judge Walker invited Ted to make the opening statement.

Ted's deep, baritone voice rang strong and true:

MR. OLSON: This case is about marriage and equality. Plaintiffs are being denied both the right to marry and the right to equality under the law.

The Supreme Court of the United States has repeatedly described the right to marriage as one of the most vital personal rights essential to the orderly pursuit of happiness, a basic civil right, a component of the constitutional rights to liberty, privacy, association, an intimate choice, an expression of emotional support and public commitment, the exercise of spiritual unity, and the fulfillment of one's self.

In short, in the words of the highest court in the land, marriage is the most important relation in life, and of fundamental importance for all individuals.

Judge Walker responded with questions regarding the regulation of marriage and the issuance of marriage licenses, and then turned to the testimony we would provide regarding the harm of not having access to legal marriage in California and how domestic partnership is an insufficient alternative.

Ted outlined how the evidence he had gathered would be introduced over the course of the trial:

MR. OLSON: Plaintiffs and leading experts in the fields of history, psychology, economics, and political science will prove these three basic fundamental points that we will be addressing during the course of this trial: Marriage, that relationship, culturally and as sanctioned by the state, is vitally important in American society. Secondly, by denying gay men and lesbians the right to marry, Proposition 8 works a grievous harm on the plaintiffs and other gay men and lesbians throughout California, and adds yet another chapter—we will talk about the chapters in American and California history—to the long history of discrimination these individuals have suffered at the hands of their fellow citizens and at the hands of their government. And, thirdly, that Proposition 8 perpetrates this irreparable, immeasurable, discriminatory harm for no good. No good reason.

Ted reminded the court how recently the right to marry someone of a different race was won. When Judge Walker asked why the courts shouldn't leave the issue to the political process, Ted responded vehemently:

MR. OLSON: That is why we have courts. And that is why we have a Constitution. That is why we have the Fourteenth Amendment.

When individuals who may not be the most popular people, who are different than we are, are treated differently under the Constitution, when they are excluded from our schools or when they are put in separate schools, or when they are not allowed to marry because of the color of the skin of the partner of their choice is different, they come to the courts. And time after time the courts have addressed these issues, and time after time the courts have addressed those issues notwithstanding that very, very point. Leave it to the political process.

We wouldn't need a constitution if we left everything to the political process, but if we left everything to the political process, the majority would always prevail, which is a great thing about democracy, but it's not so good if you are a minority or if you're a disfavored minority or you're new or you're different. And that's what happens here.

What Prop 8 does is label gay and lesbian persons as different, inferior, unequal, and disfavored. It says to them, your relationship is not the same. And it's less approved than those enjoyed by opposite-sex couples. It stigmatizes gays and lesbians. It classifies them as outcasts. It causes needless and unrelenting pain and isolation and humiliation.

We have courts to declare enactments like Proposition 8 that take our citizens, our worthy, loving, upstanding citizens who are being treated differently and being hurt every single day, we have courts to declare those measures unconstitutional. And that is why we are here today.

When it was the proponents' turn to present their opening arguments, Mr. Cooper did his best to convince the court that excluding the right to marriage from gays and lesbians was justified and was, in fact, the moral high road. We did our best not to roll our eyes or make "hrrumph" sounds as he regaled the court with passage after passage of rhetoric in his Southern drawl, referencing old-world social concepts of marriage and suggesting that we were threatening to "dilute marriage."

MR. COOPER: To whatever extent, your Honor, the traditional and overriding purpose, and that is the procreative and responsible procreation purposes of marriage, are diluted and marriage as a pro-child social institution is diluted or weakened.

We listened and waited anxiously for Mr. Cooper to finish, knowing that our testimony would follow the opening statements, with Jeff going first, followed by Paul, then Kris, and then me.

Jeff was called to the stand by David Boies. Jeff stated his name, and then responded to basic questions about his age and upbringing. A native of New Jersey with one (married) brother, he was clearly devoted to his family of origin. His parents had been married for more than forty years and were in attendance that day, proud as punch of their son. Jeff had worked his way up the ladder at AMC Entertainment, starting right out of college twenty-one years earlier. He didn't remember a time before he knew he was gay, but he spoke of the caution he exercised in sharing that knowledge with others well into his twenties and living in California, far from the threat of schoolyard bullies. He described Paul as the love of his life, his voice clenched as he explained why he wanted to marry Paul and how he thought marriage would enhance their lives and make them a legitimate family.

Jeff left the stand as Paul was called as the next witness; they met with a quick kiss. As Jeff sat down beside us, I squeezed his hand in appreciation and acknowledgement of the emotional experience. Paul spelled his name for the court reporter and then answered the questions about age and background. In his late thirties, Paul was on home territory, a San Francisco native. Coming from a divorced family, he was one of three children; he had a master's degree from UCLA and worked in the fitness industry. He responded to questions about his desire to marry Jeff, describing him as his "best advocate and supporter in life" and explaining that they felt that marriage was an important first step in starting a family. Paul described himself as a "natural-born gay," but one who came out to others gradually and who had endured his fair share of harassment and discrimination. As a younger man, he had convinced himself that he had to accept being bullied by strangers, that it was up to him to protect himself. He described how the notorious campaign for Proposition 8 had fueled his desire to fight for equality, referring to the offensive ad campaign that we had all seen on television.

David introduced a piece of media as evidence in the trial, a ProtectMarriage.com video called *It's Already Happened*. The opposing counsel objected to the evidence, but the objection was overruled by the judge, and we all watched the video, which promised to "protect our children," a common theme in the Prop 8 campaign and included in the language on the ballot measure. Kris and I clenched our hands and our jaws, glancing at Spencer and Elliott, who were sitting with Kris's mom in the row behind us. Having worked in and around the child welfare system, Kris and I both knew what children needed protection from, and it certainly wasn't any of us.

We had all been prepared for cross-examination, but only Paul was put to the test on the witness stand. Mr. Raum peppered Paul with questions about when young children should learn about sex, insisting that Paul take a position on whether first graders should have sex education in school. David objected, but he was overruled. Mr. Raum went on to make a connection between hypothetical sex education for first graders and the fact that Paul had previously stated he had a problem with the Prop 8 advertisements that proclaimed a need to "protect children." Mr. Raum insisted that the ads didn't specifically claim that same-sex couples were "bad." Paul fired back that indeed they did, by insinuating that children needed protection from "us." From him.

Jeff hadn't been cross-examined, but Paul had. We didn't know if this trend would continue, and we wouldn't know until we each had our turn.

Kris was called to the stand. She squeezed my hand and rose and crossed the room. All eyes were on my dearest as she took her seat. Our eyes met for an instant, and I willed her the calm that she would need as she faced the court to pledge her dedication to speak "the truth, the whole truth, and nothing but the truth."

CHAPTER 24

Perry v. Perry

Kris

When Ted called "plaintiff Kristin Perry" on day one of the trial, I had more than an inkling of what might be in store, thanks to the deposition process. After taking the oath and sitting down, I looked out at the row I had just left and saw my empty spot next to Sandy. She smiled the way she does when she's worried. Just behind that row, Spencer and Elliott were sitting between my mom and Cleve Jones, the human rights and LGBT activist who had become a legend in the LGBT community in San Francisco and across the country. They, too, had worried smiles. At the end of that bench, Rob and Michele Reiner gave me confident nods, and Chad, Kristina, Lady Olson, and Dustin Lance Black were perched on the edge of their bench, hoping I could match the spellbinding testimony Jeff and Paul had delivered. It had been heartfelt and deeply personal and moved everyone to tears. Jeff and Paul had so genuinely expressed their love for each other and their dream of living as a married couple that no one could deny the authenticity of the commitment they had to each other. As soon as Ted started asking questions, I focused on answering him. Even though I could see Chuck Cooper and his team frowning at me on one side of the room and Ted Boutrous, David Boies, and others from our team on the other, I looked only at Ted as I answered each question.

MR. OLSON: Would you tell us briefly about your background; where you were born, just a brief summary, your age, your educational background? Just a brief summary, please?

KRIS: I was born in Illinois, but my parents moved here with me when I was two years old. So I have lived in California since I was two years old and I'm 45 years old now.

I've grown up—I grew up in Bakersfield, California. I attended grammar school, middle school, high school there. And then I moved away to go to college at U.C. Santa Cruz. And from there I went to San Francisco State to get my Master's Degree in social work, and I have worked in the Bay Area ever since.

MR. OLSON: Describe without—you don't have to identify the name of your employer, but you—you work for a government agency. I would like you to describe the work that you do, your profession?

KRIS: My entire career I have worked in the field of child protection, child development, family support. I started out as a child abuse investigator in a Bay Area county, and from there I moved into prevention services for families that were at risk. I became a supervisor and a program manager and then later on became the executive director of a county agency that supported at-risk children, zero to five.

And at this time I am the executive director of a statewide agency that provides services and support to families with children zero to five.

MR. OLSON: So how long have you professionally been engaged in the occupation of working with children?

KRIS: For almost twenty-five years.

MR. OLSON: On behalf of government agencies of the State of California, did I hear that correctly?

KRIS: I have spent my entire career working for the government.

MR. OLSON: What is your relationship with plaintiff Sandra Stier?

KRIS: Sandy is the woman I love, and we live together in Berkeley.

MR. OLSON: And what is the composition of your family. Is it just the two of you?

KRIS: No. Sandy and I live together in Berkeley with our children. We have a blended family. We both brought two sons into our relationship. And Sandy's children are college age and my children are high school age.

MR. OLSON: When did you meet Ms. Stier?

KRIS: Sandy and I met in, I think, 1996 while we were both working at the same place.

MR. OLSON: And describe how that relationship—again, in general terms, how did that relationship grow and what did it grow into?

KRIS: Well, I remember the first time I met Sandy thinking she was maybe the sparkliest person I ever met and I wanted to be her friend, and we were friends for a few years. And our friendship became more and more. It became deeper and deeper over time. And then after a few years, I began to feel that I might be falling in love with her.

MR. OLSON: And did it work out that way?

KRIS: And it did work out that way. I did fall in love with her, I did.

MR. OLSON: And how did she feel about you?

KRIS: She told me she loved me, too.

MR. OLSON: We will be asking her to verify that.

KRIS: Okay.

(Laughter.)

MR. OLSON: How would you describe your sexual orientation?

KRIS: I am a lesbian.

MR. OLSON: And tell me what that means in your own words? What does it mean to be a lesbian?

KRIS: Well, for me what it means is, I have always felt strong attraction and interest in women and formed really close relationships with women, and I have only ever fallen in love with women.

And the happiest I feel is in my relationship with Sandy and—because I'm in love with her.

MR. OLSON: Do you feel that that's something that could change, that you could have—could you have been in the past interested in that same kind of bonding with men or do you feel that that would be—I know this is somewhat compound, or do you feel that that could turn into—that could develop in that way in the future?

JUDGE WALKER: Let's see. Which question do you want her to answer?

(Laughter.)

MR. OLSON: Do you feel that in the past you could have developed that same kind of bond with a man?

KRIS: I was unable to do that. I, as I said, grew up in Bakersfield, California and it was in the 70's and 80's. And all of my friends, as we were getting older and they were beginning to date, became more and more interested in boys. And I recognized that that was something that would have been the best thing for me to do if I could.

And I did date [a] few boys, because it was . . . easier, you know. Then I would have a date to go to the prom too, or I could go to a party, too.

But as I got a little bit older, it became clear to me that I didn't feel the same way my friends did about boys and that there was something different about me.

MR. OLSON: Do you feel that you were born with those feelings, with that kind of sexual orientation?

KRIS: Yes, I do.

MR. OLSON: Do you feel it could change in the future? Do you have a sense that it might somehow change?

KRIS: I'm 45 years old. I don't think so.

(Laughter.)

MR. OLSON: Why are you a plaintiff in this case?

KRIS: Because I want to marry Sandy. I want to have a stable and secure relationship with her that then we can include our children in. And I want the discrimination we are feeling with Proposition 8 to end and for a more positive, joyful part of our lives to begin.

MR. OLSON: What does the institution of marriage mean to you? Why do you want that?

KRIS: Well, I have never really let myself want it until now. Growing up as a lesbian, you don't let yourself want it, because everyone tells you you are never going to have it.

So in some ways it's hard for me to grasp what it would even mean, but I do see other people who are married and I—and I think what it looks like is that you are honored and respected by your family. Your children know what your relationship is. And when you leave your home and you go to work or you go out in the world, people know what your relationship means. And so then everyone can, in a sense, join in supporting your relationship, which at this point I can only observe it as an outsider. I don't have any firsthand experience with what that must be like.

MR. OLSON: Does it matter that the state is announcing that this is a relationship officially recognized by the State of California, marriage?

KRIS: Yes.

MR. OLSON: And is that part of something that goes into why you want this to happen for you?

KRIS: I want it to happen for me because I do everything else I can think to do to make myself a contributing, responsible member of this state. And the state isn't letting me feel happy. It's not letting me experience my full potential, because I am not permitted to experience everything I might feel if this barrier were removed.

MR. OLSON: Did you and Ms. Stier ever attempt to be married?

KRIS: We did.

MR. OLSON: Tell us what happened, when that was and exactly what your experience was?

KRIS: [. . .] I proposed to Sandy without any way of knowing that everything that's developed regarding gay marriage in California . . . I did it as a way to express my personal interest in marrying her.

MR. OLSON: Tell me about your proposal. What happened?

KRIS: Well, it was around Christmas and we live in a part of Berkeley that's sort of hilly and we live near this big rock called Indian Rock. And if you get up high enough on it and you sit there, you can see everything in the Bay Area laid out in front of you. And I knew I wanted to propose to her there because we could always walk back there and sit there if we wanted to.

So I took her on a walk. She didn't know I had a ring, and we sat down on the rock and I put my arm around her and I said, "Will you marry me?" And she looked really happy, and then she looked really confused. And she said "Well, what does that"—well, she said, "Yes." And then she said, "Well, what does that mean? How will we even do that?" And then we had to invent it for ourselves. We had to figure out what to do.

MR. OLSON: . . . So what did you and—I'm going to call her Sandy. What did you and Sandy do to then invent the relationship that you were hoping to have with her that you had proposed?

KRIS: We started with basically trying to figure out the day we would like to be married and the place and who we would like to have join us and how we might—what we might say to each other. So we just started the planning.

And as we were in the midst of doing that, private family and friend ceremony planning, we learned that the City and County of San Francisco, they were permitting same-sex marriages, that was while we were in the middle of planning.

MR. OLSON: This was early in 2004—

KRIS: That's correct. Uh-huh.

MR. OLSON: . . . And you learned in some way that the mayor of the City of San Francisco had authorized the issuance of marriage licenses and the performance of marriage in San Francisco; am I stating that correctly?

KRIS: Yes.

MR. OLSON: That was in the early part of 2004?

KRIS: Yes. For us it was February of 2004.

MR. OLSON: And what—did you act on that information?

KRIS: I did. I—Sandy and I both were reading about it in the newspaper and we talked about whether or not we would want to—would go to San Francisco to have this marriage and then continue with our other plans, and that's what we decided we wanted to do.

So we made an appointment and we went to City Hall. And we brought all of the boys and my mom and we were married in City Hall.

MR. OLSON: And how did you feel about that marriage coming about in the City Hall in San Francisco at that time?

KRIS: Well, as amazed and happy as I could ever imagine feeling. And I said a moment ago that I—I never let myself imagine it happening.

So in some ways the feelings I had were new to me. I didn't really know what they were. And I am still confused by these experiences because they are not the ones that have been—I haven't let myself want to feel them.

So I have a sense that—it's almost an other-worldly experience of like floating above the ceremony and saying, "Oh, that's me getting married. I never thought that would happen."

MR. OLSON: Did you then, after that ceremony, go forward with this private ceremony that you had planned?

KRIS: We did. We continued those plans. Because only a few—our kids and my mom attended the ceremony in City Hall, we wanted to continue with the other ceremony so that more people could come and we could see everybody.

MR. OLSON: Did you have a party, a ceremony and an exchange of vows?

KRIS: We did. We did. We planned an afternoon in Berkeley where our friends and family had joined us, and we had a small ceremony, and then we all came inside and there was a big celebration.

MR. OLSON: How many? How many people?

KRIS: There were 100 guests.

MR. OLSON: What month was that?

KRIS: It was August 1st.

MR. OLSON: Of 2004?

KRIS: Yes.

MR. OLSON: After that, was there a decision by a California court having to do with the ceremony that you entered into in San Francisco at City Hall?

KRIS: Yes. A few weeks after our August ceremony, the state Supreme Court ruled that the San Francisco weddings were invalid.

MR. OLSON: What was your reaction when you heard that?

KRIS: Well, the part of me that was disbelieving and unsure of it in the first place was confirmed. That, in fact, I really—almost when you're gay, you think you don't really deserve things.

So it did have this sense of, well, you know, I really didn't deserve to be married.

MR. OLSON: Did you receive notification, official notification that your marriage was null and void?

KRIS: Yeah. The City and County of San Francisco sent us a letter after they—after the ruling, and it was a form letter and our names were typed at the top. It said, "We are sorry to inform you that your marriage is not valid and we would like to return your marriage fees to you. Would you like them in a check or donated to charity?"

And so that was the—that's when we knew for sure we weren't married in San Francisco any more.

MR. OLSON: And what feelings did that evoke, that experience?

KRIS: I'm not good enough to be married.

MR. OLSON: Sometime in 2008 the California Supreme Court rendered a decision, I think it was May of 2008, that marriage could be obtained by same-sex individuals irrespective of sexual orientation; do you remember that decision?

KRIS: I do.

MR. OLSON: What did you feel when you heard that the California Supreme Court said that you had a constitutional right to marry the person of your choice?

KRIS: I—I was elated to hear it. I really was. And I know Sandy was, too, because we talked about that ruling when it happened.

And after we had known about it for a little while, we started to hear our friends talk about their plans to get married, and we were very excited for them.

And then, of course, we asked ourselves, would we get married again? And it didn't take more than a—really, a few minutes for us to—it was unanimous that we couldn't— we couldn't bring ourselves to do it again right then.

The experience in 2004 had really—we hadn't really recovered from it. And it didn't feel at that time, given [. . .] the Supreme Court ruling [. . .]. And we had experienced the impermanent solution before and we decided not to go forward at that time.

MR. OLSON: Were you aware that people were organizing an effort to overturn that California Supreme Court decision?

KRIS: Yes. I was aware there was a campaign starting.

MR. OLSON: What became Proposition 8, you were aware that there was effort going on to put a measure on the ballot to overturn the California Supreme Court decision?

KRIS: I remember media reports of—groups or individuals saying, we disagree and we'll have to take action, and the sort of beginnings of what resulted in a ballot initiative.

MR. OLSON: And that was a ballot initiative that came on the ballot in November of that same year, is that correct?

KRIS: Correct.

MR. OLSON: Now, what was it like for you to be a citizen to watch and listen to the campaign to overturn that California—can you just relate your reactions to what was going on around you in the political world on that subject?

KRIS: Well, I mean, I am just—I'm a California resident, so I could see evidence of the campaign. I commute on a local highway and I would see the bumper stickers every day.

I did see some of the television ads. One in particular I remember. I saw some posters on people's lawns, but that was about it.

MR. OLSON: What did you—you say you saw one ad in particular. What do you remember about that?

KRIS: Umm, well, it struck me as being sort of an education-focused ad because there was a moment where they showed the Ed Code in the ad.

MR. OLSON: The Education Code?

KRIS: The California Education Code, which I am sort of interested in. So that got me interested in that ad. And it did talk about needing to protect your children from learning about gay marriage in school. That was the gist of the ad.

MR. OLSON: How do you feel did you feel about that? You work with children every day.

KRIS: I do. Well, I work on their behalf. I—I remember feeling that the ad was attempting to create a sense of fear and worry in me, and that the solution to that would be to vote Yes On 8. It was kind of a—kind of a this-for-that kind of a feeling. They kind of simplified this complex thing about relationships into a bad thing. And then they said if you want to fix a bad thing, do this. And I felt essentially that it was very simplified.

MR. OLSON: As a parent, did you have a reaction to the Proposition 8 campaign?

KRIS: Uh-huh. I did. I felt that it didn't represent how I feel about my children or their friends; that I feel compelled all of the time to be protective of them with-out thinking.

   And so this message was that maybe I was in a group of people who wouldn't be protective of children, and it didn't match with the way I feel about them.

MR. OLSON: Did you feel that voters were being warned that they needed to protect their children from you?

KRIS: Yes, I did. And I felt like I was being used; that my—the fact that I—you know, I am the way I am and I can't change the way I am was being mocked and made fun of and disparaged in a way that I—I didn't really have any way to respond to it. I just had to know that people felt that way.

MR. OLSON: Do you, as you go through life every day, feel that—the other effects of discrimination on the basis of your sexual orientation?

KRIS: Every day.

MR. OLSON: Tell us about that.

KRIS: Well, when I was an adolescent and beginning to become more and more aware of my sexuality, I struggled to
feel like everybody else, to look and feel like everybody
else.

And for it to even be a struggle in the first place was
hard. And I was well aware of the comments and jokes that
were circulating through my school all the time, and some
of them were directed at me.

As I got older and clearer about who I was and I could
say I was a lesbian out loud, that would be met at times
with criticism or skepticism.

And what I want to say about me and being out is, you
know, I go to great lengths to not have that happen. I
don't want to draw people's criticism. In fact, quite the
opposite. I would really like people to like me.

So since I know I have this trait that I can't change
that people don't like, I go to great lengths to have
other traits people do like. So I put a significant amount
of time and energy into being likable. . . . So if, for
example, I'm on a plane and somebody comes up and I have
saved a seat for Sandy, but she is not there yet and they
say, "Is that saved?" I say, "Yes." And they say, "For
whom?" And I say, "For my partner." And they say, "Could
you please move that so I can sit here?"

Or if we are in a restaurant or in a store and we
travel through the store together, people want to know if
we are sisters or cousins or friends.

And I have to decide every day if I want to come out
everywhere I go and take the chance that somebody will
have a hostile reaction to my sexuality or just go there
and buy the microwave we went there to buy without having
to go through that again.

And the decision every day to come out or not come out
at work, at home, at PTA, at music, at soccer, is exhaust-

ing. So much of the time I just choose to do as much of that as I can handle doing in any given day.

MR. OLSON: Was coming out something that took a long time for you to do? Was it difficult?

KRIS: It was sort of gradual, but probably not so long. I think probably by the time I was 18 or 19 I did know that, I was able to talk to myself about that and then I could tell other people over the next few years.

But it is what you often hear lesbians and gays say. I feel like once I realized that about myself, then I could say, I think I have been gay from the beginning. But it was a gradual process at first.

MR. OLSON: You have had to explain this to your children?

KRIS: Yes.

MR. OLSON: Was that difficult?

KRIS: Well, they don't know me any other way. So—you know, it's different, probably, if you were living as a heterosexual person, but [I] have always been their mom and in their entire lives I have been out, so . . .

MR. OLSON: Have you and Sandy entered into a registered domestic partnership in California?

KRIS: Yes. . . . That was in August of 2004.

MR. OLSON: Was that easy to do? Does California make it simple?

KRIS: Yeah. It was a—I think it was a form.

MR. OLSON: That you submit to the state?

KRIS: That we—we completed it. I think we had to have it notarized and then we mailed it in.

MR. OLSON: What does domestic partnership mean to you compared to marriage?

KRIS: Well, we are registered domestic partners based on just legal advice that we received for creating an estate plan. So we saw a lawyer who works with couples on those things and we completed a number of forms; a durable power of attorney, last will and testament, and she recommended we also do the domestic partnership agreement at the same time. So there were just a number of those kinds of documents that we completed.

MR. OLSON: You regard it as something of a property transaction or estate planning transaction?

KRIS: It was—well, that's when—we did ours during that process and it was—I believe it has some unique features, that it was a little different than durable power of attorney or a will, and so we completed it.

It allows us to access each other's health benefits and some other benefits through our employers.

MR. OLSON: Is it as good as marriage?

KRIS: Well, to me, they are not the same thing at all. You know, I viewed the domestic partnership agreement as precisely that, an agreement, a legal agreement, and in some ways memorializes some of our responsibilities to each other.

But it isn't the same thing as a celebration or something we—we don't remember the day it happened or invite people over on that day.

We just did that as part of the things we did as a couple to protect ourselves since we can't get married.

MR. OLSON: One of the issues that the court is going to have to deal with is how is that domestic partnership relationship different to you than marriage, and why is it that you want marriage so much when you have this opportunity?

KRIS: Well, I don't have—I don't have access to the words that describe my relationship right now. I'm a 45-year-old woman. I have been in love with a woman for 10 years and I don't have a word to tell anybody about that. I don't have a word.

MR. OLSON: Would the word do it?

KRIS: Well, why would everybody be getting married if it didn't do anything. I think it must do something. It appears to be really important to people and I would really like to use the word, too, because it symbolizes maybe the most important decision you make as an adult, who you choose. No one does it for you. [. . .] You want to feel that it's going to stick. And that you will have the protection and the support and the inclusion that comes from letting other people know that you feel that way.

MR. OLSON: Do you think it would matter in your neighborhood in your community that you would be able to say that you and Sandy were married? Would it cause people to treat you differently?

KRIS: I think it would be an enormous relief to our friends who are married. Our straight heterosexual friends that are married almost view us in a way that—I know they love us, but I think they feel sorry for us and I can't stand it.

You know, many of them are either in their second marriage or their first marriage, but nevertheless, they have a word and they belong to this institution or this group.

And I can think of a time recently when I went with Sandy happily to a football game at the high school where two of our kids go and we went up the bleachers and we were greeted with these smiling faces of other parents sitting there waiting for the game to start. And I was so acutely aware that I thought, they are all married and I'm not.

MR. OLSON: It sounds to me like your heterosexual friends don't feel threatened if you were to get married; that same-sex marriage doesn't sound like it threatens them?

KRIS: No. The friends we have, I think, would feel better about their marriages if we could be married, too. They would feel like they get to help support our family in a way that is familiar to them, makes sense to them.

Right now they are a little bit unsure, just like we are, of what we all should be doing because we are outside of any sort of tradition. It's just sort of this thing we invented that no one but us understands.

MR. OLSON: You have heard the argument, I think probably in various different places, that allowing you to get married to a person of the same sex would damage the institution—the traditional institution of marriage; do you agree?

MR.RAUM: Objection, your Honor. Calls for expert testimony.

JUDGE WALKER: Sustained.

MR. OLSON: Have you discussed with Sandy the impact on the marriage relationship itself if you were to prevail in this lawsuit?

KRIS: Yes, of course we have. We have talked about it. And Sandy has been married before and so, you know, I really envy her having had that experience.

But we both believe that there would be a settling in and a deepening of our commitment if we could get through this, instead of feeling instead like it's everybody else's decision.

MR. OLSON: Did you in—prior to the filing of this lawsuit, seek a marriage license?

KRIS: Yes.

MR. OLSON: What happened? Describe that?

KRIS: We went to the Alameda County Recorder's Office in May, having reached the point where we wanted to see if there was a permanent solution to this problem and wanted to know in a more concrete way whether—how Prop 8 was being enacted.

And we, indeed, pulled a number, filled out a form and waited for our turn. And the clerk that day, we sat down in front of her and she opened up her computer and looked at the form we were trying to get and she—her eyes got really big and she looked at us and she said, "I'm sorry, but there are reasons why I don't think I can do what you are asking me to do, but I'm not comfortable not doing it. So I'm going to go get my boss. He is going to have to do it."

So she left the cubicle, and she went upstairs, and there was a long delay, and she came downstairs with her supervisor.

And he had written down this Prop 8, the statute, I think, and he read from it. And he was very nervous and very upset and very, I'm sure, worried that we would be upset as well, which we were. And he said after reading the statute, "I'm very sorry that I cannot give you this license. That I hope some day I can and I hope you will come back."

MR. OLSON: Have you thought about the impact upon you, of you and Sandy and your relationship of bringing a lawsuit and being a plaintiff in a civil rights case and what's that like?

KRIS: I have been thinking about it a lot lately. And to be—well, Sandy and I really like our life where—we live in our house and we see our kids and we see our friends. We don't want anything to change about our life. In fact, we would really like our life to just get better and better.

And when I think about whether or not what we want to have happen would make it possible for other people to have that happen, that makes me really happy, but it, most importantly, comes from a place of just wanting our lives to feel better than they do right now.

MR. OLSON: If the courts of the United States ultimately decided that you and other same—persons seeking to marry someone of the same sex could indeed, did indeed, have the constitutional right to get married, do you think that would have an effect on other acts of discrimination against you?

MR. RAUM: Objection, Your Honor. Speculation.

JUDGE WALKER: Close, but objection overruled. State of mind. You may answer.

KRIS: I believe for me, personally as a lesbian, that if I had grown up in a world where the most important decision I was going to make as an adult was treated the same way as everybody else's decision, that I would not have been treated the way I was growing up or as an adult.

There's something so humiliating about everybody knowing that you want to make that decision and you don't get to that, you know, it's hard to face the people at work and the people even here right now. And many of you have this, but I don't.

So I have to still find a way to feel okay and not take every bit of discriminatory behavior toward me too personally because in the end that will only hurt me and my family.

So if Prop 8 were undone and kids like me growing up in Bakersfield right now could never know what this felt like, then I assume that their entire lives would be on a higher arc. They would live with a higher sense of themselves that would improve the quality of their entire life.

MR. OLSON: Thank you, your Honor. I have no further questions.

JUDGE WALKER: Very well. You may cross-examine, Mr. Raum, is it?

MR. RAUM: Yes, your Honor. No questions.

JUDGE WALKER: Very well. Ms. Perry, you may step down.

When I reflect on the day I testified, I remember an aha! moment, when the mash-up of memories shaken loose by the Gibson Dunn lawyers, the terror of testifying, and the gift of being a plaintiff cascaded down on me, and I realized I had been coping my entire adult life. "You can't expect to be accepted, you won't be married, you'll never have children." I had told myself those things over and over, and so had everyone else. The reinforcing cycle of discrimination and self-discrimination had been looping my whole life. On the stand, I suddenly thought, "Enough. Enough coping. Enough settling. Enough making me easier for everyone else."

I could picture the three-year-old me, the eight-year-old me, the sixteen-year-old me, every one with a huge weight on her shoulders. Keeping a secret she didn't know or understand, afraid of losing the love of her family, of being rejected by her friends. By fighting to be unseen and unheard, I didn't grab love when others did. I didn't hold my head high—I looked down. I didn't see a future with my children and spouse; I thought I'd always be single and alone. If I could have dreamt of the good stuff, could have imagined what was possible, I might have known how to have more of it in my life.

I had covered up my embarrassment and humiliation for years, and it was painful for my loved ones to hear these experiences without censoring or sugarcoating. I felt like a huge weight had been lifted from me—but I knew well there was still so much more to come.

Fighting for the right to marry was fighting for the right to believe in love and hope. When I stepped down from the stand, Ted silently touched my shoulder as I joined my family. My boys were crying; my mom looked proud and heartbroken at the same time. Sandy reached out to hug me. It was a slo-mo moment. How had the lawyers known I was so invested in coping and that I had to be honest with myself to testify authentically? How did I suddenly see my past and my future at the same time? How did I get the courage to say, publicly, "You all have something but I don't and it's humiliating to sit here knowing you know that about me and there's nothing I can do about it."

The case was called *Perry v. Schwarzenegger*, but on that day, for me, it was Perry v. Perry, and Perry won.

CHAPTER 25

The Witness Stand

Sandy

Watching Kris give testimony was amazing. She calmly and succinctly answered each question, eloquently and with a vulnerability that provided depth to her story. I was so impressed by her ability to articulate her experiences and publicly speak about the most painful parts of her life. And to do it with such grace. She recalled the pain of feeling different, the fear of rejection, and the desire to find love and build a family.

The courtroom was riveted as Kris reflected on a life that might have been, on the person she might have become had she not borne the shame of discrimination. Her eyes glistened with tears as she left the witness stand, the proponents wisely declining to cross-examine her. The only sounds were the muffled sniffles of those in the room, including Spencer and Elliott, who had rarely seen their mother so vulnerable and exposed. This would mark a turning point in their lives, and they became noticeably more protective of both of us after that day.

At last it was my turn. My stomach had been in knots all day, but my focus was on the job at hand. I would answer every question as clearly and succinctly as possible. My preparation with Ted had revealed my inclination to talk too much, to use "too many words," as Kris would say. I was determined to use just the right amount of words without shortchanging my testimony, to tell the truth but to offend no one. I took a deep breath and sat down on the chair, facing the room, Judge Walker to my right.

To calm my nerves, I focused on Ted, blocking out the rest of the faces, especially the proponents' counsel and Brian Raum, of whom I had no fond memories from my deposition. I stated my full name, Sandra Belzer Stier. I had long since traded my birth middle name of Jane for my maiden name of Belzer, having chosen to keep the last name I shared with my boys.

At forty-seven, I was the oldest of the plaintiffs, a fact not lost on Kris, who referred to me laughingly as a "cougar." I described growing up on a farm in Iowa, attending the University of Iowa, and then moving to California. We went quickly through the composition of our blended family, my two biological sons, Kris's biological twins, and their general whereabouts in school.

Ted asked when I understood that I was a lesbian, and I responded that it was in my midthirties, after being married to my then husband for a number of years. I briefly talked about that marriage, how it had started well but ended badly. He asked about my knowledge of homosexuality as a child in rural Iowa. I shared the reality of my simple, sheltered upbringing on the farm, going to school in a homogenous small-town environment where I wasn't exposed to gay people or even the concept of being gay until I was a teenager.

Ted asked me to describe meeting Kris, how our relationship developed, and how my marriage ended. I told him about the joy of falling in love with her and the many factors that contributed to my divorce. He asked if my sexual orientation was the reason for my divorce. In fact, it was not. My marriage had fallen apart long before I fell in love with Kris, but the divorce happened after. It was messy, but I couldn't stay in my marriage and be happy, Kris or no Kris. It had failed, like marriages sometimes do. I responded to Ted's insistent questions about that marriage and the concept of love.

SANDY: I had a hard time relating to the concept of being in love when I was married to my husband. And while I did love him when I married him, I honestly just couldn't relate when people said they were in love. I thought they were overstating their feelings and maybe making a really big deal out of something. It didn't really make sense to me. It seemed dramatic.

You know, when you grow up in the Midwest and in a farming family—which is a really unique way to grow up, if anybody knows much about that—but there is a pragmatism that is inherent and it's part of the fabric of life and an understated way of being that is just pervasive in terms of your development.

And I remember as a young girl talking to my mom about love and marriage and she would say, "You know, marriage is more than romantic love. It's more than excitement. It's an enduring long-term commitment and it's hard work." And in my family that seemed very true.

So I really thought that was what I was kind of signing up for when I got married; not that it would be bad but that it would be hard work and I would grow into that love, and that I needed to marry a good, solid person and I would grow into something like my parents had, which was really a lovely marriage and still is.

Seemingly satisfied with my description of my first marriage, warts and all, Ted pressed on about my relationship with Kris and how I knew I was gay. After all, couldn't I change? Was I really gay?

SANDY: Well, I'm convinced, because at 47 years old I have fallen in love one time and it's with Kris. And our love is—it's a blend of many things. It's physical attraction. It's romantic attraction. It's a strong commitment. It's intellectual bonding and emotional bonding.

Ted asked about our 2004 marriage and the celebration with friends and family, how the revocation had impacted us, and why we had decided to wait until we had a clear path to a permanent legal marriage before walking down the aisle again. Judge Walker interrupted to address the issue of the state's role in regulating marriage, asking me directly how I would feel about the removal of the word "marriage" in the legal process.

JUDGE WALKER: Let me ask you this: If the state were essentially to get out of using the term "marriage" and admitting persons of the same sex or opposite sex into what it called a "domestic union," "spousal relationship," whatever name you want to use, but not "marriage," wouldn't that put you on the same plane as others who have the same relationship even though they are of opposite sex?

SANDY: I believe it would. Because there wouldn't be anything different.

Right now we are being treated differently and if the state stopped, I guess, issuing marriage licenses and nobody else picked up the task that could exclude us, then we would have the same access. And if we had the same access, I would feel like we are being treated equally.

JUDGE WALKER: Even though the term "marriage" was not used?

SANDY: Right. Because then marriage wouldn't be something that anybody got to claim as a legal status.

I guess you would have to also look at the people who were already married and would they still have marriages.

But if marriage were not a legal status sanctioned by the state or any type of government in our society, then, I guess, I wouldn't have to worry about not having access to it because nobody else would either.

I believed there were a number of ways to provide equal access to the many legal and financial benefits that marriage affords, and I was appalled that the institution of marriage itself was the vehicle to so many rights. Single people, abandoned children, mothers—there are many cases to be made for an entire redo of the marriage construct, or rather the benefits and protection construct, but we were in court for the right for same-sex couples to access marriage, and we soon returned to the particulars of that subject.

After a few questions about my reaction to the Prop 8 campaign and media blitz, Ted turned toward questions of parenting, asking, "Would your boys be better off with a man in the house?"

I was ready for this kind of question, and I understood why it was asked, but I couldn't help but catch my breath because I knew what great parents Kris and her ex-partner had been to the twins and how mightily my own boys struggled with the loss of their father. I responded:

SANDY: The best thing children can have is parents who love them. That's the most important thing. And I know I love my children with all my heart. Kris loves our children with all her heart. And that's what I believe to be the best thing for them, to be loved.

I glanced briefly at the twins, their backs rigid and their eyes fixed on me. They were loved. They were loved by their three moms, one by birth, one by adoption, and me, their stepmom. They were loved by their grandmother. At this moment, sitting next to Kris's proud mother, Laura, they were the picture of admiring sons. My own boys weren't in the audience that day. I didn't want them to witness an ugly cross-examination should that occur, and they wanted to avoid any involvement with the media, so we had decided that they would attend another day. My own parents and siblings were a world away in Iowa, suburban Chicago, and eastern Ohio.

Ted's final question was more general, asking simply, Why fight for this right? Why file this case?

MR. OLSON: Tell us what it means to you, as a plaintiff in this case, if you were to be successful? How it would change your life?

SANDY: Well, I think it would change my life dramatically. The first time somebody said to me, "Are you married," and I said "Yes," I would think, "Ah, that feels good. It feels good and honest and true."

I would feel more secure. I would feel more accepted. I would feel more pride. I would feel less protective of my kids. I would feel less like I had to protect my kids or worry about them or worry that they feel any shame or sense of not belonging.

So I think there are immediate, very real and very desirable personal gains that I would experience. And, of course, close family.

But on a different level, you know, as a parent you are always thinking about that other generation, that next generation, because you are—they are in your house. So you are constantly thinking about the world that you're— the society you are in, what are you doing for them? And are we building a good world for them? And I really want that.

I want our kids to have a better life than we have right now. When they grow up, I want it to be better for them. And their kids, I want their lives to be better, too.

So I really do think about that generation and the possibility of having grandchildren some day and having them live in a world where they grow up and whoever they fall in love with, it's okay, because they can be honored and they can be true to themselves and they can be accepted by society and protected by their government. And that's what I hope can be the outcome of this case in the long run.

And that's what I did hope for. A better world for our kids. And our kid's kids. And your kids. I want them all to live on the "higher arc" that Kris longed for. The freedom to love yourself and the freedom to love whoever you want. The freedom to choose.

My testimony complete, I walked to my seat, stopping briefly to hug Ted, his embrace punctuated by a whisper of kind and reassuring words. I took my place by Kris, my body rigid from the anxiety and worry of the cross-examination that didn't happen and painfully self-conscious of the many ears and eyes in the room that had witnessed such a personal story. I clenched Kris's hand as tears welled up in my eyes, and I struggled to regulate my breath.

Later that day, I showed Kris a text I had received from an angry relative of my deceased husband, chastising me for referencing him in my testimony. Apparently, the transcripts had hit the Internet at record speed. Ted had asked about my first marriage, and I had responded as minimally as I could, simply stating that my ex-husband had died from complications of alcoholism. Testimony isn't optional when you're on the witness stand, even when the truth is painful.

We finished the day giddy with relief that our testimonies were over. After a brief press conference, Kris and I and Jeff and Paul piled into a car and broke into laughter and cheers. The weight was off our shoulders, at least for the night. After we dropped off Jeff and Paul, Kris and I made our way back to Berkeley, stopping off at a favorite brewpub for a pint of beer and our own debriefing.

We slept soundly that night and headed back to court the next day to watch the beginning of a lengthy parade of expert witnesses. They were coming from all over the world to testify on issues of parenting, political influence, the history of marriage, sociology, economics, psychology, and the impact of discrimination. There would be rigorous examination and cross-examination, and by the end, we would feel like we had a PhD in marriage equality. It was time to buckle up and listen.

Heading to Judge Walker's court.

CHAPTER 26

Full-Court Press

Kris

For the next eleven days, Jeff, Paul, Sandy, and I sat on the hard wooden bench in the front of the courtroom while our attorneys covered the full gamut of issues, establishing a record that would be essential if the case was appealed.

The argument started with a history of marriage by scholar Nancy Cott, who testified to the importance of the institution of marriage to individuals, couples, and families by noting that "when slaves were emancipated, they flocked to get married. And this was not trivial to them, by any means." My favorite part of her testimony came during direct examination by Ted Boutrous regarding emancipated slaves and marriage:

MR. BOUTROUS: Can you tell me about—give me a couple of examples of those features?

MS. COTT: Yeah. Well, first of all, marriage, the ability to marry, to say, "I do," it is a basic civil right. It expresses the right of a person to have the liberty to be able to consent validly.

And this can be seen very strikingly in American history through the fact that slaves during the period, the long period that American states had slavery, slaves could not marry legally.

MR. BOUTROUS: Why were slaves barred from marrying?

MS. COTT: Because as unfree persons, they could not consent. They did—they lacked that very basic liberty of person, control over their own actions that enabled them to say, "I do," with the force that "I do" has to have. Which is to say, I am accepting the state's terms for what a valid marriage is.

A slave couldn't do that because the master had over-all rights over the slaves' ability to disport his person or to make any claim. The slave could not obligate himself in the way that a marriage partner does obligate himself or herself.

MR. BOUTROUS: What happened when slaves were emancipated?

MS. COTT: When slaves were emancipated, they flocked to get married. And this was not trivial to them, by any means.

They saw the ability to marry legally, to replace the informal unions in which they had formed families and had children, many of them, to replace those informal unions with legal, valid marriage in which the states in which they lived would presumably protect their vows to each other.

Professor George Chauncey, a historian who specializes in LGBT history, described how previous government campaigns had attempted "to demonize gay people as dangerous sexual deviants and child molesters." During his testimony, I understood for the first time how important it was that Sandy and I were plaintiffs. We were parents; I had worked as a child abuse investigator and social worker for more than twenty years; she worked to improve systems and services for low-income families. We represented the opposite of the type of people the other side said we were. They said we harmed children and we wanted to harm opposite-sex couples. Nothing could have been further from the truth. Dr. Chauncey's description of the history of discrimination in the United Sates helped clarify the depth of the problem the LGBT community had in fighting Prop 8 at the ballot box.

MR. BOUTROUS: Dr. Chauncey, before we go into the sub-stance or the details, if you will, of your opinions, could you just give the court a brief summary of the expert opinions that you're going to offer to the Court today.

DR. CHAUNCEY: Well, most broadly, I guess, my reading of the historical record is that lesbians and gay men have experienced widespread and acute discrimination from both public and private authorities over the course of the 20th century. And that has continuing legacies and effects.

This has been manifested in the criminalization of sexual intimacy and association; the discrimination in public accommodations, in employment; censorship of images about gay people and speech by gay activists; stereotyping and demonization of lesbians and gay men. And that all this has been drawn on and reinforced sustained patterns of prejudice and hostility.

He went on to analyze campaign material from the Yes on 8 campaign to show how it played on the same message and that that animus was unfounded.

Helen Zia, an Asian American scholar, testified about the profound importance the right to marry her wife, Lia Shigemura, had been not only in transforming her view of her own relationship but also in unifying their two families into a stronger, more loving family.

[SAN FRANCISCO CITY ATTORNEY] MR. CHOU: Just two questions. When Mr. Raum interrupted you, you were going to continue saying something. Do you want to finish?

MS. ZIA: Yes. I'd like to say, in talking about the fact that our families came together even though our marriage had been invalidated, it was really the difference, night and day, between being domestic partners and being married. Even symbolically married, even though it had been overturned.

It was as though we had tasted—that we had been prisoners in a closet; that we had been deprived of something; that we had been told to sit in the back of the bus and accept this kind of lesser status of domestic partners.

And, suddenly [. . .] our marriage was invalidated. [. . .] And that during that six months, our families really had a transformational moment that I think did transcend the sadness that we felt. But it didn't take away from the loss. We still recognized we lost something very important. But in terms of their relating to each other, it was quite a different way from when we had domestic partnership.

You know, the idea that we would be families, that we—for a brief moment in time we experienced a feeling of—of—of what equality is, what—instead of having to go to the fountain that is just for gay and lesbian people, here we could go to the fountain that formerly said heterosexuals only. And we tasted the water that was sweeter there. And our families experienced that.

And so, yes, the—our—at the time of our wedding celebration, our marriages were legally invalidated. But we had already begun a process of our families coming together in a way that did not happen in the prior 11 years that we had been domestic partners.

MR. CHOU: Thank you. Nothing further, Your Honor.

Professor Gary Segura, an expert in political science, said that no other minority group in America—including undocumented aliens—has been the target of more restrictive ballot initiatives than gay men and lesbians. Dr. Segura was one of the few expert witnesses who was clear that he was gay and was unapologetic on that point.

He underwent extensive cross-examination as the other side attempted to establish that the LGBT community does have significant political power:

MR. BOUTROUS: In analyzing the political power of a particular minority group, is it also appropriate to look at the vulnerability of the favorable outcomes that have been achieved?

MR. SEGURA: Well, I'm not sure it's—it's necessarily the case in all circumstances, but it's certainly the case

for gays and lesbians because of the role of ballot initiatives.

So in a number of jurisdictions, most of the western
part of the United States, and parts of the east, as well,
laws passed by the legislature or laws passed by even
city and county legislatures are able to be overturned by
popular plebiscite.

Or there's a process where citizens can just have a
law voted on through the initiative process. And initiatives have been used to roll back legislative gains by
gays and lesbians over and over again.

In fact, between 1990 and the middle part of the
2000s, there's been probably like 150—not even counting
the same-sex marriage votes, there's been like 150 votes
on gay and lesbian—usually, on gay and lesbian antidiscrimination protections. And they lose about 70 percent
of the time.

MR. BOUTROUS: Now, when you're looking at political power
on a particular issue, is it also a factor to—that you
consider the importance of the issue to the gay and lesbian community, or whatever minority group you're talking
about? Is that another factor you apply when you're looking at favorable outcomes?

MR. SEGURA: Well, sure. I think we would want to look at
the subject matter of any piece of legislation.

So, for example, in California, there's now a standard clause, a standard antidiscrimination clause, that's
attached to the end of many pieces of California legislation. And they might have to do with state licensing
requirements on some profession or some type of business,
or whatever. And then at the end they say "shall not be
discriminatory."

I wouldn't call that a victory for gay and lesbian
rights, because it's not clear that gays and lesbians
were, you know, actively working for, you know, rights in
insulation contracting or, you know, some other sort of
licensing issue.

We want to focus—when we want to focus on estimating political power, we want to focus on the things that are important to the group whose power we are trying to assess.

MR. BOUTROUS: Would marriage qualify as one of the salient important issues that would serve as a marker?

MR. SEGURA: Yes.

MR. BOUTROUS: Speaking of markers, in your expert opinion, what are the markers of political powerlessness?

MR. SEGURA: So, there were two types of markers I talked about in my report.

The first are sort of manifestations: Can we look at the results of power or powerlessness? And then the second were the causes or the factors that might contribute to those results.

MR. BOUTROUS: Why don't we start with the manifestations of political powerlessness of gays and lesbians in the United States.

Could you give us an example of one manifestation that supports your opinion regarding the powerlessness of gays and lesbians?

MR. SEGURA: Sure. The first thing I would look at is the— is the absence of statutory protection or the presence of statutory disadvantage. So if—if there are laws hurting you and there are no laws helping you, that would be evidence that you have a lack of power.

. . .

MR. BOUTROUS: So how does the lack of participation or representation in high ranking and other government positions undermine political power of gay men and lesbians?

MR. SEGURA: Well, for starters in many parts of the country elected officials have absolutely no problem speaking about gays and lesbians in a way that you could not imagine them speaking about any other member of the electorate.

So in addition to gay and lesbian concerns not being considered meaningfully, for example, in the U.S. Senate, there are members of the United States Senate who, in public speeches, have compared same-sex marriage to marrying a box turtle. There is a member of the Senate who has a hold on a judicial nomination because the nominee attended a lesbian commitment ceremony.

Senator Coburn has gone on record saying that the gay and lesbian agenda is the greatest threat to freedom in the United States today.

And a Senator from South Carolina, when he was elected to the Senate said during the course of his campaign that gays and lesbians shouldn't be allowed to teach in the public schools.

It's difficult to imagine an elected official saying such a thing about, really, almost any other citizen group in the United States.

Several other experts followed, including Dr. Ilan Meyer, an expert in public health, stigma, and stress, who testified about the strain of "nonevents," putting a finer point on my testimony of working hard to prevent awkward or uncomfortable situations from happening and how hard I tried to avoid wanting to be married because I believed I would never be married.

DR. MEYER: There is another type of stress that is a little different and maybe a little harder to understand as to why it is a stress. And those have been termed "nonevents." Which means nothing happened.

And the reason why a nonevent can be stressful is because it is something that was expected to have happened; so the fact that it didn't happen, in this case, also requires adaptation or adjustment.

So, for example, if I've been working in my job for a certain number of years, and I expected after a certain amount of time I would receive a promotion, but I didn't receive that promotion, that could be a nonevent, in a sense, because nothing happened but it was something that I expected and others expected.

It's not just any kind of expectation. So, you know, if I bought a lottery ticket and did not get the prize, would not be the same type.

It is something that is normal to expect to happen at a particular time. Usually, we are talking about milestones over a lifetime. And, certainly, marriage will be one of those types of expected events. Having children.

If you ask little children, that will be the kind of thing that they will tell you about what might happen to them in the future: I will marry. I will have children. I will be a grandparent. Things like that, that are easily understood in our society.

Dr. Gregory Herek argued that policies like Prop 8 encourage social stigma, harassment, and hate crimes against LGBT people. He testified that there is no evidence that conversion therapy is effective in changing a person's sexuality. Such "therapy," he commented, "sends a harmful and false message to young people that homosexuality is a disorder," and this message leads directly to more discrimination. During cross-examination, he asserted that "sexual orientation is a combination of attraction, identity, and behavior, and that the complexities researchers face in defining sexual orientation are no different than those they face in defining other characteristics such as race."

It was around this point in the trial—days into it—that Sandy and I started receiving menacing calls at home. An anonymous caller had found our number in the phone book and started harassing us at all hours. He started to call earlier and earlier in the day. I would yell to Spencer and Elliott not to answer, but sometimes they didn't hear me—instead they heard the caller hissing into the phone, "You stinking dykes. Marriage is between one man and one woman only. God set it up that way and that's the way it's gonna be. It's really disgusting that you are raising kids, and you can tell those faggots doing the case with you that I hope they both die of AIDS."

We reported the calls to the Berkeley police department and changed our number. We learned several weeks later that the same caller had been calling Nancy Pelosi, the Speaker of the US House of Representatives, and harassing her about pending health care legislation. Those calls led authorities to him and landed him in jail. Coming at the same time that experts were testifying about the high rate of hate crimes against LGBT people, the calls were deeply disturbing. Sandy and I felt physically threatened in our home—the calls seemed worse than the random name calling and hate-filled signs and protesters outside the courtroom every day.

Jerry Sanders, the Republican mayor of San Diego, testified with his lesbian daughter present about how he had come within a few hours of signing a ban on same-sex marriage in San Diego, believing that domestic partnership was good enough. He had come to his senses when he realized that this policy would discriminate against his daughter and her partner, both of whom he loved very much. His candor about the process he had gone through to reach acceptance was moving, and there was not a dry eye on our side of the courtroom when he described the anguish and embarrassment he felt upon realizing what he had almost done to his own family.

I noticed something unusual that day. After the mayor testified, during a trip to the restroom, I passed Debbie Cooper, Chuck Cooper's wife. She was in court every day, listening intently to the testimony. On this day, though, she smiled at me as I passed her in the narrow aisle in the courtroom. We'd spent dozens of hours just a few feet away from each other, but we'd never greeted each other. I respected the fact that she was there to support her husband, and I knew from Ted and Lady Olson that the Coopers had been friendly and kind to them. Lady was from Kentucky, the Coopers were from

Alabama, and they were all lawyers in Washington, DC. What I felt that day was a sense that Ms. Cooper respected our right to be there and to fight for what we believed was right.

Mr. Cooper was faintly equivocal when it came to casting the LGBT community as aberrant or amoral. His arguments tended to focus on the rights of the voters of California, honoring the majority in an election, honoring tradition, and maintaining traditional marriage to support children who needed both a mother and a father. And like us, a lot of people in the courtroom remembered the day when Judge Walker asked Mr. Cooper what harm there would be to heterosexual couples if same-sex couples were allowed to marry, and he had answered, "I don't know. I don't know, your Honor."

Near the end of the trial, economists and psychologists took the stand to share volumes of data on how much healthier and wealthier married couples are compared to unmarried couples or individuals. Experts on parenting and families testified about the positive effects of two-parent families. Michael Lamb, a developmental psychologist from Cambridge University, shared a hefty body of literature that focused on the adjustment of children with gay and lesbian parents. Matt McGill examined him:

MR. McGILL: Dr. Lamb, did you [. . .] hold the view that children need a family structure with a male parent to adjust well?

DR. LAMB: You know, when I began my career in the early 1970s, that was widely believed to be true. And so when I began my research, it was with the presumption or prediction that this was likely to be the case.

My first research was concerned with exploring the attachments that young babies form to their mothers and fathers. And I explored in that early research the differences and the ways in which [. . .] mothers and fathers behaved and asked whether those differences, in fact, were important, whether they did show that children needed to be raised by a masculine as well as by a feminine parent.

The results of both my research and, more significantly, the larger body of research that developed since the early 1970s has made clear that that initial prediction was incorrect.

And we have now as a field come to the conclusion that I stated earlier that what makes for an effective parent is the same whether or not you are talking about a mother or a father, and that children do not need to have a masculine-behaving parent figure, a father, in order to be well adjusted.

MR. McGILL: Is there any support for the view that children need to have a female parent to adjust well?

DR. LAMB: No. The same is true with respect to that.

MR. McGILL: How long has it been accepted as the consensus view within your field that the three factors you described earlier, as opposed to family structure, are the factors that most affect child adjustment?

DR. LAMB: I think the fields began to coalesce around and to focus on these issues from the early to mid-1980s. And I would say that by the beginning of the 1990s, this would have been the overwhelming consensus in the field.

MR. MCGILL: And if I could get into Cambridge and take a class in developmental psychology, is this what I would be taught today?

DR. LAMB: It is.

Dr. Lamb explained that children raised by gay and lesbian parents are just as likely to be well adjusted as are children raised by heterosexual parents. Moreover, he noted that the children of same-sex couples would be even likelier to be well adjusted if their parents were able to get married. He made the point that children don't respond as much to a masculine or a feminine parent as they do to a loving, supportive parent. That point, combined with the evidence from economists that married couples fare better than unmarried couples, painted a picture long understood by opposite-sex married couples: you'll weather the challenges of parenting and life in general if you have a partner who is committed to you and your children and you are protected by the state.

After our side rested, the defense called only two witnesses: Professor Ken Miller from Claremont McKenna College and David Blankenhorn of the Institute for American Values. Professor Miller's testimony that the LGBT community in California had political power and did not require protection could not withstand the withering assault of David Boies. Professor Miller argued that all the major newspapers in California and a majority of state politicians all strongly opposed Prop 8, which did not affect the fact that a slim majority of voters supported Prop 8. David methodically walked him through the history of voter initiatives in California and led him to contradict his evidence during direct examination, pointing out that the LGBT community did not have the means necessary to win a statewide ballot measure aimed at denying them the right to marry.

Under cross-examination, defense witness David Blankenhorn turned out to be an asset for our side! He revealed that he believed the principle of equal human dignity applied to gay and lesbian Americans and that "we would be more American on the day we permitted same-sex marriage than we were on the day before." (A few years later, Mr. Blankenhorn would write an op-ed piece in the *New York Times* admitting that he had incorrectly argued that same-sex couples should not be married.) David knew Mr. Blankenhorn had contradicted himself in his books but not in a way that many people would detect. David saw that Mr. Blankenhorn was most interested in the role of fathers in children's lives. That focus was supported by his research into family structure, parenting, and child development. When David connected the child development research already entered into evidence and Mr. Blankenhorn's interest in good parenting, whether by biological or adopted parents, Mr. Blankenhorn was painted into a corner. The only way out was to relent, to admit that all loving parents help children, regardless of gender or biological connection. If those same parents could be married, it would be even more beneficial to the child.

The trial ended on January 25, 2010. Almost five months later, we would return to the courtroom for closing arguments.

Leaving federal court, day one.
Left to right: Chris Dusseault, Jeff, Paul,
Sandy, and Kris.

CHAPTER 27

If You're Not Laughing Every Day, You're Not Paying Attention

Sandy

Because our testimony was over on the first day of trial, the remaining days were educational and inspiring, gut-wrenching and infuriating, and sometimes simply tedious. Our emotions ran the gamut each day, as we heard from insightful witnesses and revisited incendiary propaganda. Judge Walker maintained a brisk pace, his sharp wit keeping everyone on their toes, injecting humor as he nudged recalcitrant witnesses or verbose lawyers to get to the point.

After a few days, I had a new malady, a physical discomfort that can only be caused by hard bench time. I've done a few hundred hard bench hours in my life, but in one-hour segments with healthy doses of standing and kneeling (ouch) and singing. Now we were bench-bound for seven or eight hours a day, with brief reprieves for lunch in the court cafeteria. Our bums were numb. So was my mind at some points, as our (brilliant and amazing) expert witnesses were cross-examined by markedly less brilliant defense counsel.

I invented a new fitness regime that I called "court yoga." Court yoga is unique in that when it is practiced properly, it is undetectable by others. Intended to relieve the numb bum, it involves isolating muscles and holding them in tense and uncomfortable isometric positions while silently counting to a large whole number, like sixty, or twenty if the position is hard to maintain. This yoga must be practiced in total stillness, with regular breathing and a motionless face. When switching positions, a small smile and shift of the head is acceptable, but labored breathing is not. Court yoga is designed to mitigate numbness, tolerate dumbness, and keep one alert and appropriately serious.

I was practicing the first of many court yoga poses for the day, careful to hide them from my dearest, who would clench my leg at the first sign of my practice. Game on, sister; I was a pro, and I would not be discovered. Undeterred, I shifted my eyes to the other side of the court as I shifted poses. I scanned the crowd, looking for familiar faces, trying to read the expressions of people I did and didn't recognize. I saw Chuck Cooper's wife and their daughter. They had friendly, though somber, faces. I was lost in thought for a moment, wondering what was going through their minds during these tense arguments. Were they proud of Mr. Cooper's role, or perhaps not? His striking brunette daughter looked a generation younger than we were; surely, she had gay friends and found this situation awkward.

On one of the last days of the trial, the crowd on the other side of the court was joined by Maggie Gallagher, the chair of the board for the antigay National Organization for Marriage and an ill-tempered conservative. She abandoned her shoes and propped her *bare feet* on the back of the bench in front of her. Ewww! Someone had not read Miss Manners. Taken aback, I nudged Kris and Chad, motioning with my eyes for them to look over. News traveled down our bench as we all took in the view. Her indiscretion was short-lived, however, as a court officer approached to inform her of a pesky court rule about having shoes on one's feet and keeping said feet somewhere near the floor. I knew immediately that this would be my favorite moment of the day.

We were nearing the end of the trial, but it wasn't over. Kris had grown increasingly punchy; we were both weary from the daily drill and anxious about how much time we were missing from work and with the kids. Driving to court one morning, I mused about what kind of wedding we might have if and when we actually won the case. Where would it be? Who would we invite? Kris turned to me and said, "I didn't say I wanted to marry you. I said I wanted the option to marry you." I about died laughing—that comment was proof that she was the girl for me.

On the tenth day, David Boies demonstrated his mastery of the courtroom. We had seen him in action during his direct examination of Jeff and Paul. Clear and concise, almost staccato in his approach, his steely blue eyes did little to hide the big heart we felt in his presence and we had witnessed firsthand. Today, though, he was cross-examining. After a hearty lunch of sourdough bread crust and apple pie, David would spend the afternoon cross-examining Professor Miller from Claremont McKenna College of Law. I could almost hear knuckles cracking. Today would be the day that Kenneth Miller would remember for the rest of his life. The Rolling Stones sing a song about a woman who can make a grown man cry. David is a man who can make a grown man cry.

David began his questioning with some reflections about Professor Miller's deposition, asking him to confirm that statements made at his deposition were in fact correct. They were blithely claimed to be accurate by Professor Miller, who was not yet breaking a sweat. David dug further, asking his increasingly nervous witness details about a submitted list of statements. Had he or his counsel provided them? Specifically, what items had Professor Miller provided? Did he need the list? A list was provided to the now visibly anxious witness, along with a pencil he could use to identify which he had actually made, which were provided to him, and which he couldn't remember making. He was, after all, an expert witness. It was time for him to prove the "expert" part of that designation.

Time stood still. David was like a surgeon, removing credibility from the proponents' one credentialed witness, his pale blue eyes and sharp words as exacting as any scalpel. I could feel Professor Miller's sweat run down my own neck as I watched transfixed from my safe haven on the bench while the questions relentlessly flowed. Finally, the mercy that is time delivered the professor from his perch. I almost felt sorry for him, but . . . I didn't. You'd better know what you believe in when you go up against David Boies.

On days eleven and twelve, David delivered perhaps an even more impressive performance. His cross-examination brought stunning revelations from David Blankenhorn, the prime witness for the proponents, whose statements effectively brought him to our side.

David Boies is genius that way. He not only cross-examines a witness; he forces the examination of every word, every angle, every space in between. And between the words, and between the statements, he finds the truth. He lifts it like a surgeon and brings it to light like a good Catholic priest. We were in awe of him and grateful that he was for, and not against, us. With his slightly rumpled suit, his watch clasped tightly over his monogrammed shirt cuff, he had a quirky way about him. When responding to a question or statement, he was exacting and precise, clear as a bell and unequivocal. He believes in the court and in exposing the truth. As David says, the witness stand is a lonely place to lie.

The trial ended on the twelfth and final day, at noon, after Mr. Cooper's final redirect of Mr. Blankenhorn, followed by instructions from the court on final submissions of briefs and evidence. Judge Walker thanked both parties and commended them on the quality of their work throughout the proceedings, and all parties shook hands. It was an exercise in genteel behavior that was not lost on us. It would be months before we returned for closing arguments, but the evidence was in, and we were finally out of court.

Hours later, after Kris had headed off to work and Jeff and Paul were on their way to the airport, I went to my first day of graduate school at Golden Gate University, to start work on a degree in public administration, in a classroom directly across the street from the San Francisco law offices that I now knew so well. The twelve days of trial had been an education. But time marches on, and now we had to learn some patience.

CHAPTER 28

The People's Magazine

Sandy

While we were patiently waiting for a ruling, another effort was under way. Winning at court would spell success only if we also made progress in the court of public opinion. Best known for being on opposite sides of issues, Ted and David were busy doing interviews on news shows and talk shows. *Newsweek* ran a beautiful article, "The Conservative Case for Gay Marriage."

While Ted and David were making their constitutional case in the public arena, Kris and I were asked to talk to *People* magazine. They would interview us for a story about our journey. And take pictures. In our house, which was kind of messy . . . and certainly not magazine-ready. As they took over our living room, they asked about our lives, our families, and our struggle to legally marry. I could have talked about our struggle until the cows came home, but Kris and I were determined to stay focused on a positive outcome, so we kept the struggle part to a minimum, concentrating instead on what we hoped to achieve.

We talked about why gay families are just like straight families, which they basically are, with some obvious biological differences. Are marriages between same-sex couples the same as "traditional" marriages? Not exactly; at least, ours wasn't. Our family was like a modern Brady Bunch, complete with power struggles, sleepless nights waiting for teenagers to come home, and questionable hairstyles.

Smiling, Kris and I sat at our extended dining room table calmly explaining our family and our lawsuit. Yes, we had been together for quite some time, about ten years at that point. Yes, we had married each other already. We had been married legally in San Francisco in the winter of 2004 and had celebrated our marriage in style in Berkeley that summer, but then our marriage had been rescinded. So, we still weren't married and we wanted to be. This was our chance to show America how normal gay families are, so there would be no jokes about locking up the booze (which we did), being fake married, or having hot flashes (which were a constant source of misery and a good reason to wear unflattering tank tops).

We dutifully answered questions about our relationship, our family, and our experience with the case, attempting to be charming and endearing when the opportunity arose. Were we proud to represent Californians in this lawsuit? Why, yes, we were! Did we feel like this was the right approach to the problem? Absolutely! We believed that our rights shouldn't be voted on and that our constitutional rights were being violated, and who would turn down the opportunity to work with the legal team of the century? And we meant every word we said. Our right to marry had been voted on by our fellow Californians. The California Constitution had been changed to discriminate against us. That wasn't right. Going to court was the right solution to the problem, and we were hopeful that our lawsuit would be successful in overturning Prop 8 and restoring marriage equality to California.

The writers asked more about our 2004 wedding and ceremony, and we shared photographs. When the published article attributed nine-year-old Spencer's wedding toast to Tom, our oldest, we had hell to pay. A teenager at the time of the wedding and never one for public speaking, Tom wouldn't have been caught dead standing in front of a hundred people saying, "Sandy's the perfect match for Kris, and that's wonderful." We had promised to keep the boys out of the spotlight unless we had their permission, and once again we had failed.

Disappointment was no stranger in my relationship with my kids. Why couldn't I pick them up after school? Why didn't we have a new car? Why didn't we go to Hawaii over Christmas break? Why were we so strict? Didn't we know that the other parents were so much cooler? They made their homes safe spaces for drinking and all kinds of other stuff that were . . . newsflash . . . ILLEGAL. These are the kind of conversations that went on in our house for years. Every day. So, was I sorry about the incorrect reference in the article and did I wish I could have proofread it? Yes. Was I losing sleep over it? No.

In the end, *People* made us look and sound pretty normal. Not normal enough for the cover, but normal enough to land on page 100 or so, right before the reference pages. Our story as detailed in the article was true Americana, two people in love, fighting for their rights while raising four boys. The writers left out the mundane aspects of our story—two exhausted middle-aged women with two jobs, two flights of stairs, a dusty minivan, and a seven-seat SUV, trying to wrangle four boys to adulthood without anyone getting seriously injured, expelled, or incarcerated. The writers omitted descriptions of the parking tickets on the counter and the nonorganic gallons of milk lingering in the fridge, and glossed over the piles of schoolbooks, sticky backpacks, and the smell of shin guards and sweaty cleats. No wonder *Glamour* wasn't knocking at our door.

So Kris and I were in *People* magazine. And that meant I had to let my mom know so she wouldn't be surprised if one of the church ladies mentioned it. My mom is a church lady. A go-to-church-very-frequently-and-pray-for-her-children kind of church lady. Catholic-style, which is to say laced with guilt, duty, and rules. She says rosaries for us when she thinks we are screwing up. Many a rosary has been said for me, the most likely of her children to cause her to sprint to the pews, beads in hand. She is not, however, a reader of current events magazines.

"Mom, I wanted to let you know that Kris and I are going to be in a magazine article." I spoke slowly and deliberately into the phone, giving the news time to sink in.

"Oh, you are? What magazine?"

"*People*," I answered.

"*The People's Magazine*? I don't think I've ever heard of that," she responded.

"No, Mom, not *The People's Magazine*, just *People*."

"Well, I've still never heard of that."

My mom is not what you would call contemporary. She's lovely and loving and sweet as cherry pie, but in some ways she still lives in the 1950s. She would no more seek out or read *People* magazine than she would jump on a Harley and join the Hell's Angels. She had never read *People* magazine. *Readers Digest*? Now we're talking! The *Catholic Messenger*? Yes, please! I spent many a happy afternoon carefully cutting out the paper doll and outfit that came with her monthly copy of *McCall's* when I was young. But *People* magazine? Not on your life.

"Where do you get it?" she asked quizzically.

"Mom," I said in my most patient voice. "You can get it anywhere magazines are sold, like the grocery store or the 7-Eleven."

"Well, I'll try to find it." She didn't sound hopeful.

Eventually, however, she got her hands on the right copy of *The People's Magazine*. And then promptly dismissed it.

"I honestly don't think anyone will read that magazine. There's really nothing interesting in it. I don't think anyone [meaning church ladies] will know who you are or will read the article."

This was said with a sigh of relief. Although my mother loved me and accepted Kris into our family, she would have vastly preferred that we keep our relationship on the down low. I mean, was it really necessary to broadcast this information and make people uncomfortable?

"Mom," I asked on one of my frequent visits, "are you embarrassed that we're in the case?"

I asked this after she had said she didn't think anyone in Iowa would know it was me in the case because I had changed my name years earlier when I married my husband.

"Yes . . . I am, but I feel badly about that, and I wish that I didn't."

That is the essence of my mom. She speaks her truth, and it didn't hurt to hear those words so much as it filled me with empathy for her. I asked her to tell me more about those feelings, where they were coming from. A devout Catholic and a feisty Democrat, she fervently believed in fairness above all. She went out of her way to treat her four children equally and insisted on familial tranquility. No arguing or fighting allowed. We would all get along if it killed her.

We talked that day about what it was like to be her and how important respect and acceptance were for her in her small Iowa community. I understood her plight and empathized with her, knowing that change doesn't come quickly or easily to many people, especially older ones. I wanted her to find her own strength and resolve in standing up for what is right, and she did believe that we were fighting for the right thing. Focusing on that kernel of truth, we got through that difficult conversation. She agreed that if Kris and I were successful, it would help improve other people's lives, and that acknowledgement was gold.

In the many conversations Kris and I have had about using our story to change hearts and minds, I have often thought about the church ladies of Iowa, remembering that sometimes people just need a little time to accept change. If *People* can help people make that change, then bring it on. Maybe the large print *Readers Digest* can do the next story!

CHAPTER 29

Closing Arguments

Sandy

On June 16, 2010, five months after the trial ended, we were back in court for closing arguments, greeting each other like cousins at a family reunion. We were pros at getting to court, scanning the courtroom for people of interest, surreptitiously conveying joy or dismay with subtle facial expressions, and finding the best snacks in the cafeteria. David and Ted had warned us that the case would take time, but we were stunned at how slowly it moved, even more so when the lawyers insisted that we were making stellar and rapid progress.

The proceedings started in a familiar way, each lawyer introducing himself or herself to the court with a courteous "Good morning, Your Honor." The court is nothing if not civil. Judge Walker was characteristically humorous, responding:

Well, this is an impressive array of legal talent.

(Laughter)

Welcome back. Delighted to have you back. Obviously, the hiatus that we've had, the period of the presentation of the evidence to the present is not anything that I would have wished or hoped for. I was hoping that we could get this case in before present. But it may be appropriate that the case is coming to closing argument now. June is, after all, the month for weddings.

As so many times before, Judge Walker elicited a chuckle from the crowd. As we settled into the opening statement of closing arguments, Ted's deep voice silenced the murmur:

May it please the Court. We conclude this trial, Your Honor, where we began. This case is about marriage and equality.

The fundamental constitutional right to marry has been taken away from the plaintiffs and tens of thousands of similarly-situated Californians. Their state has rewritten its constitution in order to place them into a special disfavored category where their most intimate personal relationships are not valid, not recognized, and second rate. Their state has stigmatized them as unworthy of marriage, different and less respected.

Ted continued for some time, referencing the expert testimony of the trial several months prior, connecting dots along the way, exposing discrimination for what it was:

It is revealing, it seems to me, that the deinstitutionalization message is quite different from the thrust of the proponents' Yes on 8 election campaign. That, in the words they put into the of all California voters, focused heavily on: Protect our children from somehow learning that gay marriage is okay. Protect our children from learning that gay marriage is okay.

Those are the words that the proponents put in the ballot—in the voter information guide that was given to every voter.

That was not a very subtle theme that there is something wrong, sinister, or unusual about gays, that gays and their relationships are not okay, and decidedly not suitable for children, but that children might think it was okay if they learned about gays getting married like normal people.

For obvious reasons, the "gays are not okay" message was largely abandoned during the trial in favor of the procreation and deinstitutionalization themes.

And after promising proof that platform, people might stop marrying and cease procreating if Proposition 8 were overturned, the proponents switched course from that as well, and affirmatively argued that they actually had no idea and certainly no evidence that any of their prog- nostications would come to pass if Proposition 8 were to be enacted.

Their counsel asserted, in his words, "The reality is that you will hear nothing but predictions in this trial about what the long-term effects of adopting same-sex marriage will be on the institution of marriage. It is not possible," he said, "to render reliable and certain judgments on these things."

Judge Walker interrupted with questions that sparked a vol- ley of responses. Ted defended his position, bringing in not only testimony from the trial but also findings from prior cases and references to opposing counsel's statement:

And proponents' counsel said—it came down to this— "Same-sex marriage is simply too novel an experiment to allow for any firm conclusions about its long-term ef- fect on societal interests. They just don't know." That is the essence of the case as it comes to the end of the trial and to the closing arguments. They just don't know whether same-sex marriage will harm the institution of heterosexual marriage.

And I submit that the overwhelming evidence in this case proves that we do know. And the fact is that allowing persons to marry someone of the same sex will not, in the slightest, deter heterosexuals from marrying, from staying married, or from having babies.

In fact, the evidence was from the experts that elimi- nating invidious restrictions on marriage strengthens the institution of marriage for both heterosexual and homo- sexual persons and their children.

Was it reasonable to limit marriage only to those who might potentially procreate? If so, what means would be reasonable to enforce such a limitation? The questions exposed the absurdity of the procreation argument. Ted continued to peel back the argu- ments of the proponents one by one:

The latest words from the proponents, counsel for the proponents is, "We don't know. We don't know whether there is going to be any harm."

And I would submit that, "We've always done it that way," that "It's a traditional definition of marriage," which is something that "We've always done it that way," is the same—is the corollary to the "Because I say so."

It's not a reason. You can't have continued discrimination in public schools because you have always done it that way. You can't have continued discrimination between races on the basis of marriage because you have always done it that way. That line of reasoning would have prevented the Loving marriage. It would have justified racially segregated schools and maintaining subordinate status for married women. We heard a great deal about that relationship from Dr. Cott.

So the constitutional right to marry is fundamental. The constitutional right to be able to be in a relationship with a person of the same sex is a fundamental constitutional right. And in a sense, the State of California is burdening both of those—burdening in a very severe way that hurts individuals and it doesn't do any good to prevent those persons from getting married, because the evidence was also overwhelming in this regard.

Heterosexual people are not going to stop getting married. They are not going to abandon their marriage and they are not going to stop having children because their next-door neighbor has a marriage that's a person of the same sex. That is not going to happen. The evidence said that wasn't going to happen.

Ted's eloquence was not lost on the onlookers. You could hear a pin drop. His baritone voice clear and his speech measured, he concluded his passionate argument by illuminating the core reasoning behind the concept of "preserving" the institution of marriage:

Preserving the institution of marriage. We've improved the institution of marriage when we allowed interracial couples to get married. We have improved the institution of marriage when we allowed women to be equal partners in the marital relationship. We have improved the institution of marriage when we didn't put artificial barriers based upon race. And we will improve the institution of marriage and we will be more American, according to Mr. Blankenhorn, when we eliminate this terrible stigma.

We were winning. We had to be winning. Kris and I squeezed each other's hands, sharing furtive smiles with wide eyes. Ted was knocking it out of the park. How could we not win? Ted had stripped bare every single argument the proponents had made and had pointed out that even their witness ended up agreeing that we kind of had a point. That day was a good day, a very good day. Although the lawyers continued on their path of cautious optimism, I felt sure that we would be victorious.

But we would have to wait. We anxiously waited for the ruling, afraid to leave town lest the ruling come down while we were gone. We hunkered down for the summer, ready to cross the Bay Bridge at a moment's notice when we got the call.

In early August, we got the call.

Ted, David, Sandy, and Kris, San Francisco, 2010.

CHAPTER 30

The Ruling

Kris

Lawyers had told us over and over again how quickly our case was moving to its conclusion, but it felt like an eternity to us. Days became weeks, weeks became months. Finally, on August 3, the phone rang. Adam Umhoefer from AFER was on the line to say that Judge Walker would rule the next day. Fear and doubt assailed us. I felt less certain of the outcome than the day Ted Olson delivered his remarkable closing argument. Had our witnesses really slammed the door shut on the proponents of Prop 8? Was it crystal clear to Judge Walker that gay people were indeed harmed by Prop 8? Had we convinced him that thousands of children were suffering under Prop 8?

Ted's words had been so powerful, but some of the arguments from the other side were also potent. Were we interfering with the religious rights of some? Would the people of California have found their way to a democratic solution soon? It felt like the weight of the decision to pursue a federal remedy was bearing down on all of us as we timidly prepared to travel to meet the team and hear the outcome.

The day of the ruling, we gathered in cold and foggy San Francisco at the offices of Gibson Dunn. After more than a year of swimming as fast as we could to understand the legal process, learning how to share our story with the media, and juggling apprehension and optimism, we were finally going to hear if we had won or lost. As always, Ted and Lady Olson had arrived early and were there to greet everyone. Gradually, the team assembled: Ted and Helen Boutrous, Chris and Sarah Dusseault, Jeff and Paul, Chad Griffin,

Kristina Schake, Rob and Michele Reiner, Adam Umhoefer and the entire AFER staff, and last but certainly not least, David and Mary Boies. The team told us that, win or lose, we all would head to Los Angeles after the ruling to attend a rally in West Hollywood, where many of the supporters of the case would be gathered.

Suddenly, there was a flurry of activity. David appeared in the hall, wearing a stern expression, and gently guided Sandy, me, Jeff, and Paul to a corner conference room. Everyone noticed and asked where we were headed. David explained that he had just received an embargoed copy of the ruling. Ted was reading it as fast as he could, and they had permission to share the ruling with the plaintiffs prior to the public release. Everyone looked happy and let down at the same time. We followed David's instructions and entered the conference room. Ted was there, tie slung over his shoulder, head down. David dove into his copy while we stood there silently. Finally, David looked up, tears welling up in his eyes, and said, "We won."

We smiled, cried, embraced, exhaled. Amazing. Perfect. Just as we were about to jump up and down and celebrate, David said, "Do not make any noise, the others can't know the outcome until ten a.m." We squeezed our eyes hard to fight back the tears, bit our tongues, and like so many times before, waited.

Ted and David reeled off some of the highlights. Judge Walker had ruled in our favor, overturning Prop 8 based on the due process and equal protection clauses of the Fourteenth Amendment. The judge noted that Prop 8 was based on traditional notions of opposite-sex marriage and on moral disapproval of homosexuality, neither of which is a legal basis for discrimination.

Ted and David were elated. A sweeping victory covered in more than fifty pages and eighty findings of facts, including that individuals do not choose their sexual orientation; marriage is a civil and not a religious matter; and the state has no interest in making gays and lesbians change their orientation or marry someone of the opposite sex. Ted chimed in with more findings, among them that denying marriage to same-sex couples harms and imposes costs on society, and that same-sex couples are identical to opposite-sex couples in terms of the characteristics relevant to a successful marriage and union. Later, when we read the ruling ourselves, we were overjoyed to find that the judge had included findings about gender and sexual orientation and how neither is a factor in children's adjustment or well-being.

We headed out to the larger conference room and were greeted by the team. Michele Reiner begged to know what the ruling was, while others seemed to know just by looking at our expressions. There was no hiding relief, I guess. Just as the analog wall clock turned to ten, Ted and David shared the news. Judge Walker, they said, had, among a number of other issues, pointed out that California's domestic partnership law was an inadequate solution for same-sex couples for two reasons: domestic partnerships do not provide the same social meaning as marriage and domestic partnerships were created "specifically so that California could offer same-sex couples rights and benefits while explicitly withholding marriage from same-sex couples."

Rallies in support of the decision had been planned all over California that afternoon and evening. We boarded a chartered plane for Los Angeles; when we got to West Hollywood, we were greeted by a joyous crowd. Elsewhere, California's elected officials responded positively to the ruling. Governor Schwarzenegger said that, "for the hundreds of thousands of Californians in gay and lesbian households who are managing their day-to-day lives, this decision affirms the full legal protections and safeguards I believe everyone deserves." He complimented Judge Walker's conduct during the trial, congratulating his efforts to "respect both sides of the issue equally." Attorney General Brown lauded the decision, calling it "great news for California." The mayors of San Francisco, Los Angeles, and San Diego— Gavin Newsom, Antonio Villaraigosa, and Jerry Sanders, respectively—praised the ruling. Both of California's US senators hailed the ruling as an advancement of equal rights. It was an incomparable day. We rode a wave of relief, pride, and joy—and gratitude for having had such a gifted team on our side, determined to win the legal fight but also careful to protect us and our story.

Shortly after the ruling went public, the other side held a press conference promising to appeal. They wanted to keep hope alive for those who felt our relationship was an affront to their family values.

But we knew that evidence, truth, and love were on our side. As David Boies later said, "We put fear and prejudice on trial, and fear and prejudice lost."

In His Own Words: On *Face the Nation* on August 8, 2010, David Boies said:

It's easy to sit around in debate and throw around opinions and appeal to people's fear and prejudice, cite studies that either don't exist or don't say what you say they do. In a court of law, you've got to come in and you've got to support those opinions. You've got to stand up under oath and cross-examination.

And what we saw at trial is that it's very easy for people who want to deprive gay and lesbian citizens [of their rights] make all sorts of statements in campaign literature or in debates where they can't be cross-examined. But when they come into court and they have to support those opinions, and they have to defend those opinions under oath and cross-examination, those opinions just melt away.

And that's what happened here. There simply wasn't any evidence. There weren't any of "those studies." There weren't any empirical studies. That's just made up. That's just junk science. And it's easy to say that on television, but the witness stand is a lonely place to lie. And when you come into court, you can't do that. And that's what we proved. We put fear and prejudice on trial, and fear and prejudice lost.

CHAPTER 31

A Win and a Loss

Sandy

At long last it was decision day. On August 4, 2010, we drove to meet our attorneys and the AFER team in San Francisco. We headed for the Gibson, Dunn & Crutcher law offices—no court appearance this time. Kris and I nervously dressed that morning, she in a dark suit, I in a black skirt and pink cardigan. Jeff and Paul had flown up from Los Angeles, as had the Reiners and other AFER board members. The documentary crew was on hand as well. We were so used to their presence that they faded into the background.

We settled into clusters, breaking to greet and hug each other, gripped with anxiety. Although we had all witnessed the brilliant lawyering of Ted and David, the expert testimony from our witnesses, and the reversal of opinion from our opponent's star witness, a win was far from guaranteed. We were hopeful but nervous. A win in federal court would be amazing for California and set the stage for the rest of the country; a loss would be devastating, a harsh blow to the movement, with long-lasting repercussions.

As our group grew larger, the decision came down. It was made available to our legal team before it was made public. Ted and David privately reviewed the ruling in a conference room, and then they invited Jeff, Paul, Kris, and me into the room. We cautiously entered, our hearts in our throats. Ted looked up from the stack of papers that constituted the ruling and simply said, "We won."

He and David then explained that we had won big. We had won broad. The ruling was a thorough and exhaustive set of conclusions that spelled victory with a capital *V*. David and Ted were full of emotion and joy, as were we. Misty-eyed, we hugged them and each other, but as quietly as possible. Because the release of the ruling was embargoed, it had to be kept from the rest of the team for a few more minutes. After our near-silent celebration, Jeff, Paul, Kris, and I exited the room and were ushered into a conference room with everyone else, our voices silent but our eyes surely giving the news away.

Ted and David joined us. The room erupted into cheers. AFER staff, lawyers, our fierce defenders and funders, photographers and journalists, and everyone within earshot hugged and kissed each other as they understood what had happened, laughing and crying, beaming with joy. It was a beautiful moment and a shared victory like no other.

So many people had worked for this day, sacrificing time, money, energy, and even friendships to focus on winning marriage equality for residents of the state of California. Ted and David pointed out how beautifully the ruling was written and how impactful it would be moving forward—and that an appeal, the next step in the legal process, was highly likely.

The ruling, based on the due process and equal protection clauses of the Fourteenth Amendment to the US Constitution, concluded that California had no rational basis or vested interest in denying lesbians and gays marriage licenses and included eighty findings of fact to support that conclusion.

CONCLUSION

Proposition 8 fails to advance any rational basis in singling out gay men and lesbians for denial of a marriage license. Indeed, the evidence shows Proposition 8 does nothing more than enshrine in the California Constitution the notion that opposite-sex couples are superior to same-sex couples. Because California has no interest in discriminating against gay men and lesbians, and because Proposition 8 prevents California from fulfilling its constitutional obligation to provide marriages on an equal basis, the court concludes that Proposition 8 is unconstitutional.

REMEDIES

Plaintiffs have demonstrated by overwhelming evidence that Proposition 8 violates their due process and equal protection rights and that they will continue to suffer these constitutional violations until state officials cease enforcement of Proposition 8. California is able to issue marriage licenses to same-sex couples, as it has already issued 18,000 marriage licenses to same-sex couples and has not suffered any demonstrated harm as a result, see FF 64-66; moreover, California officials have chosen not to defend Proposition 8 in these proceedings.

Because Proposition 8 is unconstitutional under both the Due Process and Equal Protection clauses, the court orders entry of judgment permanently enjoining its enforcement; prohibiting the official defendants from applying or enforcing Proposition 8, and directing the official defendants that all persons under their control or supervision shall not apply or enforce Proposition 8. The clerk is DIRECTED to enter judgment without bond in favor of plaintiffs and plaintiff-intervenors and against defendants and defendant-intervenors pursuant to FRCP 58.

IT IS SO ORDERED.

VAUGHN R. WALKER United States District Chief Judge

Ruling in hand, we were off to press conferences—David, Ted, and Chad leading the way, with photographer Diana Walker, *New York Times* journalist Jo Becker, and film crew in tow. We did a press conference in San Francisco and then flew down to Los Angeles. It was a big day and a big win—a once-in-a-lifetime experience. While Chad spoke of the historic nature of the case and the

ruling, and Ted and David spoke of the legal argument and findings, Jeff, Paul, Kris, and I focused on what the ruling might mean
to families in California and beyond. Our court had said that all
families matter. That all families are equal. It was a momentous
leap for civil rights.

Days later, Spencer, Elliott, Kris, and I were in Provincetown,
Massachusetts, at a beach house, trying to absorb the details
of the ruling with the help of our trusted friends Nancy, the San
Francisco city attorney, and Olivia, her partner, who had helped
us navigate the case from the beginning. Out of the blue, I got a
call from one of my siblings. My dad was in the hospital. Always
the picture of health and vitality, he had been dealing with the
onset of dementia for well over a year, and he now had a serious
respiratory infection on top of it. A few days later, I headed to Chicago, where I met my brother, David, and drove six hours to my
parents' home and the hospital to help our mother make some
tough decisions.

Meanwhile, our legal adversaries, the proponents of Prop 8,
pulled an unbecoming stunt. Although they had known all along
that Judge Walker was gay, and they had agreed that he was well
suited to rule on the case, when they lost, they requested that the
ruling be vacated purely on that basis. It was a low blow, albeit
one that was ultimately unsuccessful.

As drama around the case was unfolding, so was drama in my
family. I was at work when I got the call from my brother on September 1 telling me that our dad had died. I quietly closed my office door so that my coworkers wouldn't see my tears. He had had
a beautiful life, working hard and showing his love mostly through
his actions, quietly and stoically. He would never see me married
again, but he had left this world in dignity, and I was supremely
grateful for that.

I spoke at his wake back in Iowa. I spent a few minutes talking
about how important it is to see love in the way it is presented,
addressing my boys and their cousins in particular. My dad loved

us in quiet ways, in "doing" ways. He wasn't much for words, but he made us stilts, tree swings, seesaws. He gave me a wild horse and an art easel. He taught us to swim, to work, to be tough, to be kind. To accept.

My dad died one day after my forty-ninth birthday. Kris had given me a third ring on that birthday—the ring that commemorates winning the case against Prop 8. The Perry case. It is a simple ring, a slim platinum band inscribed with the memorable date of the decision—August 4, 2010.

If Dad's dementia had not been so advanced, I like to think that he would have been proud of us for winning the case. A staunch, quiet Democrat and a gruff old farmer with faded blue overalls that matched his eyes, he had a penchant for justice. And in that courtroom, justice was served. We won for ourselves, certainly. But what mattered more was winning dignity and fairness for all people, whether they want to be married or can't even spell the word "marriage." We all deserve that dignity.

When I see that ring on my finger, I am reminded of how justice served us in Judge Walker's courtroom. And once a year or so, when I make it back to the farm, which is now owned by our neighbors, I feel the presence of my dad. In the rolling cornfields, the grazing cattle, the sagging buildings, the remnants of my childhood, I remember being a "normal little girl" with a hard-working dad who fought to hold onto his farm. And I am proud of myself and of Kris. Because we fought, too.

Jamie Lee Curtis (left), playing Sandy, and Christine Lahti, playing Kris, standing onstage during the curtain call in the Los Angeles production of 8.

CHAPTER 32

8

Kris

The high from winning in federal district court on August 4, 2010, lingered for days. Soon after the ruling came down, Sandy and I and the twins took off for a long-planned (and delayed) vacation to Provincetown, Massachusetts. We had grown accustomed to waiting . . . waiting for the trial, waiting for the ruling. What we didn't know that August as we finally let our guard down was that we would be waiting for three more years. Our ignorance was indeed bliss as we beamed at each other on the flight to Boston and the scenic drive to Cape Cod, over lobster on the deck of our vacation house, and while holding hands strolling down Commercial Street. The first night we were there, we atteneded a public reading by comedian Kate Clinton and her long-time partner, author Urvashi Vaid. We'd never met them before, but we spontaneously shared the news of the ruling with them and shared a celebratory hug.

We pored over Judge Walker's 136-page ruling, which decimated the proponents' case. His decision unequivocally declared that Prop 8 was unconstitutional, that it was discriminatory, and that it served no purpose other than to create second-class citizenship for gay and lesbian Americans.

Even though David and Ted had warned us that the other side would appeal the ruling, it came as a surprise when they did just a few days later. That took some of the wind out of our sails and made coming back to California feel less celebratory and more worrisome. That week we also heard the sad news that Sandy's father's health was declining quickly. She made arrangements to fly to Iowa rather than home to Berkeley with me and Spencer and Elliott.

The appeal was not only an emotional setback; it also brought up two nagging worries. One was that, because the state of California (Governor Schwarzenegger and Attorney General Brown) chose not to appeal Judge Walker's decision or to defend Prop 8 in trial, the defendant-intervenors (including the official proponents of Prop 8) would enter the case instead of the state, which might or might not be permitted in a higher court. The other, bigger, worry was the possibility that we might lose.

Coming back to Berkeley was difficult. Sandy was in Iowa, and I missed her. The appeal was looming, and things at home weren't easy. My memories of the victory were shrouded in the sadness of the reality that no matter how historic the ruling was, we still had to manage big challenges in our family: kids, parents, work, and a very uncertain future now that the case was on appeal.

August was full of dichotomies. We had only two kids at home, but they were busier than ever as high school sophomores. On the one hand, there was cause for celebration; we'd visit our favorite restaurants and strangers would send champagne to our table. On the other hand, the news about Sandy's dad was getting worse. People who knew us superficially might have thought that we lived a charmed existence. Victory laps and celebrations were documented on Facebook, but the reality of our lives was complicated. At work, I was met with kind and supportive friendship from some colleagues and cool silence from others. Relatives I hadn't heard from in years sent congratulations, while others grew distant. Some longtime friends sent cards and flowers; others voiced their disapproval. The vast majority of friends and coworkers, relatives, and strangers shared genuine joy over the ruling and our role in it. A handful seemed to drift away slowly; some expressed disappointment over the distance they felt from us and how our involvement in the case changed us. If there were changes, they felt more logistical than substantive. I know I could have done more to hold on to those people, but at the time

I felt somewhat overwhelmed juggling new demands with existing commitments and priorities. I wish I had taken more time to enjoy the moment and the connections with those I loved.

I wanted to mark the victory of the ruling, not the struggle. A few days before Sandy's birthday on August 31, I headed to the same jeweler who had made our rings in 2004. I chose a simple platinum band, inscribed with the date of the ruling, "August 4, 2010." I surprised her with the new ring on her birthday. Never one to pass up jewelry, Sandy happily added the new band to her engagement ring and wedding band on her ring finger. The next day, she got a call from her brother that their father had passed away.

Sandy immediately headed back to Iowa with Frank and Tom for the services, but Spencer, Elliott, and I didn't join them. Frank needed his mom and brother to himself for that trip. Being not only a blended family but also a gay blended family can tip the scales at a stressful or emotional time. Sandy's family had been accepting of me but reserved. I often felt conspicuously gay and awkward at family gatherings, not knowing how to fit in, certain that I never would, and worried that my very presence was somehow embarrassing to them. They didn't expect to have a gay daughter, sister, or mother. She rarely returned to California without hurt feelings, and she had grown weary of the defense she had to wage in Iowa. The rings she wore were a very small comfort to Sandy, but they did signify the bond of our relationship as she traveled across the country to say hello to her family and goodbye to her dad.

As fall gave way to winter, the legal pattern of hurry-up-and-wait restarted. On December 6, 2010, we heard the announcement that the US Court of Appeals for the Ninth Circuit would conduct a hearing on our case with a three-judge panel. Ted Olson and David Boies once again argued there was no legitimate government interest in denying gay and lesbian Americans their fundamental freedom to marry. For the first and only time during our court appearances, oral arguments were broadcast live; they were viewed by more people than any other appellate court proceeding in American history.

In February 2011, we learned that Judge Walker would retire. The summer before, our opponents had told reporters that Judge Walker was gay. This wasn't news to us or to them. Both sides had known all along that he was gay and that he had been in a relationship for over a decade. Yet supporters of Prop 8 filed a motion in district court on April 25, 2011, to vacate Judge Walker's decision, arguing that he should have recused himself or disclosed his relationship status, stating that unless he "disavowed any interest in marrying his partner," he had "a direct personal interest in the outcome of the case." This was disingenuous; Judge Walker had never concealed his sexual orientation. More important, the other side was accusing him of bias based on his sexual orientation.

Judge Walker's successor on the bench, Judge James Ware, seemed to be deeply offended by the proponents' claim. He heard arguments on the motion on June 13, 2011, and denied it the next day. Judge Ware wrote:

Requiring recusal because a court issued an injunction that could provide some speculative future benefit to the presiding judge solely on the basis of the fact that the judge belongs to the class against whom the unconstitutional law was directed would lead to a Section 455(b)(4) standard that required recusal of minority judges in most, if not all, civil rights cases. Congress could not have intended such an unworkable recusal statute.

Supporters of Prop 8 appealed this decision to the Ninth Circuit.

While we waited for the Ninth Circuit to reach its decision, AFER was raising money to cover the costs associated with a protracted legal battle. One of the most moving and important tools for raising not only funds but also awareness was the premiere of *8*. The play was the brainchild of Dustin Lance Black (known as Lance), who had been in our courtroom for many days. He wanted the public to know what had happened there because the Supreme Court had ruled on the first day of the trial that there would be no public airing. Lance took the transcripts of the trial and wrote *8*, a staged reading of the most poignant parts of the trial; the play was based on transcripts, journalistic records, and media interviews. Actors portrayed major players—Judge Walker, the lawyers, the plaintiffs, and the proponents.

On September 19, 2011, *8* premiered on Broadway in New York with an all-star cast, including Bob Balaban, Ellen Barkin, Matt Bomer, Campbell Brown, Bradley Cooper, Anthony Edwards, Morgan Freeman, Cheyenne Jackson, Christine Lahti, John Lithgow, and Rob Reiner. Three of our boys; my stepsister, Nancy; and my niece Georgie joined us in the audience that night. There was an unexpected surprise that afternoon while the cast was rehearsing: Judge Ware had honored our request from many months earlier to unseal the videotapes of our trial. The play *8* had been written specifically in response to the proponents' request to seal the transcript. Unfortunately, the other side immediately appealed, forcing the order to be put on hold. The videotapes remain under seal to this day.

In addition to the legal volleyball game that was ensuing, that fall, the Ninth Circuit certified a question to the California Supreme Court. (In other words, the Ninth Circuit asked for clarification of the proponents based on California law because California officials had declined to defend the law.) The Ninth Circuit panel wanted verification that the backers of the challenged initiative had "a particularized interest in the initiative's validity or the authority to assert the State's interest in the initiative's validity" that would permit them to defend the law when state officials refused to do so. David Boies had argued eloquently that the proponents had no standing and could not prove that they would be personally injured by the repeal of Prop 8, the criteria for standing, thus forcing the hand of the Ninth Circuit to get a "second opinion" from the highest court in California. Despite Boies's arguments, on November 17, 2011, the California Supreme Court ruled that the nongovernmental proponents of Prop 8 did have the legal standing to defend it. In less than one year, the case had traveled from the Ninth Circuit to the California Supreme Court and then back to the federal district court.

Attorneys on both sides had to jump through many hoops to reach the point where the only ruling they were awaiting was the appeal of our win to the Ninth Circuit.

That winter, as AFER was gearing up for the Los Angeles premiere of *8* and continuing to fund raise, the Ninth Circuit affirmed the August 2010 ruling of the federal district court that found Prop 8 unconstitutional:

Proposition 8 serves no purpose, and has no effect, other than to lessen the status and human dignity of gays and lesbians in California, and to officially reclassify their relationships and families as inferior to those of opposite-sex couples. The Constitution simply does not allow for laws of this sort.

With this ruling, the Ninth Circuit affirmed a simple, fundamental truth: *Every* American deserves the same dignity and respect and the same freedom to love, to marry, and to build a family.

Courts alert attorneys twenty-four hours in advance of issuing a ruling, so we had time to travel to Los Angeles to meet the legal and AFER teams before the ruling was delivered. We took Spencer and Elliott with us. After we had a chance to digest the details with the Gibson Dunn and Boies Schiller teams, we headed to a press conference. We were surprised to see Spencer talking to Adam Umhoefer, executive director of AFER, essentially lobbying him to let him deliver brief remarks. Spencer did a great job that day as he stood in front of a sea of cameras proclaiming his pride for his moms and talking about the importance of the ruling to couples in California and families like his. It reminded me of the toast he gave at our wedding celebration six years earlier. Now a young man, Spencer showed that same pride as he stated firmly to the press, "My parents are equal. Our family is equal."

The play *8* premiered in Los Angeles on March 3, 2012, with another star-studded cast, this one including Kevin Bacon, George Clooney, Chris Colfer, Jamie Lee Curtis, Jessie Tyler Ferguson, Jane

Lynch, Matthew Morrison, Rory O'Malley, Brad Pitt, John C. Reilly, Martin Sheen, Yeardley Smith, and George Takei. Sitting in the Los Angeles Wilshire Ebell Theater that night with Sandy, the boys, and my parents was one of the proudest moments of my life. None of our loved ones had witnessed the entire trial or read all the arguments and testimony. I felt like the boys and my parents finally understood the scale and scope of the last few years of our lives, the impact it was having on others, and the very real chance that we would ultimately win. I hate to admit it, but at forty-eight years old, I still wanted parental approval. The icing on the cake was watching my parents, Tom, Spencer, Elliott, and our niece Katie at the party after the play, which the cast joined. They congratulated us on our wins—that and the fact that AFER raised more than $2 million that night.

As expected, on July 31, 2012, the proponents appealed to the US Supreme Court. Our side responded on August 24, 2012, arguing that the Supreme Court should not take the case based on the previous rulings, not to mention the trouble the other side would have with standing. Despite those arguments, the court granted certification of our case, which was now named *Hollingsworth v. Perry* (to show who was suing whom), on December 7, 2012. (Dennis Hollingsworth was a Republican state senator at the time the case was filed. He was supportive of Prop 8 and its proponents. He was the named proponent in the same way that I was the named plaintiff.)

On March 26, 2013, nearly four years after we had been denied a marriage license by the Alameda County Recorder's Office and had first filed our case, our lawyers presented our case to the Supreme Court. The night before, as we were dozing off in our hotel in Washington, DC, Spencer ran into our room to share the news of his first college acceptance, to the George Washington University, just blocks away. Spencer and Elliott had spent most of their high school careers coping not only with homework and practices, tutors and tests, and friends and girlfriends but also with the glare of a media spotlight. None of us had ever thought the light would shine for so long. We were all eager to see that light directed elsewhere.

In front of the Supreme Court, 2013.

CHAPTER 33

Waiting for Our Rights

Sandy

March 23, 2010. Packed into a tall van, we wound our way across Washington, from our Dupont Circle hotel to the Supreme Court. On this cold, slushy day, everyone in the van was somber, lost in thought, staring at something—Jeff and Paul at their phones; Ben, Ryan, and Diana into their respective camera lenses; Jo at her notebook; Kris at the crowds gathered by the court; Chad and Adam at the various occupants of the van. I was nervous but struck by an ironic thought: we were having to fight so hard to get married when other people get married and divorced at the drop of a hat.

Inching our way to Capitol Hill, passing block after block of attached row houses that had seen their share of history, we were going to make our case for the right to be married. Arriving at the US Supreme Court to blockaded streets was surreal. The absurdity of it all was crystalized as I broke into a childhood camp song, changing the lyrics to fit the day:

> *Here we sit like birds in the wilderness, birds in the wilderness, birds in the wilderness.*
>
> *Here we sit like birds in the wilderness, waiting for our rights.*
>
> *Waiting for our rights, waiting for our rights.*
>
> *Here we sit like birds in the wilderness, birds in the wilderness, birds in the wilderness.*
>
> *Here we sit like birds in the wilderness, WAITING FOR OUR RIGHTS!*

Chad gave me a look, the one that says "really?" Kris squeezed my hand in that "Babe, please don't be . . . you know . . . " way. I knew these messages well. I am easily entertained, most often by myself. I am uptight and unhinged, judgmental but carefree, a bossy mom and a middle-aged juvenile. I am all of this woven together like three-color yarn knitted into a messy blend. My song trailed to an end as I returned Kris's look with a look of my own.

The van pulled to a stop, a half block from the court, orange cones everywhere, streets blocked by chain-link fencing. "Deep breaths. Try to be calm, focused. Take this in and remember it always. Above all, do not cry." I silently repeated these instructions to myself.

Stepping into crowds and cameras had gotten easier over the years, and I'd learned to control my emotions and let others lead. And lead they did. We were graciously helped from the van and ushered through the hoards of journalists and supporters, the shouts of the opposition making polite conversation impossible. I told myself, "Lean in but hold tight," a reminder to be present but contained. I grasped Kris's hand, calmed by the connection. Her touch regulates my heartbeat.

Old people, young people, babies, grannies. Homemade banners, rainbow flags, a sea of "HRC" (Human Rights Campaign) signs: all imploring the court and the people to support equality. To support marriage equality. To say definitively that we matter too, and that our choice for love and family is valid. The love and hope expressed by so many people overwhelmed me. Choirs singing, megaphones blaring, reporters swarming the wide sidewalk—I felt like we were on a movie set.

We climbed the marble steps of the imposing Supreme Court building to the entrance, where we were joined by Lady Olson, Ted's beautiful wife and a sunny force of nature. Tears streaming down her face, she hugged us all. We were barely able to speak, and this is not a usual thing. Soon we were joined by Spencer and Elliott, proud and upright in dark suits; Spencer sported an oversized camel overcoat that looked as though it had been borrowed from a much older relative; Elliott was characteristically light-hearted and smiling.

The night before, Chad and Adam had pulled Jeff, Paul, Kris, and me aside to let us know that three tickets for entry to the hearing had been given to the team, and they wanted us to use them for our family members. Jeff's parents, unfailing in their support, had come to DC to be on the steps with us, as had the twins. Always the gentleman, Jeff insisted that our boys get two tickets while his father got the other. Although we felt lucky to have the twins with us, I missed the presence of my own sons. They had kept a fair distance from the circus-like atmosphere surrounding the case, occasionally joining us for an event but usually declining involvement, particularly when media was present. Their ambivalence wasn't lost on me, and I felt grateful for every text or message they sent, keenly aware of the pressure they were under from some of their paternal relatives, who were adamantly opposed to the case and to our cause.

Hand in hand, Kris and I walked into the majestic building, clearing security, and stuffing our coats, bags, and phones into coin-operated lockers to ensure a smooth entry into the courtroom. We quietly filed into the courtroom and were efficiently seated in the same manner. This time, we sat with the public, no front-row view. The boys were seated in a different section from us. I was on one side of Kris; Chad was on the other, his right leg jiggling madly, his gaze intense. We were packed together like well-behaved sardines under the stern eyes of the Supreme Court security guards.

There was no chatter or laughter in this court. We whispered furtively to each other so as not to attract attention. I looked for familiar faces. Lady was seated several rows away, and we watched as Ted walked over and kissed her gently before joining his team. David and Mary Boies shared an embrace before she was seated. David had led the case during the appeal process, but Ted would take the lead at the Supreme Court, a court he knew well. Jo

Becker, the *New York Times* journalist who had been following the case from the beginning, was in the press area, intensely studying the crowd as she scribbled away. Jeff and Paul were seated too far away for us to exchange anything more than a smile. Valerie Jarrett, Senior Advisor to the President of the United States, and Nancy Pelosi, Speaker of the US House of Representatives, were directly in front of us. The energy in the room was palpable.

The audience was silent as the justices entered from behind the front drapes, taking their seats, from least senior on the edges to the chief justice in the center. I paid particular attention to Justice Sotomayor; having finished her autobiography on the flight to DC, I felt a sense of kinship with her, a shared understanding and experience of struggle, and a deep admiration for her dedication to justice. Scanning the faces of each justice, I tried to feel what they were thinking. Were they emotional about this day, this issue? Were the tides of change uplifting them to include more Americans in the dream of an equal and just society?

I wondered if they knew who we were or anything about us or if they even cared. I didn't expect them to, really, but I was curious. I saw Justice Kagan look at the audience. It seemed as though her eyes hesitated when they landed on us for just an instant, but I am optimistic by nature, with a great capacity for magical thinking. Still, my heart leapt. I saw Justice Kennedy settling into his space and was warmed by his kind face as I recalled his progressive views, as evidenced in his previous opinions protecting immigrants, inmates, juveniles, and gay rights. His opinion in *Lawrence v. Texas* had clearly shown his affinity for the autonomy of the individual:

Liberty protects the person from unwarranted government intrusions into a dwelling or other private places. In our tradition the state is not omnipresent in the home. And there are other spheres of our lives and existence, outside the home, where the state should not be a dominant presence. Freedom extends beyond spatial bounds.

Liberty presumes an autonomy of self that includes freedom of thought, belief, expression, and certain intimate conduct.

Justice Ginsburg, focused and serene, seemed to disappear behind the table, her tiny frame sinking into her oversized chair. She harkened from another era, long hair coiled into a bun above her huge white lace collar. My throat clenched just thinking about her and the voice she had given to women and minorities throughout her long and distinguished legal career, including her dissent in the *Hobby Lobby* decision, when she said:

Any decision to use contraceptives made by a woman covered under Hobby Lobby's or Conestoga's plan will not be propelled by the Government, it will be the woman's autonomous choice, informed by the physician she consults.

I noticed that two of the conservative justices seemed uncomfortable. Justice Thomas looked like he was chewing something while moving back and forth in his swivel chair, to the point of turning his back to the court. He reminded me of a student in afternoon English class, bored out of his mind. Justice Scalia appeared annoyed for some reason.

"Hear ye, hear ye." Chief Justice Roberts struck the gavel to bring the court to attention. The room was silent as the questions began. Chuck Cooper was the first to speak, followed by Ted, and then Donald B. Virrelli, Jr., the US solicitor general. David had graciously ceded his time to accommodate comments from the solicitor general, who would be speaking on behalf of President Obama and the administration.

There had been many phone calls and meetings to prepare us for this day. We knew that there would be questions, but we understood that no one could predict their content, who would ask them, or what path they might take. We had been counseled to expect the unexpected and never predict the outcome, especially to the media.

Mr. Cooper had just started his lofty opening remarks when he was interrupted by Chief Justice Roberts.

MR. COOPER: Thank you, Mr. Chief Justice, and may it please the court: New York's highest court, in a case similar to this one, remarked that until quite recently, it was an accepted any society truth for almost everyone who ever lived in any society in which marriage existed—

CHIEF JUSTICE ROBERTS: Mr. Cooper, we have jurisdictional and merits issues here. Maybe it'd be best if you could begin with the standing issue.

Standing had been an issue in our case since the state of California had declined to argue in defense of Prop 8, clearing a path for the proponents of the proposition to secure their own counsel to face the Olson-Boies team in federal court. The last time standing had dominated the courtroom was in the California Supreme Court, regarding the issue of whether our opponents had standing to represent the people of California at the appellate level. That court decided in favor of our opponents, a victory for them and an expensive legal detour for both sides.

Chief Justice Roberts was joined by Justices Ginsburg, Scalia, Kagan, Sotomayor, Breyer, and Kennedy in questions regarding standing, asking Mr. Cooper to defend his very purpose for being in that courtroom. Finally, Chief Justice Roberts allowed Mr. Cooper to proceed to the merits of his argument. Mr. Cooper was quickly challenged by Justice Sotomayor:

JUSTICE SOTOMAYOR: Outside of the—outside of the marriage context, can you think of any other rational basis, reason, for a state using sexual orientation as a factor in denying homosexuals benefits or imposing burdens

---

Standing: According to the 'Lectric Law Library (http://www.lectlaw.com), standing refers to "the legal right to initiate a lawsuit. To do so, a person must be sufficiently affected by the matter at hand, and there must be a case or controversy that can be resolved by legal action."

on them? Is there any other rational decision-making that the Government could make? Denying them a job, not granting them benefits of some sort, any other decision?

MR. COOPER: Your Honor, I cannot. I do not have any—anything to offer you in that regard.

Mr. Cooper wasn't hitting it out of the park, to use a baseball analogy. Justice Sotomayor continued to hammer him on the issue of government-sanctioned discrimination, which Mr. Cooper failed to defend.

Then Justice Kagan went straight to the core of Mr. Cooper's principal argument—procreation.

JUSTICE KAGAN: Mr. Cooper, could I just understand your argument. In reading the briefs, it seems as though your principal argument is that same-sex and [. . .] opposite-sex couples are not similarly situated because opposite-sex couples can procreate, same-sex couples cannot, and the State's principal interest in marriage is in regulating procreation. Is that basically correct?

MR. COOPER: I—Your Honor, that's the essential thrust of our—our position, yes.

The tone changed when Justice Scalia spoke, his gruff voice full of skepticism.

JUSTICE SCALIA: Mr. Cooper, let me—let me give you one—one concrete thing. I don't know why you don't mention some concrete things. If you redefine marriage to include same-sex couples, you must—you must permit adoption by same-sex couples, and there's—there's considerable disagreement among—among sociologists as to what the consequences of raising a child in a—in a single-sex family, whether that is harmful to the child or not. Some states do not—do not permit adoption by same-sex couples for that reason.

JUSTICE GINSBURG: California—no, California does.

JUSTICE SCALIA: I don't think we know the answer to that. Do you know the answer to that, whether it—whether it harms or helps the child?

MR. COOPER: No, Your Honor. And there's—there's—

JUSTICE SCALIA: But that's a possible deleterious effect, isn't it?

There was an audible gasp. I glanced at the boys, seeing their necks stiffen, as did ours. Kris's eyes narrowed into a squint, and we both straightened our spines.

JUSTICE KENNEDY: I—I think there's—there's substantial—that there's substance to the point that sociological information is new. We have five years of information to weigh against 2,000 years of history or more. On the other hand, there is an immediate legal injury or legal—what could be a legal injury, and that's the voice of these children. There are some 40,000 children in California, according to the Red Brief, that live with same-sex parents, and they want their parents to have full recognition and full status. The voice of those children is important in this case, don't you think?

The audience was rapt. Perhaps the most uplifting moment of the hearing was when Justice Kennedy mentioned that the harm that was inflicted on children with same-sex parents was the point that had persuaded him to rethink the marriage ban in California. His comments focused the country on the reality of unequal rights: numbers of American children had heard, too frequently, from their own government, that they were less than others, not good enough, not relevant, not equal. Thank you, Justice Kennedy!

As in the district court, there were amusements. Clever, witty justices who hit the nail on the head, like Justice Kagan:

JUSTICE KAGAN: Well, suppose a state said, Mr. Cooper, suppose a state said that, because we think that the focus of marriage really should be on procreation, we are not going to give marriage licenses anymore to any couple where both people are over the age of 55. Would that be constitutional?

MR. COOPER: No, Your Honor, it would not be constitutional.

JUSTICE KAGAN: Because that's the same state interest, I would think, you know. If you are over the age of 55, you don't help us serve the government's interest in regulating procreation through marriage. So why is that different?

MR. COOPER: Your Honor, even with respect to couples over the age of 55, it is very rare that both couples—both parties to the couple are infertile, and the traditional—

(Laughter.)

Justice Kagan interrupted him, exasperation written all over her face.

JUSTICE KAGAN: No, really, because if the couple—I can just assure you, if both the woman and the man are over the age of 55, there are not a lot of children coming out of that marriage.

(Laughter.)

MR. COOPER: Your Honor, society's—society's interest in responsible procreation isn't just with respect to the procreative capacities of the couple itself. The marital norm, which imposes the obligations of fidelity and monogamy, Your Honor, advances the interests in responsible procreation by making it more likely that neither party, including the fertile party to that—

JUSTICE KAGAN: Actually, I'm not even—

JUSTICE SCALIA: I suppose we could have a questionnaire

at the marriage desk when people come in to get the marriage—you know, Are you fertile or are you not fertile?

(Laughter.)

JUSTICE SCALIA: I suspect this court would hold that to be
an unconstitutional invasion of privacy, don't you think?

JUSTICE KAGAN: Well, I just asked about age. I didn't ask
about anything else. That's not—we ask about people's
age all the time.

MR. COOPER: Your Honor, and even asking about age, you
would have to ask if both parties are infertile. Again—

JUSTICE SCALIA: Strom Thurmond was—was not the chairman
of the Senate committee when Justice Kagan was confirmed.

(Laughter.)

MR. COOPER: Very few men—very few men outlive their own
fertility. So I just—

JUSTICE KAGAN: A couple where both people are over the
age of 55—

MR. COOPER: I—

JUSTICE KAGAN: A couple where both people are over the
age of 55.

MR. COOPER: And Your Honor, again, the marital norm which
imposes upon that couple the obligation of fidelity—

The laughter faded as Mr. Cooper continued to defend his position on procreation, albeit with less-than-stellar results, and the
justices continued to challenge his statements, backing him into
a tighter and tighter corner. With just thirty minutes of time in
which to present his arguments, Mr. Cooper soon sat down, and

it was Ted's turn to speak. Ted's voice, so familiar and comforting, filled the space like the voice of God. Deep and steady, he began:

MR. OLSON: Thank you, Mr. Chief Justice, and may it please the Court:

I know that you will want me to spend a moment or two addressing the standing question, but before I do that, I thought that it would be important for this Court to have Proposition 8 put in context, what it does. It walls-off gays and lesbians from marriage, the most important relation in life, according to this Court, thus stigmatizing a class of Californians based upon their status and labeling their most cherished relationships as second-rate, different, unequal, and not okay.

CHIEF JUSTICE ROBERTS: Mr. Olson, I cut off your friend before he could get into the merits.

MR. OLSON: I was trying to avoid that, Your Honor.

CHIEF JUSTICE ROBERTS: I know—

(Laughter.)

Thus began the detour into standing that Mr. Cooper had already weathered, with questions from Chief Justice Roberts and Justices Kennedy, Alito, Sotomayor, and Breyer. After a spirited debate on the issue, which the court clearly viewed as the primary argument, Justice Kennedy invited Ted to address the merits of the case itself. Finally, we were going to hear about what really mattered. Ted redirected the court back to his opening statement, expanding upon it, which garnered an interjection from Justice Scalia:

JUSTICE SCALIA: You—you've led me right into a question I was going to ask. The California Supreme Court decides what the law is. That's what we decide, right? We don't prescribe law for the future. We—we decide what the law is. I'm curious, when—when did—when did it become unconstitutional to exclude homosexual couples from marriage? 1791? 1868, when the Fourteenth Amendment was adopted?

. . .

MR. OLSON: When—may I answer this in the form of a rhetorical question? When did it become unconstitutional to prohibit interracial marriages? When did it become unconstitutional to assign children to separate schools?

JUSTICE SCALIA: It's an easy question, I think, for that one. At—at the time that the Equal Protection Clause was adopted. That's absolutely true.

But don't give me a question to my question.

(Laughter.)

The debate continued, with Justice Scalia and Chief Justice Roberts pushing Ted on the issue of constitutionality:

JUSTICE SCALIA: It seems to me you ought to be able to tell me when. Otherwise, I don't know how to decide the case.

MR. OLSON: I—I submit you've never required that before. When you decided that—that individuals—after having decided that separate but equal schools were permissible, a decision by this Court, when you decided that that was unconstitutional, when did that become unconstitutional?

JUSTICE SCALIA: 50 years ago, it was okay?

MR. OLSON: I—I can't answer that question, and I don't think this Court has ever phrased the question in that way.

Justice Scalia had started the session looking agitated, and his agitation had increased. I could almost feel sweat fling from his glistening brow as he whipped his head back and forth between the justices and Ted, his face flushed red. We knew Ted had great respect for Justice Scalia, friendship even, but in this moment, the exchange was far from friendly. Chief Justice Roberts showed his skepticism more subtly, in words only, always calm and cool in delivery as he pushed Ted on why marriage mattered in a state that already had accepted domestic partnership.

MR. OLSON: It is like you were to say you can vote, you can travel, but you may not be a citizen. There are certain labels in this country that are very, very critical. You could have said in the Loving case, what—you can't get married, but you can have an interracial union. Everyone would know that that was wrong, that the—marriage has a status, recognition, support, and you—if you read the test, you know—

CHIEF JUSTICE ROBERTS: How do we know—how do we know that that's the reason, or a necessary part of the reason, that we've recognized marriage as a fundamental right? That's—you've emphasized that and you've said, well, it's because of the emotional commitment. Maybe it is the procreative aspect that makes it a fundamental right.

MR. OLSON: But you have said that marriage is a fundamental right with respect to procreation and at the same level getting married, privacy—you said that in the Zablocki case, you said that in the Lawrence case, and you said it in other cases, the Skinner case, for example. Marriage is put on a pro—equal footing with procreational aspects. And your—this Court is the one that has said over and over again that marriage means something to the individual: The privacy, intimacy, and that it is a matter of status and recognition in this—

JUSTICE SOTOMAYOR: Mr. Olson, the bottom line that you're being asked—and—and it is one that I'm interested in the answer: If you say that marriage is a fundamental right, what state restrictions could ever exist? Meaning, what state restrictions with respect to the number of people, with respect to—that could get married—the incest laws, the mother and child, assuming that they are the age—I can—I can accept that the state has probably an overbearing interest on—on protecting a child until they're of age to marry, but what's left?

MR. OLSON: Well, you've said—you've said in the cases decided by this Court that the polygamy issue, multiple marriages raises questions about exploitation, abuse, patriarchy, issues with respect to taxes, inheritance, child custody, it is an entirely different thing. And if you—if a state prohibits polygamy, it's prohibiting conduct. If it prohibits gay and lesbian citizens from getting married, it is prohibiting their exercise of a right based upon their status. It's selecting them as a class, as you described in the Romer case and as you described in the Lawrence case and in other cases, you're picking out a group of individuals to deny them the freedom that you've said is fundamental, important, and vital in this society, and it has status and stature, as you pointed out in the VMI case.

The questioning soon turned back to the issue of whether standing should have been granted in the first place, by the district court or the California Supreme Court, with Justice Kennedy interjecting:

JUSTICE KENNEDY: The problem—the problem with the case is that you're really asking, particularly because of the sociological evidence you cite, for us to go into uncharted waters, and you can play with that metaphor, there's a wonderful destination, it is a cliff. Whatever that was.

(Laughter.)

JUSTICE KENNEDY: But you're—you're doing so in a—in a case where the opinion is very narrow. Basically that once the state goes halfway, it has to go all the way or 70 percent of the way, and you're doing so in a case where there's a substantial question on—on standing. I just wonder if—if the case was properly granted.

MR. OLSON: Oh, the case was certainly properly granted, Your Honor. I mean, there was a full trial of all of these issues. There was a 12-day trial, the judge insisted on evidence on all of these questions. This—this is a—

JUSTICE KENNEDY: But that's not the issue the Ninth Circuit decided.

MR. OLSON: The issue—yes, the Ninth Circuit looked at it and decided because of your decision on the Romer case, this Court's decision on the Romer case, that it could be decided on the narrower issue, but it certainly was an appropriate case to grant. And those issues that I've been describing are certainly fundamental to the case. And—and I don't want to abuse the Court's indulgence, that what I—you suggested that this is uncharted waters. It was uncharted waters when this Court, in 1967, in the Loving decision said that interracial—prohibitions on interracial marriages, which still existed in 16 states, were unconstitutional.

As Ted's thirty minutes evaporated, he ended with a quote from Justice Ginsburg from the *United States v. Virginia* case about discriminatory admissions policies:

"A prime part of the history of our Constitution is the story of the extension of constitutional rights to people once ignored or excluded."

Ted was politely thanked by Chief Justice Roberts as he ceded the floor to US Solicitor General Donald Verrilli. We had been thrilled to hear that the White House wanted to present argu-

---

United States v. Virginia: In a seven-to-one decision in 1996, the US Supreme Court struck down the Virginia Military Institute's long-standing male-only admissions policy.

ments on our behalf and that the Supreme Court had granted a thirty-minute extension of the usual sixty minutes to accommodate the solicitor general.

The Obama administration, and the president himself, had been slow to come to the table of support for marriage equality, but they had at long last arrived. Vice President Joe Biden had enthusiastically stated his support some months earlier, looking surprised by his own voice as he uttered the words of support on national TV. When the president followed suit shortly thereafter, albeit with more aplomb and control, our hearts swelled with gratitude. We knew that the United States needed his leadership on this issue, and that his words would resonate in the hearts and minds of parents, employers, neighbors, children, and church ladies like my own mom. He had called for tolerance many times before, but this time he called for equality. And he sent the solicitor general, the leading attorney for the nation, to make the case.

Mr. Verrilli got about five words in before being interrupted by the court. This had been the standard for the last sixty minutes. I wondered how the presenting lawyers could stand the constant redirects, never getting to end a statement before being cut off by a justice.

SOLICITOR GENERAL VERRILLI: Mr. Chief Justice, and may it please the Court:

Proposition 8 denies gay and lesbian persons the equal protection of the laws—

CHIEF JUSTICE ROBERTS: You don't think you're going to get away with not starting with the jurisdictional question, do you?

(Laughter.)

SOLICITOR GENERAL VERRILLI: As an amicus, I thought I might actually, Your Honor. And—and, of course, we didn't take a position on standing. We didn't—

we didn't brief it, we don't have a formal position on standing. But I will offer this observation
based on the discussion today and the briefing. . . .
We do think that with respect to standing, that at this
point with the initiative process over, that Petitioners
really have what is more in the nature of a generalized
grievance and because they're not an agent of the state
of California or don't have any other official tie to the
state that would—would result in any official control
of their litigation, that the better conclusion is that
there's not Article III standing here.

The justices continued with questions on standing, which was
clearly the crux of their concern with our case—or perhaps it was
all they were willing to discuss. I felt increasingly frustrated by the
lack of attention to the merits of the case, which was the reason
we were there. The trial was supposed to be a full representation
of the facts. Where were those? Was the court waiting to hear
United States v. Windsor, the Defense of Marriage Act (DOMA)
case, the next day to address the actual harms of discrimination?

Justice Alito jumped in:

JUSTICE ALITO: You want us to assess the effects of
same-sex marriage, the potential effects on—of same-sex
marriage, the potential—the effects of Proposition 8.
But what is your response to the argument which has already been mentioned about the need to be cautious in
light of the newness of the—the concept of—of same-sex
marriage.

The one thing that the parties in this case seem to
agree on is that marriage is very important. It's thought
to be a fundamental building block of society and its
preservation essential for the preservation of society.
Traditional marriage has been around for thousands of

DOMA: The Defense of Marriage Act (DOMA), enacted September 21, 1996, was a federal
law that defined marriage for federal purposes as the union of one man and one woman
and allowed states to refuse to recognize marriages granted under the laws of other states.

years. Same-sex marriage is very new. I think it was first adopted in the Netherlands in 2000. So there isn't a lot of data about its effect. And it may turn out to be a—a good thing; it may turn out not to be a good thing, as the supporters of Proposition 8 apparently believe.

But you want us to step in and render a decision based on an assessment of the effects of this institution which is newer than cell phones or the Internet? I mean we—we are not—we do not have the ability to see the future.

On a question like that, of such fundamental importance, why should it not be left for the people, either acting through initiatives and referendums or through their elected public officials?

Give me a break, I thought. Invoking cell phones and the Internet? Spencer and Elliott had lived their entire lives with gay parents. Were those lifetimes less worthy of the full protection of the constitution? Or did you have to have a full head of gray hair to count? Hmmm . . .

The court continued to challenge Mr. Verrilli:

CHIEF JUSTICE ROBERTS: I don't want to—I want you to get back to Justice Alito's other points, but is it the position of the United States that same-sex marriage is not required throughout the country?

SOLICITOR GENERAL VERRILLI: We are not—we are not taking the position that it is required throughout the country. We think that that ought to be left open for a future adjudication in other states that don't have the situation California has.

JUSTICE SCALIA: So your—your position is only if a state allows civil unions does it become unconstitutional to forbid same-sex marriage, right?

GENERAL VERRILLI: I—I see my red light is on.

CHIEF JUSTICE ROBERTS: Well, you can go on.

Mr. Verrilli did go on, for a number of minutes, surprising in a court of strict rules and red lights signaling that a speaker's time is up. It was clear that he, or perhaps the president himself, was not advocating for a national victory, but taking the more conservative position of a state-by-state approach, a disappointing tactic in our eyes. He continued by distinguishing between states like California that had granted every domestic partnership right but marriage, and those that had no such laws, and by reminding the court of the harm that waiting would bring to those who would continue to be denied access to marriage.

SOLICITOR GENERAL VERRILLI: We are not taking the position that it is required throughout the country. We think that that ought to be left open for a future adjudication in other states that don't have the situation California has.

The argument here about caution is an argument that, well, we need to wait. We understand that. We take it seriously. But waiting is not a neutral act. Waiting imposes real costs in the here and now. It denies to the—to the parents who want to marry the ability to marry, and it denies to the children, ironically, the very thing that Petitioners focus on is at the heart of the marriage relationship.

CHIEF JUSTICE ROBERTS: But you are willing to wait in the rest of the country. You saying it's got to happen right now in California, but you don't even have a position about whether it's required in the rest of the country.

Mr. Verrilli finished his argument by going back to equal protection, referencing the *Loving* case and the cost of waiting. He struck a nerve with Chief Justice Roberts, a devoted father, and a rapid dialogue ensued:

SOLICITOR GENERAL VERRILLI: And the fourth point I would make, and I do think this is significant, is that the principal argument in 1967 with respect to Loving and that the Commonwealth of Virginia advanced was: Well, the social science is still uncertain about how biracial children will fare in this world, and so you ought to apply rational basis scrutiny and wait. And I think the Court recognized that there is a cost to waiting and that that has got to be part of the equal protection calculus. And so—so I do think that's quite fundamental.

CHIEF JUSTICE ROBERTS: I—it seems to me that your position that you are supporting is somewhat internally inconsistent. We see the argument made that there is no problem with extending marriage to same-sex couples because children raised by same-sex couples are doing just fine and there is no evidence that they are being harmed. And the other argument is Proposition 8 harms children by not allowing same-sex couples to marriage. Which is it?

SOLICITOR GENERAL VERRILLI: Well, I—I think what Proposition 8 does is deny the long-term stabilizing effect that marriage brings That's—that's the argument for—for marriage, that—

CHIEF JUSTICE ROBERTS: But you also tell me there has been no harm shown to children of same-sex couples.

SOLICITOR GENERAL VERRILLI: California—there are 37,000 children in same-sex families in California now. Their parents cannot marry and that has effects on them in the here and now. A stabilizing effect is not there. When they go to school, they have to, you know—they don't have parents like everybody else's parents. That's a real effect, a real cost in the here and now.

Mr. Verrilli ended by clearly stating the need for equality, if not fully delivered by the Supreme Court as a result of our case, then soon. By reminding the court of the cost to children and families of not allowing same-sex marriage, he struck a chord that resonated profoundly with me. There was harm done every day to children and families in our country as the result of this discrimination. It had to be stopped. If not now, when?

Mr. Cooper was invited back to the podium for some final words. He implored the court to let the political process in the state of California to play out, both with Prop 8 and with any future acts, stating:

MR. COOPER: It is an agonizingly difficult, for many people, political question. We would submit to you that that question is properly decided by the people themselves.

I didn't see our right to be married as a political issue at all. And I sure hoped the court didn't. We had witnessed a spellbinding ninety minutes, but I felt acutely disappointed by what was missing from the discussion. The bulk of the time had been spent arguing whether or not our case should have been granted in the first place, with a weird detour into procreation and the possibility of requiring fertility for marriage. It was unsettling, yet we were optimistic. Our arguments were simply stronger.

Kris and I walked out of the building that afternoon to a sea of enthusiastic supporters, their excitement drowning out the chants of those who had come to protest. We were ushered into a crowd of reporters. I didn't want to focus on anything but the momentous experience we had just had; my desire to savor those moments—the words spoken by Ted in front of the justices—and to sear them into my memory far outpaced my interest in the press. Kris and I each spoke for a minute or two, thanking people for their overwhelming support.

The next day, after we got the boys off to the airport so they could return home, Kris and I decided to join the huge crowd gathering outside the Supreme Court building to be a part of the support and anticipation unfolding around the DOMA hearing, in which the court would likely find the Defense of Marriage Act invalid, resulting in the federal government recognizing same-sex marriages in those states that had them. The AFER team had encouraged us to keep a low profile and avoid the media, which we were more than happy to do. But miss the excitement of being in front of the courthouse for DOMA? No way. We were determined to be a part of the crowd that we had waved to the day before. Donning puffy coats and sunglasses, we headed to the Supreme Court steps to join the sign-waving and cheering people who had taken over not only the steps but also the plaza in front, the sidewalks surrounding the building, and every square inch of grass nearby. Some people had camped for days in the drizzly weather for a chance to witness the arguments. As people lined up to enter the court, Kris and I wound through the crowd, marveling at the energy of the mass of people, squeezing each other's hands in appreciation of the experience. Few people recognized us, and we were delighted with our relative anonymity. We cheered and waved madly an hour later as plaintiff Edie Windsor and her counsel, Roberta Kaplan, exited the court and came down the stairs to the same mad love we had enjoyed the day before.

We walked away from the court that day keenly aware of the momentous occasion. If DOMA were struck down—and it seemed certain it would be, based not only on our lawyers' opinion but also on that of the media—*and* if our case won on the merits of the arguments rather than on the basis of standing, our entire country would have marriage equality. If our case won on standing, then California would be the winner and would likely lead the way for further victories in other states, once other bans were challenged in court. Kris and I walked away from the Supreme Court, past the Capitol, and down to the Newseum, the news museum. In front of the Newseum is a permanent exhibit that shows the front page of every major newspaper in the country for that day. Every newspaper had a story about our case on the front page. Every single one.

Bundled up against the cold winter air, we made our way back to the hotel on Dupont Circle to again start the process that we had become so accustomed to. We began to wait. Our final wait, for a final decision.

CHAPTER 34

A Good Day for Marriage Equality

Sandy

Senioritis. The twins had it in spades, as did their entire class. The excitement of prom having subsided, the final weeks of high school flew by as we headed to graduation, which felt bizarrely in step with the Supreme Court ruling. A Supreme Court ruling is a tricky thing. Although we had a clear schedule for graduation activities, we had no such luck with the court. The Supreme Court could rule on one of many days, and what case will be ruled on what day was a mystery not only to us, but also to the lawyers, the press, and the general public. Our lawyers had a method of predicting when the ruling would likely be delivered, and they were banking on one of the later dates, right before the court went on summer break, but they were also ready for the ruling to come in earlier. And they wanted us to be present when it happened. How could we imagine not being there?

The time frame for the ruling to come down was wide; the ruling could come on a Tuesday, Wednesday, or Thursday over several weeks. We couldn't possibly be in Washington on every possible date, although we were asked to come and be there on the most likely dates. In those weeks before the end of the court's calendar, we made several quick trips to the nation's capital to be in or near the court in the event of a ruling.

On one of those trips, Kris and I went to the Supreme Court and stopped for a moment on the building's steps to enjoy the peace, quiet, and grandeur of the scene on a day that the building was closed. Kris pulled me close, took a tiny velvet box from her pocket, and asked me to marry her "for real," which we both knew meant legally. Forever. The proposal was romantic, the ring a reminder that we were on the verge of a new phase in our lives that had so long eluded us. We were optimistic the deal would soon be sealed. A lovely complement to the other three rings that signify our marriage, this ring is a simple platinum band with five small diamonds, representing a Supreme Court majority. We kept the ring in its box, however, in anticipation of the ruling.

While we were juggling work schedules and burning through our vacation days traveling back and forth between Berkeley and DC, the boys and their friends were getting fitted for graduation gowns—red for boys, white for girls. Oh, the girls. We were increasingly misty-eyed, anticipating how much we'd miss our boys, as well as the girls who often hung out at our house, giggling madly as we teased them about school drama, misfit teachers, and the latest social media aggravations. Because we had never had girls of our own . . . sniff . . . we loved those beautiful girls as much as the gaggle of boys we had come to know so well over the years.

The court didn't rule the week before graduation. We didn't really expect that it would, but that meant that graduation day became a possible ruling date. Kris and I didn't give it a second thought. We would be at graduation, come hell, high water, or Supreme Court rulings. If we missed being in DC for the ruling, we would be disappointed, but missing commencement was unthinkable.

The morning of graduation, Ryan White was at our house shooting video of the boys getting ready to walk across the stage. By that point, Ryan had become a member of the family—he was one of our boys. He was finishing filming for *The Case Against 8*, a film that would be released some months later, a collaboration with Ben Cotner and Rebekah Fergusson and produced by HBO.

We were so used to Ryan's presence, including his ravenous appetite for snacks and occasional requests for rides, that he had become part of the fabric of our lives. He captured the moment that day when the boys backed out of the driveway, a little too fast and not really watching for cars, in the red Volkswagen convertible we had bought from Kris's dad.

Our hearts swelled with pride as Spencer gave one of the major speeches at the graduation ceremony, and Elliott beamed from his seat with the other soon-to-be graduates. It was the end of an era, a twenty-one-year run of parenting school-age boys. I couldn't believe we were finally at this point. Things were about to change—including our address, because we were also packing up our Berkeley home for a move to Washington, DC, so Kris could be closer to her new job. She had just been appointed executive director of the First Five Years Fund, a nonprofit advocacy organization that works to expand access to early childhood education for children in poverty; I was putting the wheels in motion to work at the US Department of Health and Human Services.

Graduation behind us, we turned our focus again to the case. We joined Jeff and Paul days later in DC to wait for the ruling that had eluded us all summer. We were full of hope that the Supreme Court would rule in our favor—and on the merits of the argument. Such a ruling would bring marriage equality to all Americans. It had been clear at the hearing in March, though, that some of the justices were focused on the issue of standing, which would make a decision more limiting. And we dared not even consider the possibility of losing—that thought was simply too painful.

Soon it was the final week that the court would be in session. With no ruling on Tuesday, we knew that Wednesday, June 26, 2013, would be the day that both the *Perry* and DOMA rulings would be announced. It was "gay day" at the Supreme Court, and the turnout was spectacular. Once again, the line to get in the court snaked around the corner, and the front of the building was a mob scene, made festive by signs, horns, and enthusiastic well-wishers enjoying a lovely early summer day, full of hope for justice. We joined the AFER team and David Boies on the steps of the building, missing Ted, who couldn't be there because he had a court appearance elsewhere.

We made our way into the building, a more familiar process this time, put our bags in the lockers, and took our seats in the courtroom. Seats were filled in an orderly fashion under the watchful eye of the court security officers, who made it clear that any noise or fidgeting was forbidden. What they couldn't stop were my frequent hot flashes, which seemed to be coming more often than ever. I would suddenly turn beet red, followed by a fervent desire to shed layers of clothing and to use just about anything to fan myself, followed by a clammy intermission before the cycle started again. As we sat waiting, Kris sweetly reminded me that I was sweating too much—always a welcome comment.

The packed room came to order. After delivering a ruling on the first case of the day, one that was relatively low profile, the court announced its decision in the DOMA case—and what a spectacular decision it was.

Authored by Justice Kennedy, the ruling was an enormous victory. Plaintiff Edie Windsor, who wasn't able to be present, was victorious thanks to the able counsel of Roberta Kaplan. I had met Edie many years earlier at a film screening of *Edie and Thea: A Very Long Engagement,* a documentary about her forty-one-year relationship with her wife, Thea, and I was a fervent fan. The epitome of committed, Edie had taken loving care of Thea during Thea's terminal illness. Edie and Thea had been married, but Edie was saddled with estate taxes because their marriage wasn't recognized by the federal government, a by-product of DOMA. When the announcement was read that DOMA was overturned in a five-to-four decision, the courtroom was full of quietly jubilant people.

The ruling was specific and clearly in line with what we were hoping for in our own case:

DOMA's principal effect is to identify a subset of state-sanctioned marriages and make them unequal. The principal purpose is to impose inequality, not for other reasons like governmental efficiency. Responsibilities, as well as rights, enhance the dignity and integrity of the person. And DOMA contrives to deprive some couples married under the laws of their state, but not other couples, of both rights and responsibilities. By creating two contradictory marriage regimes within the same state, DOMA forces same-sex couples to live as married for the purpose of state law but unmarried for the purpose of federal law, thus diminishing the stability and predictability of basic personal relations the state has found it proper to acknowledge and protect. By this dynamic DOMA undermines both the public and private significance of state-sanctioned same-sex marriages; for it tells those couples, and all the world, that their otherwise valid marriages are unworthy of federal recognition. This places same-sex couples in an unstable position of being in a second-tier marriage. The differentiation demeans the couple, whose moral and sexual choices the constitution protects. [. . .] and whose relationship the state has sought to dignify. And it humiliates tens of thousands of children now being raised by same-sex couples. The law in question makes it even more difficult for the children to understand the integrity and closeness of their own family and its concord with other families in their community and in their daily lives.

Surely, the DOMA win indicated that good news was coming our way. Our spines were straight as we held our breath in anticipation. *Hollingsworth v. Perry* was finally announced; it was the final ruling of the year. Kris and I gripped hands tightly, hoping for an indication of a merits-based ruling. The decision was delivered by Chief Justice Roberts, a sign that standing would likely be the focus of the ruling. And indeed it was.

Holding: The proponents of California's ban on same-sex marriage did not have standing to appeal the district court's order invalidating the ban.

Judgment: Vacated and remanded, 5-4, in an opinion by Chief Justice Roberts on June 26, 2013. Justice Kennedy filed a dissenting opinion, in which Justice Thomas, Justice Alito, and Justice Sotomayor joined.

ROBERTS, C. J., delivered the opinion of the Court, in which SCALIA, GINSBURG, BREYER, and KAGAN, JJ., joined. KENNEDY, J., filed a dissenting opinion, in which THOMAS, ALITO, and SOTOMAYOR, JJ., joined.

CHIEF JUSTICE ROBERTS delivered the opinion of the Court.

. . .

We have never before upheld the standing of a private party to defend the constitutionality of a state statute when state officials have chosen not to. We decline to do so for the first time here.

Because petitioners have not satisfied their burden to demonstrate standing to appeal the judgment of the District Court, the Ninth Circuit was without jurisdiction to consider the appeal. The judgment of the Ninth Circuit is vacated, and the case is remanded with instructions to dismiss the appeal for lack of jurisdiction.

It is so ordered.

JUSTICE KENNEDY, with whom JUSTICE THOMAS, JUSTICE ALITO, and JUSTICE SOTOMAYOR join, dissenting.

In other words, Judge Walker's ruling had been upheld.

We had won!

We were thrilled with the victory, and although we were disappointed that it would help only California, we had done what we set out to do. California now had marriage equality, but many people in many states didn't, because the Supreme Court had passed on an opportunity to rule on the merits of the case and take advantage of the full body of evidence our trial had produced.

And while the uptick of states that did support marriage equality was encouraging, a handful of states was unlikely to extend this right on their own and would need the courts to step in. We knew that it was unlikely that there would ever be a trial or such a thorough presentation of the facts again, and it felt wrong for that information to be ignored in the ruling. The Supreme Court had certified the case; Ted had presented the facts, but there would be no ruling on the merits of the argument.

It was a win, albeit a bittersweet one.

As we exited the court, wide-eyed and full of emotion, we met our team in the hallway. Lady Olson joined us, full of joy and congratulations. I was reeling from disappointment that the court had dodged the merits issue on our case, even though we had a victory on our hands. I felt it was wrong to take the case and then refuse to actually hear it. Lady insisted that the win was a solid one, urging me to embrace the joy of our victory. Like us, she was missing Ted, and we all felt like we couldn't really celebrate until he was among us. We were ushered out of the building together, descending the grand front stairs to a cheering crowd awaiting us in the DC summer heat. We locked hands and raised our arms triumphantly in response to the love and the full realization that we had prevailed. We had started as a group of strangers: lawyers, activists, and a pair of unknown couples, bound together to prevail upon the government to protect us from discrimination at the hands of voters. We descended the steps of the court, the US Capitol in view, feeling more American than we had that morning thanks to our newly won rights.

Within minutes, we were doing interviews. Between my hot flashes, my general anxiety about the day, and the sweltering sun, I was drenched in sweat that was staining my suit an unbecoming shade of dark gray. I had decided black was too somber for the day, but I rued that decision as I held my arms tight by my side, worried that I would be a talking mop on TV that evening. Kris quietly asked me if I could stop sweating. As if.

We were quickly placed in front of cameras, suddenly talking to the press, to America, about our experience. We went from CNN to MSNBC to the next and the next. At one point, Chad interrupted to tell us that President Obama was on the phone to congratulate us personally. I mean, come on! My heart nearly stopped as tears stung my eyes. The president I so loved and admired was acknowledging us. It was one of the most poignant moments of my life.

After a bunch of interviews and what felt like a million hugs, we jumped into a car with some members of the team, took a deep breath, and started trying to catch up on the news about, and social media reaction to, the ruling. We hadn't had a moment to breathe, or drink water, or stop sweating for hours. There were dozens of messages from friends and family thrilled for us and for all of California. There was also one less kind text, from a relative of my deceased ex-husband, imploring me to "do the normal thing and change my name." I wasn't deterred from my own happiness or celebration, but I felt sad for the sender, and I was suddenly aware of the mixed feelings and responses that might await us. I called my mom as we were boarding the plane to take us back to the West Coast to let her know that we had won, at least in California. She said, in her characteristically understated way, "Well, you got that taken care of." Yes, I guess we had.

We flew with the AFER team, photographer Diana Walker, and our filmmakers on a private plane to Los Angeles to join Ted and others at a rally in West Hollywood, followed by a reception in LA with the AFER team and funders. Our Wi-Fi connection cut in and out the entire flight, as we frantically tried to keep up with the coverage while messaging families and friends. We landed in Burbank, and after a quick stop at the AFER office to change our clothes, we zoomed over to the rally. Traffic was at a standstill, so Kris and I ran a couple of blocks to make it to an MSNBC interview with Rachel Maddow, my TV idol. Because we watched her popular political show every night, I felt like we were friends with her—a one-way friendship, true, but better than nothing.

We celebrated that night. Camera in hand, Diana was with us, joined by her friend, the civil rights activist and actress Jamie Lee Curtis. They made us feel like a million bucks. My older son Tom lived in LA, and he and one of his friends joined us. Eventually, we collapsed into our bed at the New London Hotel, falling asleep in the middle of watching our interview on the *Rachel Maddow Show*. Even Rachel couldn't keep us awake.

The next day, we hopped on a flight back to Oakland. Back to our life in Berkeley, to our recent graduates, to moving boxes waiting to be packed.

Although we had won our case, the state of California still had to implement the ruling and lift the ban. Along with Jeff and Paul, we wanted to be the first couples in California to be married; our lawyers assured us that the process of lifting the ban would take several weeks, which was a relief because we had yet to figure out our wedding plans. Our heads and hearts were spinning from the last few action-packed days—months really, if not years. Tuesday we had been at the Supreme Court when the justices didn't rule; Wednesday we had been inside the court when they did rule; Wednesday night we had toasted equality at a rooftop party in LA; and Thursday we had flown home to unpack and try to find clean laundry and edible food in our house.

We woke up Friday morning in the mental fog that often descends after a big event. Kris was relieved to be working from home, no travel that day, and I decided to go into the office, even though I had told my staff and my boss that I would be out. Going to work felt like a welcome reprieve from the press and the pressure of so much exposure. Kris thought I was nuts to give up a Friday at home, but I insisted on going, wanting to end the week with a normal day and a chance to catch up on work.

I threw on a sundress and put my unruly hair into a ponytail, my least professional look, but acceptable at my office on a summer Friday. After checking in with my colleagues and giving them the skinny on our day in court, I settled into managing my email in my beautiful office overlooking the Oakland estuary, sailboats slipping in and out of the bay in full view. Just before noon, I got a call from Kris. She said she knew I wouldn't want to hear this today, but that the lawyers had called to let us know that there was a slim chance that the stay on the ruling would be lifted in a few hours—in other words that we, and the rest of gay California, might be able to get married. Today.

She was right: I didn't want to hear that. I wanted a quiet, normal day at work, followed by a quiet, normal evening at home. With pizza and a couple of beers. And I wanted time to plan our legal and perfect wedding, with all four of our boys standing with us, maybe trading the Converse sneakers for something more befitting the men they had grown into.

But we were committed to getting married the moment it was legal, and we had plenty of support from the City and County of San Francisco and the Attorney General's Office to make that happen, so we knew we had to be ready . . . just in case. Jeff and Paul were in the same situation at their home in Southern California. None of us had expected anything to happen for several weeks, having been advised that it usually takes that long to lift a stay.

I groaned somewhat unromantically and said fine, I would come home immediately to pull myself together to go to San Francisco City Hall. I slipped out of my office, swinging by the camp in the Berkeley hills where Elliott was working to pick him up. The other boys were too far away to make it.

We grabbed the most appropriate clothes we could find, not what we would have chosen if we had had time to plan our wedding. As we rode to San Francisco in a car that our legal team had sent for us, I mentally checked off items in my bag, hoping I hadn't forgotten makeup or a hair brush. We arrived at the law offices of Gibson Dunn and then began the familiar routine of waiting. Waiting for information. Waiting for Godot. We chatted about the possibility of the stay being lifted, none of us particularly optimistic that it would be that day but increasingly hopeful that it might.

By early afternoon, the lawyers decided that we should get dressed, just in case. We donned our potential wedding outfits in the ladies room. Our random closet pulls turned out to be complementary. Both dressed in silver-gray outfits, Kris and I looked like we had planned the occasion better than we had. My hair, however, refused to look remotely coiffed; I looked less like a well-groomed bride and more like I had just returned from a brisk jog around the block.

We decided to go over to City Hall to wait it out. Kris texted her mother to let her know that we might be getting married soon. It turned out that she was spending the day in the city, so she made a beeline for City Hall. We waited in a black SUV for about fifteen minutes in front of City Hall while a makeup artist hired by AFER attempted to make us look bride-like, and Ryan popped in and out of the vehicle with his camera. At around two p.m., our friend Bruce Cohen knocked on the SUV's window. When we rolled it down, he told us that the stay had been lifted.

We would be getting married—now.

We entered City Hall and were joined by activist Cleve Jones; Chad Griffin, who had first enlisted us; screenwriter Lance Black; *New York Times* journalist Jo Becker; and Bruce. Ryan, clad in shorts, filmed our entourage. While we applied for a marriage license, California's attorney general, Kamala Harris, was on the phone ensuring that Jeff and Paul's license would be granted in Los Angeles, where they would be married shortly after us. Flowers were provided by the ever-ready AFER staffers: white rose bouquets for both Kris and me and a corsage for Elliott, who was tall and handsome in a navy blue suit. The moment felt surreal: I fought back tears thinking of how much I had wanted to have all our boys with us when we were finally married.

Kamala led us upstairs to a large marble balcony surrounded by tall stately columns in the atrium of City Hall. Standing near a bust of Harvey Milk and with Elliott as our witness, we repeated our vows and our commitment to one another, affirming our love for always. Kris placed the fourth ring on my finger.

Kris has never looked more beautiful to me than on our final legal wedding day. Her beauty in that moment eclipsed even the earliest days of our relationship. Her eyes grabbed mine with a fierce love. A forever love. She said "I do" with finality, as did I. We finally did.

After being pronounced "spouses for life," we pulled our boy to us and faced a growing crowd of well-wishers, their cheers punctuated by the San Francisco Gay Men's Chorus, who had spontaneously joined the merriment and were serenading us with fervor. Holding hands, we wove our way through the crowd of beautiful strangers, hugging them, thanking them for their sweet words, humbled by their tear-streaked faces.

That evening we celebrated with half of our AFER family in a suite at the Clift Hotel, surrounded by food courtesy of room service, our shoes kicked to the corners of the room, our feet up on chairs.

The next morning, Kris and I made our way back across the bay to Berkeley to meet our friends Carrianne and Gina for breakfast at Venus Café, a local favorite that serves organic hippie food. We were well into mounds of Meyer lemon pancakes and fresh-squeezed juice when glasses of champagne started to arrive. We hadn't anticipated the recognition and love we would feel from strangers. For days, this was a common occurrence: people we knew and people we had never met would stop to thank us and hug us; a bottle of bubbly would arrive at our table; drivers who recognized us as we walked down the street would honk their horns.

The commencement of weddings was serendipitously timed with the celebration of celebrations, Pride Week in San Francisco. As one of the historic epicenters of gay life, San Francisco hosts an annual Pride parade that is one of the largest and most riotous in the country—and the parade was on Sunday. Jeff and Paul flew up to join Kris and me as honorary marshals. Kris and I were perched on the back of a beautiful, baby-blue antique Cadillac convertible. We were followed by marchers, including Elliott and a bunch of his high school friends, gay and straight alike. We wove through the parade route stunned at the record turnout, people waving and cheering as far as the eye could see. We waved and cheered right back, yelling "Thank you!" over and over again. What a day!

And then Monday arrived. By this time, I had missed so much work, *so* much work. My Catholic guilt was in overdrive, and I felt like I should walk in and immediately apologize for my sparse attendance. That morning, as I entered the office, I couldn't believe my eyes. My colleagues had spent the better part of Sunday decorating in celebration of our victory. Posters of our San Francisco City Hall wedding and our car in the Gay Pride parade lined the walls. Balloons filled the air, pink plastic tablecloths covered the surfaces of file cabinets and conference tables, and a big wedding cake was the focal point of the office. By noon, coworkers from all over the building were pouring into the office kitchen, bringing meatballs, salads, tacos, and cookies. I was deeply touched by the thoughtfulness of my colleagues and uncharacteristically emotional in my thanks to them; their faces reflected such pride and joy for us.

Kris and I had often talked about how we would celebrate our "real" wedding. We had plans for beautiful wedding outfits; we envisioned our four boys, now men, standing with us, our families at our sides, friends near and far joining us for a big party. Our real wedding was much different, but it was perfect. Our guests were strangers; our reception was room service in a hotel. But we were legally married, at long last.

The next weekend we did host a celebration at our house, the festivities lasting well into the night. Tom, Frank, and Elliott were there; Spencer was there in spirit only. Many of our friends and even a few relatives made it. People brought food and drink and commandeered our grill. Singer-songwriter David Berkeley serenaded us. Thanks to the absence of media, I traded in my heels for

Birkenstocks and my suit for shorts. Kris was dressed in a typical weekend outfit of shorts, a button-down denim linen shirt, and white Converse sneakers. We all enjoyed good food and even better beer on our patio by the creek. I looked across at Kris, laughing with our boys, her arms slung over friends' shoulders. We had had our fair share of heartache and struggle, but it paled in comparison to the joy, the love, and the laughter of that perfect day. It had been thirteen years since we had become a family. Thirteen years, and finally we were legally a family.

Amen. Amen to that.

CHAPTER 35

Two Steps Forward, One Step Back?

Kris and Sandy

As of this writing, we are officially a (slightly) older married couple. Our boys are grown, our home a quieter and quite cleaner place than in the past. We have shifted our entertaining from feeding bunches of hungry boys to dining in or out with friends. We miss the boys, but we enjoy "us."

We've also enjoyed many full circle moments since our case went before the Supreme Court: being with our friends Carri-anne and Gina and their twin boys when they applied for and received their marriage license at the Alameda County Clerk-Recorder's Office from the same sweet clerk who had been forced to deny us ours, and, many months later, officiating at the wedding of our friends Jen and Jen in Virginia, where inter-racial marriage was struck down fifty years earlier and where they now could be legally wed.

Although the *Perry* case ended, the marriage equality de-bate continues, fueled in part by the work of people we became so close to throughout the case. Ryan and Ben completed their documentary, *The Case Against 8,* with the help of HBO and some brilliant editing and originally scored music. Although Ryan and Ben were our almost-constant companions during our court battle, because they were so much younger than us, and because we knew basically nothing about the art of filmmaking, we didn't take their efforts too seriously. We thought they were adorable and clever, and we had no doubt they would produce something wonderful, but when they showed us the first cut of the film, we were moved to tears. It is a masterful piece of work, the story of our four-plus years of legal battles condensed into a very moving 152 minutes.

In 2014, *The Case Against 8* was released; we saw it about 152 times. Okay, maybe not quite that many times, but still more than we would have imagined as we attended film festivals and screenings, often joining the directors and our co-plaintiffs for conversation onstage afterward. Although not all our boys could attend our second legal wedding, they did all attend the San Francisco premier of *The Case Against 8* when it headlined the annual San Francisco Frameline Film Festival that year. That night, we celebrated with those beautiful boys of ours and stood on stage after the screening with our lawyers, Jeff and Paul, and of course Ben and Ryan. Even after all the viewings, we still cannot hear the opening score without choking up. The film was a gift to us, an artifact of a life-changing experience that we will someday share with our grandchildren. Someday—no rush there.

The case itself—the legal arguments and the case's progression through the system—were also beautifully captured in two books, one by Jo Becker, *Forcing the Spring*, and one from the lawyers' perspective, *Redeeming the Dream* by Ted and David. Those books and the new information we learned in the aftermath of the events helped us gain a deeper understanding of the complexities of the case that we had been so intimately involved in, leading us to an even greater appreciation for the team and the sacrifices so many people made. Our admiration for the legal team and the AFER family has only grown over the years. And we are so grateful to Diana Walker for capturing with her camera the essence of the journey.

The shift in the courtroom of public opinion was exemplified spectacularly by two individuals who had opposed us during the trial. David Blankenhorn wrote a *New York Times* piece in June 2012 declaring that he had had a change of heart and now supported marriage equality. Then, in 2014, we were invited to the home of Chuck and Debbie Cooper. They reached out to us through Jo Becker in the wake of learning that their own daughter, Ashley, was gay and engaged to her girlfriend. We had a lovely dinner with the Coopers, finding common ground in the very simple concepts of love and family and being regaled by Chuck's Rolling Stones impressions. We're still on the opposite side of the fence on many issues, but Chuck adores his daughter. He proudly danced with Ashley at her wedding and has embraced her new wife into their family. Loving your child unequivocally is the single most important thing any parent can do.

Two years to the day after our Supreme Court ruling came in, the Supreme Court ruled on a group of cases from Michigan, Ohio, Kentucky, and Tennessee. Those six cases represented thousands of families struggling for the same rights that most people take for granted. The Supreme Court ruled in favor of those families, bringing marriage equality to those few states that had refused to guarantee it on their own. Finally, the United States of America had a united response to marriage. Our children's children, we dared to hope, would grow up in a more just and equal society than Kris and I had.

Having relocated to Washington, DC, Kris and I became locals, living just blocks from the Supreme Court, where we had been lucky enough to be a part of history. On June 26, 2015, Kris and I drove past a rainbow-lit White House to join Ted and Lady for an intimate dinner in Georgetown, where we toasted love, family, and equality.

We the people had won.

Or had we? As of this writing, with a new American president newly enthroned in the White House, that old America—the one that had made being gay a crime and had decreed same-sex marriage a legal impossibility—is trying to reassert itself. Like a monster in a B-movie that everyone thought had finally drowned, it's risen from the swamp and is once again lurching forward, its outstretched arms determined to grab someone or something.

And one of its targets seems to be same-sex marriage. With the recent turning of the political tide, uncertainty now hangs over the future of not only the Supreme Court but also the entire federal bench. Our challenge started in one state and wended its way through three layers of federal courts before the final ruling. It's not hard to imagine, in the not-too-distant future, an initiative banning same-sex marriage landing on a ballot in another state. A majority of voters could pass that initiative into law, and the federal judges who would hear the same-sex marriage argument would not agree with the decision in our case, and neither would the judges above them. It took a legal dream team and more than a decade to achieve marriage equality in California—only one of the continuing battles in the fight for equal rights in our country.

The war is not even close to being over.

Timeline of Our Case against Prop 8

November 8, 2008	Proposition 8 passes.
May 23, 2009	*Perry v. Schwarzenegger* is filed.
October 13, 2009	Summary judgment hearing: Judge Walker decides to have a trial.
January 11, 2010	First day of trial (and day of testimony). The trial lasts thirteen days.
June 16, 2010	Closing arguments heard.
August 4, 2010	District court ruling: *Perry* wins. A few days later, defendant-intervenors file a notice of appeal to the Ninth Circuit.
January 4, 2011	Ninth Circuit asks the California Supreme Court to decide whether intervenors have the right to appeal.
September 6, 2011	California Supreme Court hears oral arguments on the intervenor issue.
November 17, 2011	California Supreme Court rules that intervenors have the right to appeal.
February 7, 2012	Three-judge panel upholds the district court ruling. *Perry* wins again.
July 30, 2012	Proponents appeal the case, now called *Hollingsworth v. Perry,* to the US Supreme Court.
December 7, 2012	Certiorari is granted. This means the Supreme Court agreed to hear the case.
March 26, 2013	The Supreme Court hears oral arguments in *Hollingsworth v. Perry.*
June 26, 2013	The Supreme Court upholds Judge Walker's ruling.

CREDITS

Pages 2, 10, 20, 37, 38, 44, 60, 78, and 86: authors' private collections.

Page 94: Karin Hildebrand Lau / Alamy Stock Photo.

Page 98: Cloudpix.

Pages 106 and 218: REUTERS / Alamy Stock Photo.

All other images by Diana Walker. We are very grateful to Diana for giving us her permission to use these photographs.